Keeping the Harvest

HOME STORAGE OF VEGETABLES & FRUITS

Nancy Thurber &
Gretchen Mead

GARDEN WAY PUBLISHING
CHARLOTTE, VERMONT 05445

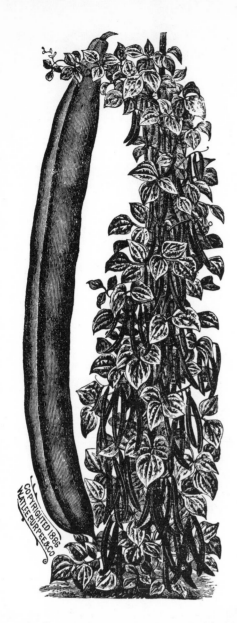

Printed in the United States by George Little Press
ISBN 0-88266-068-3 (pbk)
       0-88266-055-1 (hardcover)

ILLUSTRATIONS

Photographs and line drawings used in this book were supplied by the following contributors, whose help we gratefully acknowledge:

Photographs

Natalie Abodeely: 10, 14, 15, 16, 17, 18, 19, 21, 22–23, 29, 34–35, 44–45, 47, 51, 108, 119, 123, 126–27, 135, 138, 154–55, 162, 165, 172

Addison County Independent (Middlebury, Vt): p. 54 (bottom)

Burlington Free Press: pp. 52 (bottom), 53

Peter Coleman: pp. 3, 150, 191

Charles Cook: pp. 8, 64, 74, 76, 90, 97, 104, 117, 146, 183, 184, 187, 192

Donald Hanson: pp. 91, 176, 177, 178-79, 180

Grant Heilman: p. 180

Jerry Jones: pp. vi, 9, 158, 168, 173, 198.

Julia Oesterle: pp. 52 (top), 53, 54, 55

Line drawings

Except as otherwise noted, all line illustrations shown are included by permission of W. Atlee Burpee Co., Warminster, PA 18991 and R. H. Shumway Seedsman, 628 Cedar Street, Rockford, IL 61101, whose help we sincerely appreciate.

Grateful acknowledgment is also made for line drawings used by permission of The Bettmann Archive, Inc., 36 East 57th Street, New York, NY 10022.

The Bettmann Archive: pp. 4, 49, 51, 111, 194, 195

Charles Cook: pp. 61, 185

Charles H. Joslin: 2, 27, 31, 39, 40, 42, 43, 57, 67, 77, 79, 82, 86, 88, 94, 95, 101, 106, 107, 109, 110, 112, 113, 114, 115, 116, 125, 130, 132, 133, 142, 148, 149, 164, 174, 183, 197

Douglas Merrilees: pp. 6, 12, 14, 28, 33, 34, 46, 140, 141, 145, 170-71, 188, 189, 190

Cover photo by Jerry Jones

Designed by David Robinson

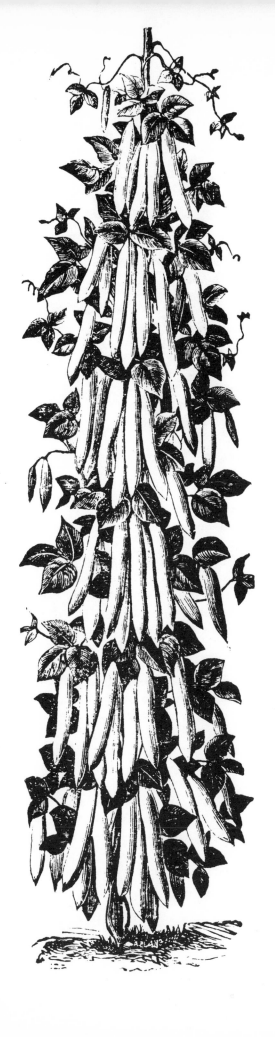

Contents

Preface

Preserving and storing food in the home has been coming back into its own the past few years. The fairly obvious reasons are the constantly climbing costs of foods, their doubtful quality and our knowledge that chemicals are added to many. Because of these things, hundreds of thousands of families are turning back to the basics of gardening and storing the foods they grow.

The successful and thrifty gardener often has an overabundance of fresh vegetables and fruits, either by design or accident. Our grandmothers knew exactly how to cope with this, but in the last two generations the "art" of food storage has been neglected and often forgotten. Now it has to be relearned from books, but with the addition of new, improved methods and techniques that our grandmothers never knew. We do urge you to use these modern, tested methods to avoid spoilage, which at the least is wasteful and at the worst dangerous.

This book is for the beginner who is just deciding which of the methods to use. It also is for the experienced and confident cook looking for a quick reference guide. We have tried for as much clarity and accuracy as possible because food storage involves the health of our families. We've tried to help you decide which methods best preserve the nutrients in your produce and which are most economical in terms of both time and money.

Only tested methods are recommended, and there is a strong emphasis on new techniques that have proved far safer than many older ones. But shortcuts and ways to improvise whenever practical are presented, too. The accompanying photographs and drawings are intended to take the uncertainty and mystery out of food processing and make it genuinely a simple and practical operation.

We have tried to look at food preservation from the standpoint of a typical gardener and homeowner, emphasizing those methods most commonly used and best adapted to available space, time and pocketbook. Canning and freezing are given primary emphasis. Root cellaring, drying and salting are treated thoroughly but as supplemental means of preservation.

Anyone who can cook can preserve foods; and if you have a little space you can store it. We want to encourage the beginner, for the rewards and satisfaction of having a cupboard or freezer full of your own fruits and vegetables is well worth the effort. It is a creative and constructive use of home time, and it will pay off in dollars and cents. By becoming a little more self-sufficient, too, growing more of our own foods and using what's available in season and not letting it go to waste, we all will be helping to overcome the ever-present threat of a world food shortage.

So, the best of luck, and good eating.

Gretchen Mead
Nancy Thurber

Acknowledgments

We want to give a special thanks to all the people who helped make this book possible: to the many people at the University of Vermont who gave us technical information, suggestions, and pointed us in the right direction, especially Joyce Livak, Alice Coffey, and Winston Way; to Dick Raymond, who shared with us his ideas on harvesting and preserving developed during a lifetime of gardening; and to the many home economists and horticulturists of the U.S. Extension Service.

We also would like to thank the various seed companies and the canning jar manufacturers who have researched and experimented in the field of home food preserving, for the benefit of all of us.

We are grateful, too, to Mary Twitchell, who, with good humor and helpful contributions, typed and retyped this manuscript.

We are indebted to our many friends and relatives who shared their recipes and preserving ideas with us, especially Bebe Wood, Mary Thurber, Ethyl Atkins, and Marion Palmer; and to our editors, Walter Hard and David Robinson for their helpful criticism and patience.

Credit is especially due to Jerry Jones, Don Hanson, and Natalie Abodeely, who spent many hours taking the photographs of step-by-step preserving, and to the many friends of Garden Way who sent us their hints and ideas.

A special note of thanks also goes to Roger Griffith, who cheerfully supplied many of the little boxed "hints" and recipes that appear throughout.

Finally, we thank our families, who kept their senses of humor and gave us encouragement while we were writing this book.

Chapter 1 Planning Ahead

If you have ever stayed up until 2 AM on a hot summer night cutting and freezing corn, or been turned down by the neighbors when offering them just one more bushel of extra cucumbers, you will understand why, when "raising your own," good garden planning is essential. With careful planning, you can provide just enough of the fruits and vegetables for "in season" eating and winter storage. Non-gardeners will also find this chapter helpful in estimating what, when, and how much to buy for their home preserving needs. In addition, equipment such as jars, freezer containers, and a pressure canner should be purchased well in advance of the season while they are still plentiful. It can be downright discouraging in August to be faced with a bushel of tomatoes rotting on the porch because the stores have run out of canning jar lids. Whether you are a gardener or not, you can never be overprepared for the summer deluge of local and home-grown produce.

What Method to Choose?

There are many methods of storing and preserving foods. Common storage or "root cellaring" is the simplest method. If you live in an area with a cool or cold climate, you can store many vegetables for several months in a cold cellar or any space with the appropriate atmosphere. This method requires no preparation and can be used for the root vegetables (onions, carrots, beets, potatoes), winter squash, pumpkins, cabbage, and fruits such as apples. *Dried* foods such as beans, split peas and the grains require only darkness and a cool, dry spot protected from the 3 M's—*mold, moisture,* and *mice.*

Other methods include canning, freezing, pickling, salting, fermenting, drying and making jams or jellies.

Freezing is the easiest and can be used for almost any fruit or vegetable. There is very little loss of nutrients compared with other methods, but freezing does involve the most expensive equipment and the continuing use of electricity.

Canning by "boiling water bath" is the tried-and-true method to preserve high-acid foods like fruits and pickled vegetables.

Pressure canning is necessary for the majority of other vegetables, such as beans, peas, corn and beets, which are "low acid." Low acid foods also may be preserved by freezing, drying, salting, fermenting or pickling. Choosing a preserving technique will depend on the equipment you have available or can afford to buy. In later chapters you will find the information and equipment necessary for each method. A discussion of the effects of the different methods of preserving on the nutrients in the foods is included.

If you do not have a garden, you can pick produce at local farms and orchards, buy specials at supermarkets, or check roadside stands for good, fresh foods. It is also possible to buy in bulk from food cooperatives and farm supply stores. The tables in this chapter will show you what to look for in cultivated foods and when, as well as how much to buy.

Wild berries, fruits, "edible weeds," and asparagus are yours for the picking in some areas, the property owner permitting.

When to Plant

A friend of ours, in her first summer of serious gardening and preserving, planted her green beans in May despite frost warnings and the wet clayey soil so typical of this part of New England. She was feeling very proud of herself because her neighbor—a more experienced gardener—had yet to put a bean in the ground by the first of June. But her pride turned to vexation when in the heat of August she found herself trapped by a hot stove, blanching bushels of beans. And her neighbor? She was at the beach while the hot sun was maturing her later beans, to be preserved in early September when the kids had returned to school and the weather was cooler. The moral of this story is to plan ahead!

With a little forethought you can control the time of maturity and quantity of vegetables in your garden. Your plantings should be made so that you are not left with gaps when there are no vegetables to eat or preserve, also that you are not overwhelmed later with more than you can possibly handle. Your enjoyment of preserving will depend on how well you plan the seasonal progression of your produce. Small batches are not as discouraging as bushels.

Harvesting can start with rhubarb and asparagus in May and continue into November with chinese cabbage and parsnips. Depending on the climate, some vegetables can winter over in the garden for year-round harvest. Stagger the planting of other vegetables to maximize yield and minimize preserving bottlenecks during the summer months.

Canning and freezing actually start in early January with the arrival of seed catalogs. Study them carefully. Many new hybrids are designated as especially good for canning or freezing.

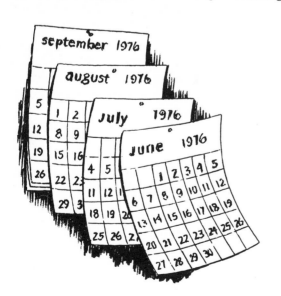

You may wish to choose a few new varieties each year. Sometimes you will hit on a family favorite, or at least increase your knowledge for next year. But be realistic. Take into account your family's likes and dislikes. It is easy to get carried away with the glossy pictures. If your family will not eat a certain vegetable, you will have wasted your time and garden space. Save your garden plan from year to year. If you also record the varieties and how well each did, you will be spared from making the same mistakes and be at least partially assured of the same successes.

When to Pick

Of all the lessons we have learned from our garden, the most important has been that *when a crop is ripe it should be picked and eaten or preserved as soon as possible.* If you don't, you will have overripe, poor-quality vegetables and fruit that won't be improved by preserving. What is second-best fresh is third rate processed.

If you've ever grown zucchini, for example, you know what we mean. These summer squashes are most tender and delicious when six to eight inches long. If you pick them all at that size, your plants will continue to produce until frost. However, if you turn your back on that plant for even a few days, you will have overgrown, tough-skinned monsters which must be peeled, and the seeds and soft core removed before they can be used. At the same time there will be fewer tender little squash since the plant has now produced its seeds. And that's the primary purpose of most annual plants—to produce seeds for the next generation. When this has been accomplished, it ceases producing fruit. We don't mean to imply that large zucchini are useless; on the contrary, the thick flesh can be cut into cubes and used to form the base of many casseroles. In addition zucchini can be substituted for ripe cukes in tongue and other pickles. However, wait until the end of the growing season before letting the zucchini grow.

It is important to remember to pick all your vegetables when just ripe so that you will have a

continuing harvest; let them go by a few days and in the long run you will have fewer, less appetizing vegetables. Knowing this, you may want to put in fewer plants, encouraging maximum production from your rows and preserving in small quantities over several weeks. If your plants ripen all at once, many may go by because you cannot concentrate enough time on preserving in such large quantity.

This is particularly true of summer squash, cucumbers, spinach, beans, broccoli, and asparagus. It is not so true with plants that set only a certain number of fruit, such as corn and the root crops. You'll get only one carrot or turnip per seed no matter what you do. Certain vegetables such as winter squash and pumpkins will need to mature completely on the vine before being picked if they are to store well.

3

In the case of vine crops like pumpkins, winter squash and melons you may even want to discourage their vine growth so more energy will be devoted to fewer large fruit. If so, pinch off the fuzzy ball at the end of the vine. This stops the plant from spreading. Also pick off some of the blossoms. This will limit the number of fruit and thereby encourage the growth of a few bigger ones. Mammoth pumpkins weighing 100–200 pounds are grown in this way. Only one fruit per vine is allowed to ripen, and that one is coaxed with fertilizer or even is "milk-fed" to grow enormous.

Size, however, is not usually an important goal with the vegetables you plan to keep for winter use. Giant tomatoes make attractive slices on the summer table, but they have to be cut up to fit into a mason jar. The smaller varieties are more practical. Green and yellow wax beans are best when pencil thin (not yet knobby with maturing beans), crisp and tender when snapped. Extra-large carrots and beets may impress the neighbors, but they tend to be tough and tasteless. For fresh eating and for storage, the smaller "table size" are preferred.

NUTRITIONAL EFFECTS OF FOOD PROCESSING*

One important consideration in deciding which methods of home food preservation to use is the effect each method has on the nutrients in the food. There is evidence that the greatest losses in vitamins and minerals often result from the way the food is prepared in the home for eating.

The actual vitamin content of some table-ready foods may be very similar no matter how they were preserved. For example, a bowl of peas placed steaming on the table will contain 35–45 percent of its original, "raw" vitamin C content whether it was prepared from fresh peas (45 percent), frozen peas (40 percent) or canned peas (35 percent).

Water-soluble vitamins, such as vitamin B_1, riboflavin and niacin, tend to be lost by "leaching" or dissolving in the cooking water. Losses of the fat-soluble vitamins (A, D, E and K) and vitamin C, on the other hand, are more likely to occur during heating and storage in the presence of air.

In general, the overall effect of heat processing destroys the factors in cereal grains, peas and beans that make them hard to digest, so that the proteins and carbohydrates in these foods become better utilizable by man.

Another factor that affects the vitamin and mineral content of foods, no matter how they are preserved, is the natural differences in the

KEEP IT FRESH

To achieve the very best in quality in your canning or freezing, pick garden produce at the last minute, when you're all ready to process it.

Corn is perhaps the most critical item. Even if it's stored at 40° F., in one day half its sweetness will have turned into starch.

If you can't get to the processing at once, chill the foods immediately to as close to 32° F. as you can get them. Strawberries, for instance, "respire" (lose quality) ten times as fast at 40 degrees as they do at 32. Even apples sitting for one day in 70 degree heat lose as much life as they would at 32 F. in a week.

Take along a pre-chilled cooler chest if you go shopping for garden-fresh produce at a farm market. Then it won't lose so much on the hot ride home.

Best of all, if you can, have the water boiling on the stove before you go out to the corn patch to pick.

4

raw foods because of genetic variations, climatic conditions and maturity at harvest. For example, carrots may vary a hundred-fold in their concentration of carotene (provitamin A), and samples of fresh tomato juice have shown 16-fold differences in vitamin C. Vegetables grown in different parts of the country will vary in acidity and mineral content because of soil differences.

Here are some of the known nutritional losses from each type of food processing:

Blanching. Blanching before freezing and drying foods inactivates the enzymes that would otherwise gradually destroy the color, flavor and some nutrients of the food during storage. Blanching in boiling water will lose more nutrients than blanching with steam. For example, steaming spinach will cause the loss of up to 10 percent of vitamins B_1, B_2 and C and niacin; while blanching in boiling water for 2¼ to 5 minutes may cause losses of up to 35 percent of these vitamins. Minerals are not destroyed by the heat, but they may be lost by leaching into the blanching water.

Canning. Most vitamins, except riboflavin and niacin, break down when heated, so losses in heat processing for canning can be expected. Riboflavin will break down when exposed to light, which is one reason for storing canned foods in the dark.

Foods that form a dense pack in the canning jar, such as greens and strained pumpkin (which require a long processing time in order for the heat to reach the center of the mass), will lose more of their vitamin content than will the more liquid vegetables such as tomatoes.

The water-soluble vitamins in canned foods will become evenly distributed throughout the solids and liquids in the jar soon after canning. Since liquid may make up about 1/3 of the contents, that means 1/3 of these vitamins will be lost unless the liquid is consumed with the food solids or is used in soups and gravies.

The storage temperature of canned goods makes a difference in long-term retention of some nutrients. At cold temperatures (below 65° F.) very little loss occurs. Warmer temperatures may cause losses of vitamins. For example, the vitamin C in canned tomato juice may be reduced by 25 percent when stored at 80° F. for a year, while about 10 percent of vitamin A will be lost. Thiamine is preserved at 65°

F. but at 80° for one year there may be losses of 15 percent in canned fruits and 25 percent in canned vegetables.

Drying. The process of drying preserves a percentage of most vitamins, except those lost when blanching is used. However, during a long period of storage, major losses of vitamins A, C, and E may occur in foods dried at home because they are stored in the presence of oxygen. Commercially dried foods that are vacuum packed or packed in nitrogen will retain more of their vitamins over a period of time.

Freezing. Freezing does not significantly destroy any vitamins except vitamin E and pyridoxine (B_6). Processing losses that occur are primarily the result of blanching the vegetables before freezing. Frozen foods will retain most of their nutrients if kept at a constant temperature of 0° F. or less. At temperatures above 15° F. the easily-oxidizable vitamins will be gradually lost. For example, one-half of the original vitamin C in asparagus, peas and lima beans will be lost during storage at 15° F. for 6 months. Over a longer storage time some losses occur even at 0° F. For example, beans, broccoli, cauliflower and spinach may lose from ⅓ to ¾ of their vitamin C when stored for a year at 0° F.

All this would indicate that the differences in food preservation methods will be substantially counteracted and the losses kept to a minimum by:

1. Preserving only garden-fresh, ripe produce.
2. Using heat in processing for no more than the recommended time.
3. Storing canned foods in a cold, dark place; frozen foods at 0° F. or less.
4. Cooking foods for the table as briefly and with as little water as possible.
5. Making use of all cooking and blanching liquid either with the food cooked or in soup stock and gravy in order to save the nutrients dissolved in it.

---

*Information taken from the Institute of Food Technologists' Expert Panel of Food Safety and Nutrition and the Committee on Public Information, "Scientific Status Summary," October 1974; and United States Department of Agriculture, *Conserving the Nutritive Values in Foods,* USDA Home and Garden Bulletin #90 (Washington, rev. Jan. 1971).

How Much to Grow

The tables that follow will help you decide how much of each vegetable to plant for preserving. For summer use you can make additional plantings. With the vegetables that mature quickly you can plant small quantities of the earliest varieties, to mature toward the beginning of the season for table use. Later, plant a larger storage crop to ripen near the end of the summer or early fall. For example, depending on your climate, you could put in a few of your onion sets as soon as the ground can be worked. These are for summer eating. The rest should be planted so as not to ripen before they can be stored for winter. If you try to store them during the warm weather of late summer or early fall, they will rot in or out of the ground. But watch out! If you hope to get storage onions from seed, they should be planted as early as possible, as it takes almost four months for them to reach adequate size.

Cabbage is another example. In the spring, set out only a few plants of the early varieties for your summer cole slaw needs. Wait until early summer to plant the later varieties which you

plan to store. Otherwise they will ripen long before the harvest season, and you will have cabbages cracking in the sun that are choice targets for the cabbage worms. The later, longer-growing varieties of most vegetables are usually the strongest *and* have the best flavor and storage qualities.

The vegetable planning chart, Table A, shows how much of each vegetable you can harvest from 100-foot rows, and how much seed is needed to plant these rows. Tables in Chapters 2 and 3 show how many quarts of canned or frozen vegetables you can expect per pound or bushel of produce. These tables should be helpful whether you grow your own or buy in bulk.

The "days to maturity" column of the vegetable chart will help you plan when to plant each type of vegetable for winter use. Decide when you want to *harvest* the crop, and using the number of days to maturity, count backwards. For example, you may be planning a vacation in August and want a crop such as beans to ripen either before or after that time. So that the beans will not mature while you're gone, you should plant them in several batches, one to ripen a week or two before you leave, another a week or two after. Some varieties mature in about 50 days. If you are going to be away August 8–15, you could plant one batch before June 10 which should ripen by the last week in July. The next planting should be three weeks later (July 1) in

A cold frame can help you start your garden earlier, for tasty fresh vegetables for the table. These diagrams show how a cold frame is made.

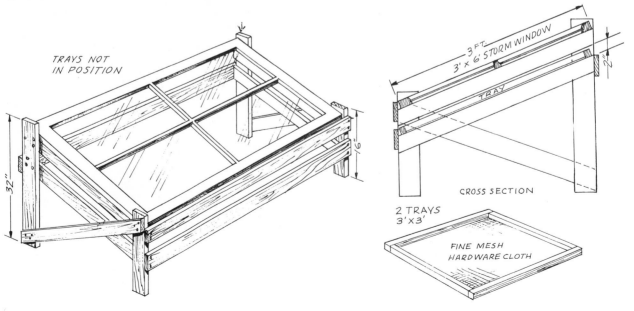

6

TABLE A — VEGETABLE PLANNING CHART

Vegetable Variety	Earliest Planting Time* 1	2	3	4	Days to First Harvest and/or Maturity	100-Foot Single-Row Planting — Seeds or Plants Needed	Yield Picked Pound or Bushel	Vitamins Rich In	Two Best Methods of Preserving
Asparagus	R				After 2 yrs.	65 1-yr. old crowns	30# spears	B₁ C	freeze, pressure can
Beans, Dry (kidney, navy, soldier, etc.)		S			65-100	1#	*	B₁, B₂, E, protein	dry storage, pressure can
Beans, Lima-Bush			S		65-80	¾#	(64# in hull)	B₁, B₂, C	freeze, pressure can
Beans, Lima-Pole			S		80-95	½#	2 bushels	B₆, niacin	dry storage, pressure can
Beans, snap, green & wax- Bush		S			50-60	¾#	2 bushels	B₁, B₂, C	freeze, pressure can
Beans, snap, green &wax- Pole		S			60-70	¾#	(60#)	B₁, B₂, C	freeze, pressure can
Beets		S			50-65	102	2 bushels (104#)	A₁, B₂, B₆, C (tops)	storage, pressure can
Broccoli	T				50-80	65 plants	60#	A, B₁, B₂, C	freeze
Brussels Sprouts	T				65-75	65 plants		B₁, B₂, C	freeze
Cabbage	T				60-90	65 plants	65 heads +	B₆, C (raw)	storage, sauerkraut
Cantalope			S		75-100	1 pkt.	60 melons	A, C	freeze
Carrots		S			55-80	½ oz.	2 bushels (100#)	A	storage, pressure can
Cauliflower	T				65-80	50-70 plants	50-70 heads	B₁, C	freeze
Celery	T				100-150	200 plants	200 bunches	E	storage in ground or cellar
Chard, Swiss		S			45-55	202	3 bushels (54#) +	A, B₂, C	freeze, pressure can
Collards	T				65-85	65	3 bushels (54#) +	A, B₁, B₂, C, niacin	freeze, pressure can
Corn			S		60-95	1#	6-8 doz. ears	B₁, niacin, E	freeze, pressure can
Cucumber			S		50-70	1 pkt.	1½ bushels	C	pickle
Eggplant				T	80-90	1 pkt.	100 eggplants		freeze in casserole
Okra			S		50-55	2 oz.	1000 pods	B₁,B₂,B₆,C, niacin	freeze, pressure can
Onions	S				85-200	½ oz.	200-400		storage
	sets				35 +	8-10 lb.	scallions &	green tops	pickles
				T	35 +	400 plants	onions or 4½ bushels	A, C	
Parsley		S			50 +	½ oz.	*	A,B₁,B₂,C, niacin	freeze, dry
Parsnip		S			120-150	1 oz.	75-100#	B₁	keep in ground or storage
Peas, Green	S				50-80	1#	2 bushels (60# in pods)	B₁, B₂, C, E, niacin	freeze, pressure can
Peppers				T	60-100	1 pkg.	4 bushels	A (red), C	relish, freeze
Potatoes		eyes			100-120	10# seed potatoes	3 bushels	B₁, B₆, C, niacin	storage, pressure can
Pumpkin			S		100-120	1 pkg.	300#	A	storage, pressure can
Rhubarb	R				1 yr.	35 roots	*		freeze, can
Spinach	S				40-50	1 oz.	3 bushels	A, B₁, B₂, C, iron	freeze, pressure can
Squash, summer			S		75-80	1 oz.	135 squash	C, niacin	freeze, pressure can
Squash, winter			S		85-100	1 oz.	400#	A, C	storage, pressure can
Strawberries	T				1 yr.	75-100 plants	*	C	freeze, sweet preserves
Sweet Potatoes				T	120-150	75-100	80#	A, B₁, B₆, C, E	storage, pressure can
Tomatoes				T	55-90	40-60 plants	3 bushels (160#)	A, C, E	can whole, sauce or juice
Turnip (& Rutabaga)	S				40-60	½ oz.	100#	A, B₁, B₂, B₆, C, E (greens), C (root)	storage freeze greens

*Yield varies considerably. For summer eating and winter storage by a family of four, we suggest planting the following amounts:

Dry Beans — about 2 lbs.
Parsley — 1 pkt.
Rhubarb — 8 – 10 plants
Strawberries — 60 – 100 plants

Earliest Planting Time Key

(1) as soon as the ground can be worked in the spring, 20-40 days before last average annual frost
(2) early, about 10-30 days before last frost
(3) on average date of last frost
(4) when soil is warm; 10-20 days after last frost

Symbols: R = Root
S = Seed
T = Plants

order to mature around August 24. Both plantings will continue to produce beans if they are kept picked.

Successive plantings can be made all summer, so long as the last planting will mature before the first frost. Use the average annual fall frost date for your area for calculating the growing season of non-hardy vegetables such as beans, squash and tomatoes. Your hardy varieties—

A tiller can be a great help in turning under a fall crop of winter rye or alfalfa.

cabbage, broccoli, Swiss chard, etc.—can withstand many light frosts. Table B indicates which vegetables can survive the cold.

Weather & Maturity

Some crops do best in certain types of weather. Spinach and peas, for example, prefer the cold of spring, while tomatoes and melons thrive in the hot summer sun. You will have to follow nature's guide for these: plant them when they will grow best and harvest when ripe. Spinach will bolt in the heat of summer so be sure to plant enough in the spring or fall for your preserving needs.

Another factor in your garden planting schedule should be what plants you might want to have mature at the same time. For example, to make dill pickles the dill should be ripening at same time as the cucumbers are reaching the various sizes good for dills (from tiny gherkins to 5 to 6 inch spears). So make several successive plantings of dill, a few feet of row at a time, starting in early spring for summer salad use, and continuing every couple of weeks to the middle of July. Dill can be frozen when at its best stage for pickling (just before the flowers open) and used when needed; or the seeds can be dried when it matures. But the most distinctive dill flavor in pickles results when the dill flowers are picked fresh from the garden.

Some good vegetable combinations that you might want to grow for preserving together are tiny *peas* and *onions*, *corn* and *limas* (succotash), *tomatoes* and *celery*, *zucchini* and *eggplant*, with a variety of fresh herbs, such as basil

TABLE B FROST-HARDY VEGETABLES	
All root crops	Kale
Broccoli	Lettuce
Brussels sprouts	Parsley
Cabbage	Spinach
Cauliflower	Swiss chard
Celery	

Hardy Swiss chard can be harvested even after several frosts.

and oregano. For bread and butter pickles, you will need *onions* and *cucumbers;* for relishes *red* and *green peppers* and *onions* are needed together. Sweet *red* peppers are mature *green* peppers; and in order to have red and green at the same time allow all the peppers on a few of your plants to mature to the red stage, while picking green peppers as needed from the other plants. Your family may prefer other vegetable and herb combinations, so plan your garden with these in mind.

Holding Vegetables

What should you do if you buy or pick vegetables in bulk and can't preserve them immediately? Unless they are kept cold and moist, they will lose both taste and nutrients within a few hours. If you must hold vegetables, we recommend that they be washed quickly in cold water, drained, put in large plastic bags and kept in the refrigerator. Do not cut or peel them, as this hastens the loss of nutrients. Stored in this manner they should be good for one or two days, and in the case of root crops and cabbage, considerably longer. But please, for good quality, preserve your vegetables *as soon after picking as possible.*

Most fruits will keep for a while, but if they are ripe they should be kept cold until you can use them. Raspberries and other soft fruits which deteriorate rapidly must be handled gently and quickly, and preserved immediately.

Hints

Here are several hints that apply to all aspects of preserving:

1. Plan to have the right kind and amount of *equipment* ready before you start. You will need to have on hand enough jars and lids for canning, bags or containers for freezing. You will find lists of other necessary equipment for each preserving method in later chapters.

2. Always *label* your canned and frozen foods with the date, product, variety and method or recipe used. The date is important because food should be eaten within one year of processing to insure good quality. And unless you can see through the container, you'll also want to specify the contents. Nothing is more frustrating than opening dozens of food containers in a freezer in order to find the right box.

Labelling the variety will prevent you from planting an unpopular vegetable next year. If in the spring you are faced with dozens of containers of uneaten, frozen summer squash, you will realize it's not a family favorite.

3. Also *note the recipe* used for pickles and relishes and vegetable combinations so you can repeat your successes next year.

Chapter 2
Freezing — Or The Lazy Way

We simply can't imagine preserving without freezing. There are no two ways about it. Freezing is easy, fast, holds color, flavor and nutrients, is suited to more foods than canning, is safe and convenient—and is expensive in relation to other methods. Bear in mind, however, that the cost is variable, based on full or partially full operation, cost of containers, electric rates, turnover rate, and whether or not you grow your own produce.

We started with an upright, manual defrost freezer the first year that our garden was REALLY BIG. We haven't stopped appreciating it yet. Not only does it allow time to enjoy summer, which is all too short in the northern states, but also it is a convenience all year long. It holds extra pies and baked goods, leftovers, meat specials and holiday cooking. Casseroles can be frozen using oven-proof dishes lined with aluminum foil. (After it has frozen, remove the dish. Replace it when you are ready to heat the casserole.) Our freezer proves itself every time we have a cheese cake dotted with extra-large "fresh" strawberries straight from the freezer or corn in mid-winter that tastes just picked.

We have had problems of our own making. Once the freezer came unplugged by accident, ruining our early summer, frozen fruit. I cried, plugged in the freezer, cleaned up the mess and bought a screw-in plug (more later). Even with that problem, plus the expense that perhaps makes a freezer a luxury, we would never forsake it. This is not to suggest that other methods aren't good too. We make pickles, can fruit, make relishes, jams and jellies, cold store and dry food, but the freezer is the backbone of our home storage.

Maybe because of laziness the idea of washing fruit, packaging and putting it in the freezer appeals. Then there is time for a swim with the children. But, like everything else, not all of it is that simple. There are rules as with all the other methods.

What Kind of Freezer to Buy?

Most of us have a freezer section in our refrigerator. If it is within the refrigerator itself, it is too warm for anything except short-term holding.

A separate door is one step better but still not adequate for long-term storage. To insure good quality, a freezer should maintain a minimum of 0° F. For each 10° above zero, the storage life of your food will be cut in half. Keep your freezer compartment for quick-rotation foods such as ice cream and popsicles. This will save on the constant "in and out" that makes running a freezer more expensive and defrosting such a problem.

UPRIGHT

An upright freezer, which generally comes in models rated at 16 and 21 cubic feet, is easier than a chest type to find things in and takes up less floor space. On the other hand, cold spills out each time it is opened, making it slightly more costly to run. Use containers that stack well, since odd-shaped packages tend to fall out.

CHEST

With the chest freezer, unlike the upright, the cold settles in when the lid is opened. Chest freezers do take up more floor space and are considerably harder to locate packages in, but the lid can provide counter space if the freezer is conveniently located. Chest freezers come in 15, 20, and 25 cubic foot models.

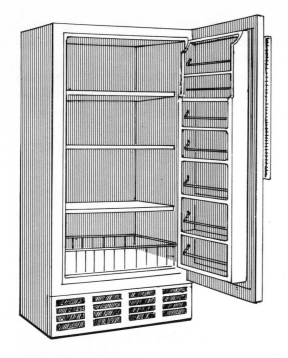

Upright freezer. Each shelf contains freezing coils on which food is placed. The inside of the door is used for frozen juices and other smaller packages.

MANUAL DEFROST

We can't say enough for a manual defrost. The expense of running one is significantly less than the automatic, frost-free models. A frost-free motor must turn on periodically to chill off the freezer each time the defrost mechanism finishes. With a manual, *you* are the defrost mechanism. We may be lazy, but not too lazy to defrost a freezer once a year. It's easy. Wait for a cold day late in the late winter when the freezer stock is low. Then you can turn the freezer down as cold as possible overnight so the food is as cold as possible. The next day turn off the freezer, unload the contents and place them out-of-doors, open the freezer door, and turn on a fan in the interior or put pans of hot water inside. I scrape with a blunt instrument, preferably the kind that comes with a refrigerator or freezer.

Frost need not build up to defrosting levels more than once a year *if* care is used. A half inch of frost indicates defrosting time. Do the defrosting before you start your summer freezing.

Wrapping frozen packages in newspaper and covering them with a blanket or sleeping bag will keep the food frozen even indoors during defrost. After defrosting, wash the interior with warm water and baking soda and wipe dry before reloading.

AUTOMATIC DEFROST

All we can say is that your freezer should be shut down once a year anyway to be cleaned.

FEATURES TO LOOK FOR

Either type of freezer should have *controls* so that temperatures can be regulated. A minimum high for quality is 0° F. For the best quality, freezers should be adjustable to −20° F. for a quick initial freeze that helps prevent large ice crystals.

Some freezers have a special *quick-freeze area.* If not, put packages to be frozen directly over the coils. A refrigerator-freezer *thermometer* is an asset, so you can quickly check your freezer's calibration.

Any freezer should have a *key* (or two or three, in case you lose keys). It's frustrating not to be able to get into your freezer.

Chest freezer. This cut-away view shows the freezing coils in the walls. These coils are on all four sides of the freezer. Wire racks roll on tracks for easier access to lower level. Freezers range in size from 10 cubic feet to 22 cubic feet capacity.

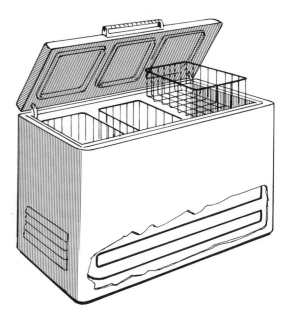

Buy a *screw-in plug,* a very minor investment that may save you countless dollars in goods. It simply keeps a plug from being pulled out accidentally.

HINTS ON USING YOUR FREEZER WISELY

Freeze realistically. Don't freeze more of anything than you can use in one year. If you know it will only be thrown away the following summer, resist the temptation to freeze several more cartons of zucchini just because it's there. Too many other things could have taken its place.

Try moving a week's supply of food from your big freezer to your freezer-refrigerator. It will keep frost build-up to a minimum.

KEEPING TRACK

To get the most value and enjoyment out of your frozen foods you have to know just what's left in store. Chest-type freezers especially defy a storage system which allows useful visual checking. And just as the new year's strawberries are ripening, you'll find a forgotten store of the frozen berries you thought had long been used up.

The only answer is an **inventory checklist,** posted by the freezer or in the kitchen. Draft it up on a large cardboard from the totals you kept while freezing.

Down the lefthand side list alphabetically by name all the fruits and vegetables you froze—meat cuts too if you wish. To the right of each food provide a square to mark off a package each time you use it. In the first square write the total you start with.

You'll need as many squares as the largest number of packages of any of the foods you froze. For instance, if you put up 40 pints of kernel corn the figure "40" goes in the first square and there are 39 squares following to be filled as you use it up.

This way you can always tell what's left of any food. You won't end up with nothing but spinach—and you won't be forgetting those strawberries.

Some people use a similar but extended chart which records the freezing, too, the build-up of inventory for each vegetable and fruit from zero. Finally the harvest and freezing are over for each item, and the squares show declining numbers as the freezer slowly empties.

If possible, you should have a full freezer at all times. The operating cost of a freezer is less at ¾ full than at ¾ empty. We heard of one woman who stuffed a sleeping bag in a ¼ full freezer so that it would operate at maximum efficiency.

Test-freeze a food that you have never frozen before to make certain you are satisfied with the quality. This will not, however, indicate its keeping ability.

HOW BIG A FREEZER FOR YOUR FAMILY?

Never, never underbuy. The cost of replacing a too-small freezer or adding a second one is excessive. Rent a freezer locker the first year to discover how much space you will need, or go by this formula:

> 3-4 cubic feet of vegetables per person:
> four-person family: 4 × 4 equals 16 cubic feet
> six-person family: 4 × 6 equals 24 cubic feet

If you raise your own meat or buy on special, allow at least six cubic feet per person. It seems wiser to buy a freezer slightly larger than you think you may need, as you are certain to find a use for the extra space.

Packaging

There is more room for flexibility in packaging for a freezer than in canning, but for maximum quality, certain criteria must be met.

Packages should be proof against air, moisture and vapor. The seal should prevent odors from being absorbed from the freezer into the food. *Freezer burn,* a condition caused by exposure to the dry air of the freezer that causes a loss of moisture, can be prevented by a good seal.

Gear your packaging sizes to family size. Pick the container size that will make one-meal servings.

Rigid containers. This means either glass jars, plastic boxes or wax-coated cardboard containers. The glass jars should be especially

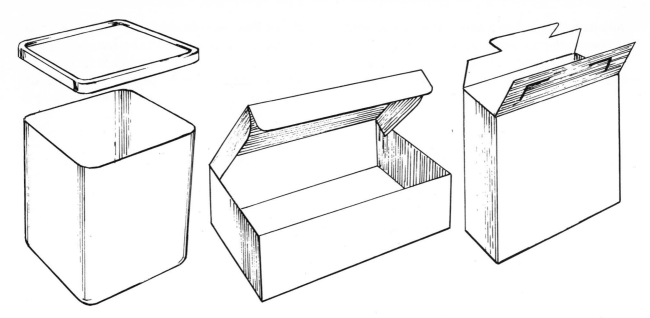

Freezer containers. The one at left is plastic with a snap-on lid and can be used for freezing anything. The center and right ones are made of plastic-coated cardboard and can be reused, but they wear out quickly. These should be used with plastic freezer bags as liners and the lids should be closed firmly with freezer tape. All come in ½ pint, pint, quart, and 2-quart sizes.

designated as appropriate for a freezer — with flared or straight sides to get out unthawed food. Always leave the recommended head space when freezing in jars. Without it they will break when the food expands during freezing. To speed the thawing of food in glass containers, put the cold jars in cold water—never hot water.

Plastic containers stack better in the freezer and store compactly when empty. They are a substantial initial investment but are handy also for storing leftovers in the refrigerator and are reuseable. Plastic-coated containers are not re-useable in the freezer. Headroom is marked on the plastic containers.

Flexible bags. These are not reuseable, as are most rigid containers, but the initial investment is much less. They are awkward to store compactly in the freezer. They will retain a more rigid form, however, when used in conjunction with reuseable boxes. Put the food in the bag, using the box as a form. Force excess air out of the bag and close with a twist tie. Freeze in the box until the package is solid. Then you can remove the box, allowing it to be used again—though if left on, the box protects the bag from tears. Label.

Never put hot food into the bags, and be especially careful to get the appropriate heavy-duty bags. They come in pint, quart, two-quart, one-gallon and two-gallon sizes. Special funnels and racks for easy filling are available.

Boil-in bags. This is a relative newcomer to the frozen food packaging field and is a luxury convenience. Special bags are filled and heat-

Appropriate freeze bags can be fitted into freeze containers. When frozen, the bag will have a rectangular shape, which makes storage easier. Then you can remove the bag and use the box again. Don't forget to label.

sealed with a sealer mechanism and then frozen. The food is heated in the bags in boiling water. There is less nutrient loss in the food because it comes in contact with water only during blanching before freezing.

Some people have experienced uneven cooking with these bags, but they are excellent for vegetables such as corn on the cob or for vegetables frozen in a sauce or with butter.

Improvised containers. Let your imagination loose and improvise. Just remember to get a good seal with pressure-sensitive tape. Scotch tape and masking tape won't do, as their stickiness releases in the cold. You can use plastic cottage cheese, ice cream, and margarine containers, reinforced with tape, but the quality

Improvise freeze containers if you wish. Just make sure they have a moisture-vapor-odor-proof seal. Seal reused containers with freezer tape. You can use canning jars if the manufacturer so specifies.

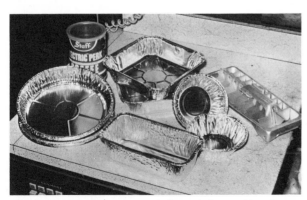
Use and re-use aluminum foil containers. Use freeze wrap and seal with freezer tape. Use coffee cans for freezing cookies. Freeze baby food in ice cube trays. Put frozen cubes in freeze containers when solid.

may not be so good as with conventional freeze containers. Freeze cookies in coffee cans. Freeze fresh fish in ice in waxed milk cartons. Put homemade baby food or puree in ice cube trays until frozen, and then place the frozen cubes in freezer bags for easy access.

Freeze wrap. To insure freshness, use the special papers and plastic wraps which are indispensable in wrapping meats, pies, bread. Seal with freezer tape. Wax paper and aluminum foil will account for a deterioration in quality.

Labeling Containers

Using an *indelible marking pen*, label with the variety, date and any other pertinent information. Keep an accurate inventory chart so you will know what is in the freezer. If you have ever been in a hurry when you froze, neglected to label, and later stood in front of your open freezer trying to find that one special package, you'll understand. Labeling becomes crucial if you've used opaque packaging. See-through plastic box lids are no substitute for labeling. Spinach looks like broccoli!

The *date* is especially important, since shelf life in freezing is more complicated than in canning. Following is a chart for shelf life. Note that the keeping quality of fruits and vegetables varies greatly.

SHELF LIFE: FREEZER STORAGE TIME

Recommended Length of Time at 0° F.

Fruits, citrus	3-4 months
Fruits, other	12 months
Vegetables (except onions)	12 months
Onions	3-6 months
Corn on cob	8-10 months
Mushrooms	8-10 months

Nothing should stay in your freezer for more than one year. If it does, you are using your freezer space unwisely.

Be sure to label your produce, whether it's for the freezer or for the shelf. Include the date, too, so you can use your stored food within the year.

What to Do
If the Power Fails

When the power fails, *don't* open the freezer door. Resist the temptation to peek. A closed freezer will keep food frozen for two days if full, for one day if half full. In most cases the power will return before then. If not, keep the freezer covered with blankets. If available, put in 25 pounds of dry ice on cardboard (using gloves), or move your frozen food to a food locker or a friend's freezer, first wrapping it carefully.

If the food has started to thaw before the power returns, what can you refreeze? *Refreeze only those foods that still have ice crystals.* This will be food at a temperature of 40° or below. Look at and feel the food. Food with no ice crystals is said to be defrosted and should not be refrozen—with the exception of bread. If fruit is still cold, however, it can be refrozen with a marked decrease in quality. Label it again and use it first.

Bacteria that cause spoilage in food are not destroyed by freezing—only kept inactive as long as the food is stored at 0° F. Should the food thaw, the bacteria will start to grow and food poisoning is possible. You should throw the food away.

If the freezer itself fails, check your warranty as many will cover a certain portion of your food loss.

DRY ICE

For years home freezer owners have been advised if all else fails to pack chunks of dry ice into their freezers. Fifty pounds of it should hold an average freezer load of food at zero for 36 hours.

The problem is where to find the dry ice, which is solid carbon dioxide that melts (turns to gas) at **minus** 110 degrees F.

In case of a prolonged power failure or non-functioning freezer, dry ice might be the best remedy, so locating a source ahead of time is a good idea. Most often it is used by ice cream manufacturers and medical laboratories.

Handle dry ice **very carefully**—with thick gloves. Its extremely low temperature will damage bare skin instantly.

What to Freeze

If you have all the preserving options available, freezing will be only part of your food storage plan. You should freeze only what freezes best. Potatoes will cold cellar, tomatoes and relishes will can , apples will dry, while the bulk of your vegetables, fruits, and all your meat will freeze.

But if your freezer is small, you will have to be even more selective. Pick only things that definitely have an edge on quality when frozen.

Applesauce is as good canned and quicker to use on short notice, but you would definitely freeze strawberries. Broccoli, Brussels sprouts, and cauliflower discolor and become stronger in flavor when canned, so freeze them. On the other hand, beets change texture when frozen, and radishes, lettuce and green onions just don't freeze. Be selective and think out your priorities.

For variety in preparation of beans, try French-style. Use the slotted end of a peeler, pressing beans through lengthwise.

Once you have decided on your choices, choose your varieties. Check seed packages and seed catalogues for the varieties that freeze better than others. For instance, Freezonia peas are especially adapted for freezing.

How to Freeze

1. Select only prime quality produce. Only the best is good enough, and freezing won't improve the quality. Process vegetables as quickly as possible. Freeze fruit only when you would eat it fresh, when the flavor is matured completely.

2. Use the most sanitary conditions and equipment.

3. Organize your equipment and work area, as well as your time. Although freezing takes far less time and equipment than canning, you don't want to be interrupted by a last-minute trip to the store.

4. Sort for uniform size, as this makes for better appearance and consistent blanching and cooking.

5. Prepare as for fresh cooking. Wash or scrub thoroughly. Peal and/or slice as needed. Blanch (steam) or scald vegetables and cool them quickly in ice water. (Blanching times are given in specific instructions.) Use an ascorbic acid preparation to prevent discoloration, if desired (see more about this later).

6. Fruits can be packed with or without sugar or in a sugar syrup.

7. Package promptly, expelling as much air as possible from the container. Allow headspace since foods expand, but leave as few air

pockets as possible. A dry pack needs no headroom.

8. Label and place in your freezer's "cold zone" for as quick a freeze as possible. Don't put more than one layer and be sure that the packages are not touching each other. Your freezer should be filled with no more than it can freeze solid in 24 hours—about two to three pounds per cubic feet of freezer capacity.

9. To use vegetables, don't first defrost. The vegetables already are partially cooked, so they need only be cooked a short time or until tender. Add a ½-inch of water, cover and boil. Fruits don't need to be defrosted completely. A few ice crystals will prevent the fruit from becoming limp. For more information on freezing fruits refer to Chapter 5.

Freezing Fruit

Few items are as easy to preserve or as rewarding in quality as fruit. And almost all fruits are suitable for freezing. The requirements and rules are simple.

Pick or process *small quantities.* The first time we picked at a local farm we developed a temporary loathing for strawberries after doing dozens of quarts at one time.

All fruit should be *ripe* when preserved, as opposed to vegetables which are at their best slightly immature. (This is because the sugar in vegetables turns quickly to starch as they ripen while the starch in fruit breaks down into sugar. The sugar is what pleases the palate.)

A mellow flavor in peaches, plums, figs and some berries is acquired by letting them sit at room temperature to mature overnight. Apples may require several days to develop maximum flavor. Pears usually are picked green and allowed to ripen in the dark for several days.

All fruit should be sorted for uniformity to make an attractive product. Slightly bruised or overripe fruit makes excellent jelly. Freeze only those fruits that you would want to eat fresh.

FREEZING STRAWBERRIES

1. Sort and wash ripe, red strawberries.

2. Remove hulls and green spots. Wash again.

3. For sugar pack, add ¾ cup sugar to 1 quart of fruit.

18

4. Mix thoroughly.

5. Pack into containers, leaving ½ inch headroom. Seal, label, and freeze.

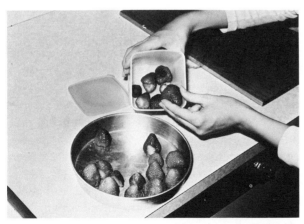

6. For whole, perfect strawberries, flash freeze on a metal sheet. Transfer when solid to freeze containers.

Prepare fruits much as you would for the table. (Consult the individual directions for each kind.) Wash the fruit *gently* in *cool* water to minimize damage. Don't let fruits soak in the water, or they become waterlogged.

Many fruits darken quickly when they are peeled, especially peaches and apples, so you may want to use an anti-oxidant. This is provided by ascorbic acid (Vitamin C) which comes as tablets or crystals, available at drug stores. The crystalline form is easier to use. Dissolve the powder in cold water according to directions:

In syrup pack: add the dissolved ascorbic acid to the syrup before adding it to the fruit.

In sugar pack: before adding sugar, sprinkle the ascorbic acid solution over the fruit.

In unsweetened pack: sprinkle the ascorbic acid solution over the fruit and mix before packaging.

ASCORBIC ACID POWDERS

"Fruit Fresh" ascorbic acid powders are made of ascorbic acid, sugar and silica aerogel. Directions simply require sprinkling the granular powder over the fruit before packaging. These powders are very convenient but not quite as effective as ascorbic acid solutions. Lemon juice is a simple substitute for the two commercial agents but is not quite as effective and lends a lemony flavor to fruit.

SUGAR: TO USE OR NOT?

Fruits can be packed several ways, depending on their eventual use. Adding sugar helps to hold the color and bring out the flavor, but if you are trying to cut down your consumption of refined sugar it can be left out or other natural sweeteners such as honey can be tried. A syrup pack often is used for desserts or fresh use, while a dry or unsweetened pack is generally used for cooking, as in pies or jellies. Sugar syrups can be made of any density, but a 40 percent syrup generally is recommended. It is made up of three cups sugar to four cups water, yielding 5½ cups. Dissolve the sugar in either hot or cold water

19

and use the syrup cold. It can be made ahead of time and stored in the refrigerator. Sour fruits may take a heavier syrup while mild-flavored fruits need a lighter syrup. (See chart.)

SYRUPS FOR USE IN FREEZING FRUITS

Type of Syrup	Sugar (in cups)	Water (in cups)	Yield of Syrup (in cups)
30% (thin)	2	4	5
40% (medium)	3	4	5½
50% (heavy)	4¾	4	6½
60% (extra heavy)	7	4	7¾

OTHER SYRUPS

Sugar syrups also can be made by dissolving the sugar, using the same amounts as above, in fruit juice extracted from less perfect fruit. The flavor will be superior to a sugar and water syrup. Honey or corn syrup can be substituted for the sugar in either water or juice. If you replace only a quarter of the sugar with an alternative sweetener there will be little flavor change. Above that the difference will be more noticeable. Experiment!

Cover the fruit completely with syrup. Most fruits will float, so crumple wax paper and place

HEADROOM IN FREEZING FRUITS AND VEGETABLES

Dry pack:
For straight-sided or flaired containers:
    Pints: ½ inch   Quarts: ½ inch

For regular mouth:
    Pints: 1 inch   Quarts: 1 inch

For wide mouth: with shoulder:
    Pints: ¾ inch   Quarts: 1 inch

Syrup, puree or liquid:
For straight-sided or flaired containers:
    Pints: ½ inch   Quarts: 1 inch

For regular mouth:
    Pints: 1½ inch   Quarts: 1½ inch

For wide mouth with shoulder:
    Pints: 1 inch   Quarts: 1½ inch

it between the top of the syrup and the lid, to keep the fruit below the surface during freezing. Remove the wax paper when thawing the fruit for use.

An unsweetened pack calls for cutting and washing the fruit, draining, and putting it directly into containers or covering it with ascorbic acid solution or the fruit's own juices.

Dry or sugar pack refers to sprinkling sugar over the fruit and mixing *gently*. Then it can be left for several hours to draw out a syrup.

Flash freezing is reserved for super-quality fruits. Wash extra large, perfect fruits, drain *well* and place them on a metal sheet, separated from each other. Place the sheet in the coldest area of the freezer until solid. Then package in rigid containers. Used semi-thawed, they will retain their shape. The fruit will separate easily in case you need only a few at a time. They make excellent decorations for cakes and pies.

Most fruits are best packed in rigid containers so that the shape is retained. Seal, label and freeze.

Avoid iron utensils which may darken fruits, using stainless steel or enamel ware instead.

Don't overlook buying already-frozen fruits from local stores that sell in large quantity containers. They can be canned in smaller quantities or broken apart (such as blueberries) and frozen in more convenient-sized portions. These stores often offer good buys, too, on citrus fruits sold fresh by the case.

Freezing Vegetables

If you have ever bought fresh green beans from the supermarket in mid-winter and then compared them with your own frozen green beans, the merits of freezing should be obvious. Using the proper procedure, there is no comparison in quality. Following are general directions for freezing vegetables. For specific details on each vegetable refer to Chapter 4.

First, check the seed catalogues and seed packages to be sure you have chosen a variety that freezes well.

Second, pick only the tender, young vegetables ready for table use or even slightly

FREEZING CORN

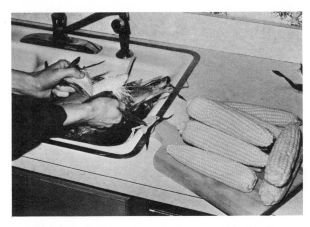

1. Husk corn and remove silk from strictly fresh ears. Process quickly.

4. For corn-on-the-cob, pack into freeze bags after blanching and cooling, expelling as much air as possible. Seal, label, and freeze.

2. For whole-kernel corn, blanch for 4 minutes in boiling water. For corn-on-the-cob, blanch small ears 7 minutes, medium ears 9 minutes, and large ears 11 minutes.

5. For whole-kernel corn, cut kernels from the cob at about ⅔ their depth.

3. Cool immediately in cold water. Drain well.

6. Pack into containers, leaving ½ inch headroom. Seal, label, and freeze.

younger. Nothing but the best is worth freezing. If you must pick or buy before you are ready to freeze, put the vegetables in the refrigerator or spread them out in a well-ventilated area.

Third, wash the vegetables thoroughly by rinsing, repeatedly if necessary, and using a vegetable brush, one of the indispensible kitchen gadgets. Lift the vegetables out of the water rather than draining out the water, which allows the dirt to settle back on them. Don't let them soak so long that they become waterlogged. Sort according to size and keep only the best. Generally, prepare the vegetables as you would for table use.

Fourth comes *blanching*. This always produces puzzled looks among novices, but it's really simple and essential. It means scalding the vegetables either by steaming or by immersing them in boiling water, the easier method.

Blanching sets color and stops the action of the enzymes which otherwise will continue to mature the vegetables in color and flavor beyond the optimum. Blanching also helps to retain vitamins. Consult the specific instructions for blanching times, as they vary from vegetable to vegetable. Only peppers and herbs do not require blanching.

In a large kettle bring one gallon of water to a rolling boil. Prepare no more than one pound of vegetables at a time. Put the vegetables in a wire basket or other device which will allow all the vegetables to be removed at the same time—to avoid overcooking. Count your processing time from the *return* of the rolling boil.

SOME THAWING-COOKING TIPS

Frozen bread, muffins, cakes and waffles can go from the freezer right to the warming oven or toaster, *McCall's* Magazine advises. Fruits also, that will go into preserves or cooked sauces, can be used frozen, and of course frozen vegetables usually are cooked that way.

When it comes to meats and poultry it's best to thaw them slowly in the refrigerator, though big birds or thick roasts may be cooked frozen, allowing 15 to 20 minutes extra cooking time per pound. Give frozen fish extra cooking time and steaks about 15 minutes extra per side.

FREEZING ASPARAGUS

1. Wash by scrubbing with a vegetable brush to remove any sand.

2. Cut off tough ends or snap at the brittle point. Cut into pieces or sort spears.

3. Blanch for 2-4 minutes in boiling water, depending on size.

4. Cool immediately in cold water. Drain.

5. Pack in containers, leaving no headroom. For spears, alternate tips and ends unless you are using wide-mouth containers, in which case you put tips down. Seal, label, and freeze.

MUSH

Have you been plagued some years with fine-looking frozen snap beans that turned out mushy when used? We've traced it back to two errors. The basic mistake was trying to blanch too many beans at once, with the result that the re-boil was slow and the beans were over-blanched. Then, too, we found we weren't, in these large batches, chilling them fast enough or long enough. This year they're crisp and delicious.

To steam, use a blancher or *steamer*, a kettle with a perforated insert that can hold the vegetables *above* the water. Put two to three inches of water in the bottom and bring to a boil. Put the vegetables in the insert and lower it into place. Start timing when steam appears after you have replaced the lid. Don't steam large amounts at one time. When steaming add two to three minutes to the recommended blanching times.

Remember: when giving the vegetables a final cooking for the table, the steaming and blanching have already partially precooked them.

Burns. Never underestimate the hazard of burns whenever working around a stove, and especially if you have small children. Canning and blanching both require large kettles of boiling water. Take precautions and always have first aid remedies and know-how nearby in case of an accident.

Cooling. One secret to good, crisp vegetables is *prompt cooling* to stop the cooking process. Prepare plenty of ice in advance if you plan to do a lot of freezing. Fill the sink with ice water and put the hot, drained vegetables in, swishing them around. The cooling will take approximately as long as the blanching did, but don't let them soak.

Drain the vegetables as completely as possible, even rolling them gently in towels if necessary. Proper drainage will prevent the formation of large ice crystals.

All of this requires the timing of a juggler, as there usually are vegetables being cut, blanched, cooled and packed at approximately the same time. Allow space and time, and be organized. Have help if possible. Children can help by cutting beans or shelling peas. Make it an assembly-line process.

Freezing. Put vegetables in freezer containers, allowing appropriate headroom. Vegetables expand very little after cooling, so pack firmly but not tightly. Seal and label. Put the containers in the quick-freeze area in a single layer so that they are not touching each other until frozen solid in 24 hours.

APPROXIMATE YIELD

OF FROZEN VEGETABLES FROM FRESH

Vegetable	Fresh, as Purchased or Picked	Frozen
Asparagus	1 crate (12 2-lb. bunches)	15 to 22 pt.
	1 to 1½ lb.	1 pt.
Beans, lima (in pods)	1 bu. (32 lb.)	12 to 16 pt.
	2 to 2½ lb.	1 pt.
Beans, snap, green, and wax	1 bu. (30 lb.)	30 to 45 pt.
	⅔ to 1 lb.	1 pt.
Beet greens	15 lb.	10 to 15 pt.
	1 to 1½ lb.	1 pt.
Beets (without tops)	1 bu. (52 lb.)	35 to 42 pt.
	1¼ to 1½ lb.	1 pt.
Broccoli	1 crate (25 lb.)	24 pt.
	1 lb.	1 pt.
Brussels sprouts	4 quart boxes	6 pt.
	1 lb.	1 pt.
Carrots (without tops)	1 bu. (50 lb.)	32 to 40 pt.
	1¼ to 1½ lb.	1 pt.
Cauliflower	2 medium heads	3 pt.
	1⅓ lb.	1 pt.
Chard	1 bu. (12 lb.)	8 to 12 pt.
	1 to 1½ lb.	1 pt.
Collards	1 bu. (12 lb.)	8 to 12 pt.
	1 to 1½ lb.	1 pt.
Corn, sweet (in husks)	1 bu. (35 lb.)	14 to 17 pt.
	2 to 2½ lb.	1 pt.
Kale	1 bu. (18 lb.)	12 to 18 pt.
	1 to 1½ lb.	1 pt.
Mustard greens	1 bu. (12 lb.)	8 to 12 pt.
	1 to 1½ lb.	1 pt.
Peas (in pods)	1 bu. (30 lb.)	12 to 15 pt.
	2 to 2½ lb.	1 pt.
Peppers, sweet	⅔ lb. (3 peppers)	1 pt.
Pumpkin	3 lb.	2 pt.
Spinach	1 bu. (18 lb.)	12 to 18 pt.
	1 to 1½ lb.	1 pt.
Squash, summer	1 bu. (40 lb.)	42 to 40 pt.
	1 to 1¼ lb.	1 pt.
Squash, winter	3 lb.	2 pt.
Sweet potatoes	⅔ lb.	1 pt.

Cooking. To cook, remove the vegetables from the freezer. Place about ½ inch of boiling water in a saucepan. Add the vegetables, cover and count the cooking time from the return of the rolling boil. Don't overcook. Remember they have been partially precooked. Save the water for soups and stews. That's where most of the vitamins are.

Also try oven-cooking frozen vegetables. Place them frozen in a covered dish with a little (about 1 tablespoon) water, with butter and seasonings if desired. Cook at 325° until tender (about 10 to 20 minutes depending on the vegetable).

TIMED CONSUMPTION

Most people freeze their year's supply of each vegetable within a week or two of the harvest peak. Thus every carton of peas and every pack of corn is likely to be about the same age, and there's not much point in trying to date each container and use the oldest first.

But if you freeze some crops, such as broccoli, over several months, or early and late crops of snap beans, it's a good idea to separate the batches so you can use the first-frozen items first.

Under proper conditions and packaging most vegetables keep well for a full year or more, but there is appreciable and steady deterioration of flavor and nutrition. In a general way, then, it is better to concentrate on your frozen peas and spinach in late fall, saving most of the late-frozen corn, lima beans and the like for later.

SAVING HERBS

Sure, dry some of your herbs—but don't stop there. Try some of the many other methods that can be used to catch their flavors.

Freezing them is one of the easiest and most satisfactory. Wash them well, then spread them out until they are dry and wilted. This may take several hours. Cut or chop them into the form you want them for cooking, pack them in jars and freeze. With most herbs, flavor and color are preserved. Try this first with chives and parsley, then move on to others.

Herb butters, too, can be made when herbs are most plentiful, and frozen for later use. They are handy for adding flavor to vegetables as well as for the more conventional use with bread and rolls. Chop herbs very fine, then mix with butter or margarine on a ratio of one part herbs—to two or three parts margarine, depending on your taste. Tarragon, chives, parsley and rosemary are some to try, and combinations are recommended as you become more familiar with them.

The herbs and margarine should be blended with a fork, then left in your refrigerator for a few days, to permit the flavor to spread through the margarine. Then pack it for freezing. The plastic bowls some margarine is sold in are handy for this.

Most satisfactory, of course, is not to store herbs, but to have them fresh and ready for use. Every kitchen should have a pot or two or three of herbs. Ideally, start them outside in summer, then pot them up before the first frosts. The bigger the pot, the more productive will be the herbs. For starters, try parsley, chives and basil. Give them as much sunshine as possible, keep them cut back regularly and water them and they will reward you with a constant supply of goodness.

Chapter 3 Canning

Home-canned vegetables are just as good as store-bought ones, and perhaps better when you have grown them yourself and know exactly how they have been handled and what types of pesticides and fertilizers have (or have not) been used on them. Canned foods have an advantage over frozen in that they require no expensive equipment to keep them — just a shelf in a cool, dark, dry place.

The first time that we made yeast bread it was with much hesitation and faltering, stopping constantly to read and reread what seemed endlessly complicated directions. Now we breeze through, yet without skimping on accuracy.

The same is true with canning. The first time it was time-consuming, frustrating and a little frightening, but now we do it with confidence and skill. So read through the following instructions and cautions carefully; then proceed. You will find few more gratifying sights that the rows of sparkling jars of tomatoes, pickles, relishes, vegetables and fruits.

Good planning is the secret to rewarding and satisfying canning. Be prepared with *all* the necessary utensils, ingredients and information. Set aside more than enough time so that you don't have to cut corners on processing times. Clear a large surface since canning takes space. Then organize before starting.

Jars

Jars are the canner's stock in trade. They are an investment that will repay you in the years ahead. But jars seem to come in a multitude of confusing sizes and shapes.

MASON JARS

First, let's settle the word *Mason*. John L. Mason invented the first practical canning jar in 1858. Mason jars, as such, are no longer manufactured but all such canning jars now are called Mason, denoting a type rather than a manufacturer.

Most processing times specify using pint or quart jars. They are easiest to find and seem to fit most families' needs. They come with either a wide or regular mouth. Wide mouths are easier to fill but cost slightly more than regular mouth jars. Definitely use wide mouths if you freeze in jars, so that the contents will come out before thawing.

Jars also are available in ½ pints and ½ gallons. The processing time for ½ pints is the same as that for pints. The ½ pint is ideal for jellies and relishes that are used only in small quantities. Many come with decorative lids and molded designs on the sides. They make attractive gifts of a practical size. These have seals, so paraffin is unnecessary. However, you can improvise jelly jars out of any appropriate jar and seal it with paraffin.

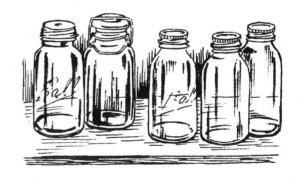

Half gallons are for large families, but they have several drawbacks. Processing times are difficult to find for ½ gallons, and dense, low-acid foods don't process adequately due to the bulk. In addition, most water bath canners are not tall enough to handle ½ gallons. If you do use them for high-acid foods in a boiling water bath, a rule of thumb is to add 10 minutes to the time required for quarts.

Canadian canning jars are available in many northern states. They come in conventional American size pints and quarts, and their lids are interchangeable with American regular mouth jars. The jars are squarish, which makes storage and stacking easy.

Anchor Hocking has recently marketed canning jars which have slightly different directions for the use of their lids. Read each manufacturer's directions carefully for slight variations.

USING TWO-PIECE LIDS

The method of using these lids, which are made by different manufacturers, is pretty much the same, but to be sure, always read the directions that come with them.

Wash the lids and screw bands in hot, soapy water, rinse, place in a pan and cover with boiling water. Do not actually place them on the stove to boil, as this would damage the sealing compound.

When the jars have been filled with foods, remove air bubbles by running a rubber spatula or knife carefully around inside the jar. Wipe off the top of the jar to be sure no specks of food will catch between the sealing compound and the glass, then screw the band on tight. The jar is now ready to be processed.

NEW TYPES OF LIDS

The shortage of canning lids in 1974 and 1975 brought a flood of new types of lids on the market — both two-piece and one-piece types, and all with rubber sealing compound.

When buying any of these, try out a few before making a big investment, since they all have not been thoroughly tested, and our experience with some has been unsatisfactory. Follow the manufacturer's directions, and avoid using those that come with none.

BAILS AND GLASS LIDS

Bail-wire-clamp or "lighting" jars are still used for canning. They have glass lids under which a rubber ring is placed to create a seal. When processing instructions say "complete seal if necessary," this is one type of jar to which they refer. After fitting the rubber ring and glass lid, put the longer of the two clamps into the slot of the lid and process the jar. Immediately *after* processing, press the second wire clamp down, thus completing the seal. To check for a good seal of wire-clamp jars, tip them over after cooling and check for leakage or air bubbles. Either is the sign of a poor seal.

USED CANNING JARS

If you are lucky enough to have found old canning jars in a family attic or a flea market, you may own valuable collector's items or some practical canning jars. Make sure which they are before canning. The blue glass jars are especially valuable, selling for prices that would have made your grandmother blush.

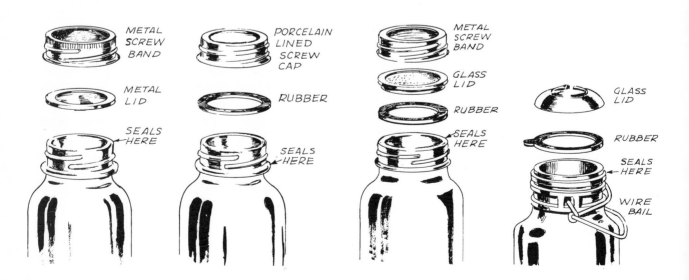

Carefully wash all jars, rings, lids, and screw bands in hot soapy water before using them in any method of food preservation.

Test the jars by running your finger around the lip. If there are any cracks or flaws, the jars are *not* up to canning standards and will not seal. However, don't throw them away if the bail clamp is sprung or loose. New bail clamps are available. Many old jars are still around for which lids are no longer being made. Don't improvise for canning. They make lovely canisters or can be used for jelly jars.

Standard Mason screw-top jars can also be used with porcelain-lined zinc cap under which a rubber ring is placed. The caps are unusual in that they can be used repeatedly if boiled for 15 minutes before reuse. However, you must always use new rubber rings. Wash the caps and new rubbers in hot, soapy water. Rinse. Keep the rubber rings wet until used.

EARLY CANNERS

In France, way back in 1806, Francois and Nicholas Appert (the latter famed also for his work in prison reform) developed methods of storing foods for up to a year in hermetically sealed containers. Initially they heated foods for varying times in corked bottles to destroy the "ferments" which cause spoilage.

The brothers established a factory for their canning work near Paris, and in 1814 published a treatise on *The Art of Preserving.* Apparently they also were engaged in production canning for the French military, and in 1820 were awarded a substantial cash prize by the government for their work supplying canned foods for the army and navy.

Before filling jars, stretch the wet rubber just enough to fit flat on the sealing shoulder of the jar. Fill the jars, leaving recommended headroom.

Remove air bubbles from jars by carefully running a spatula or table knife around between food and jar. Wipe the threads of the jars and the top of the rubber with a clean towel.

Screw the cap tight, then loosen about ¼ inch. Process immediately following instructions. Remove jars from the canner and *slowly* screw the caps tight. Let the jars cool according to standard directions. *Don't* tighten the lid again after cooling. This is another type of lid referred to when instructions say to "complete seals if necessary" after processing.

The test for a good seal is to see if the middle of the cap is depressed in the center.

You may find it difficult to find replacements for the porcelain-lined zinc caps. In addition, they are somewhat suspect because of the zinc. There is a variety of European jars and American reproductions on the market. They are very decorative, but make sure they are suitable for canning before using.

LIDS

The lids for standard, modern canning jars are two-part: a *screw band* and a *one-use lid.* The *soft compound* on the inside of the dome completes the seal. The screw band holds the new lid in place until it is sealed—after which it is unnecessary. For this reason screw bands may be removed after the cooling process. (Don't tighten *these* bands after processing.) Leaving them on is optional but is similar to leaving a pattern pinned to a dress after it is completed. To prove the point, you can actually lift the jar by the dome lid after the screw band is removed, provided you have a good seal. Once removed, store the screw bands for next year in a dry place where they won't rust. *Don't* reuse dome lids or rubber rings, however, as the rubber is good for only one sealing.

If you understand the principle behind the sealing procedure, it will be easier to see why it is so important to follow directions carefully.

When a jar of food is heated, the contents expand, forcing air out of the jar. As the contents contract during cooling, a vacuum is formed which will hold the lid in place aided by the rubber compound on the dome lid.

Sometimes the simplest questions are left unanswered. *How do you open a jar of home-canned food?* Easy, with a bottle opener, which puts a hole in the dome lid and further reminds you that it can't be used again. For jars requiring a rubber ring, pull the rubber tab. Pliers may be needed to do this. Sometimes it takes the insertion of a sharp knife between the rubber ring and the lid to break the vacuum on bail jars. This might crack the glass lid, so use care.

People often ask if all Mason jar screw bands and dome lids are interchangeable among modern canning jars of the same size mouth. Yes. If you bought jars from one company and lids from another you will have no problem.

HOW DO YOU TEST
FOR A PERFECT SEAL?

There are three tests for Mason jar seals recommended by the major canning companies.

First, you can *hear* it seal. As the jar completes the seal, each one will make a kerplunking sound. This test is only reliable if you are doing *one jar at a time.* If you have a dozen jars cooling on your counter, it is difficult to keep track of which jar is kerplunking.

Second, you can *see* the seal. The lid should curve *down* in the middle.

Third, after the jar has cooled *feel* that the lid is down and stays down.

Finally, tap the center of the lid with a spoon. It should make a clear, ringing sound if the seal is perfect.

One test for bail jars is to *tip them* to check for leakage or air bubbles, which indicate a poor seal. A better test is to release the bail wires and

pick up the jar by the glass lid. With a good seal the lid will be firmly attached to the jar. (Caution: lift only an inch or two off the counter in case the seal *isn't* good!)

WHAT DO YOU DO
IF YOU HAVE A POOR SEAL?

After the jars have cooled, in approximately 12 hours, test the seals. If the jars didn't seal properly you can re-process them *within 24 hours* of the original processing, using new dome lids — or you can eat the food. Re-processing will result in a less satisfactory product because the full canning time must be repeated. On the other hand, eating the food may not be very appealing just then either.

If your jars come unsealed later during storage, discard the contents, being sure neither children nor animals might eat them, and sterilize the containers.

THE GREAT JAR LID CRISIS

The great increase in home gardens — millions of new ones — in the middle 1970s caught the Mason jar manufacturers unprepared, and 1974 as every home canner remembers, was the year there just weren't any to be bought anywhere by early summer.

The next year there were jars enough but a real crisis in replacement lids—in spite of the fact that some 2 billion were made and marketed!

The Department of Agriculture computed that there were 18.6 million home canners that year, and the supply of more than 100 new lids per canner *should* have been enough.

A congressional inquiry and other investigations came up with the same answer: panic hoarding. "If home canners buy just the lids they need for this season, there would be enough," reported Nancy Steorts of the USDA. "However, if this hoarding continues, there won't be enough, no matter how many lids are placed on the market."

Up-to-the-minute data on the latest in replacement jar lids and re-usable lid inserts is available if you send a stamped, self-addressed envelope to LIDS, *Family Food Garden*, P.O. Box 1014, Grass Valley, Calif. 95945.

CHECKING THE LIDS

Taking a lead from the baby food manufacturers, Owens-Illinois is marketing Mason jar lids with a "Magic Button." This button in the center of the lid pulls down under vacuum and pops up very clearly if the seal isn't perfect.

RE-USING COMMERCIAL JARS

Many of the foods we buy from the store come in glass containers, some with self-sealing lids. Peanut butter, dry roasted nuts, wheat germ and pickles are just a few examples. These have lids with a rubber sealing compound. Other jars, such as for mayonnaise, appear to have the same size mouths and threads as standard canning jars, but self-sealing canning lids will not always fit on them.

We asked the USDA, some extension service people and the manufacturers of some of these people and the manufacturers of some of these jars if it was safe to re-use them for canning. They all responded with a resounding "NO," and we agree.

These jars are not heat-tempered as are canning jars, and at high heat, at irregular temperatures and under pressure there is a danger of their breaking. This would mean the loss of the food (at the least) or a nasty accident (at the worst).

So play it safe. DON'T re-use commercial jars for canning, no matter how great the temptation. You *can* use them for jellies and jams, though, which are sealed with paraffin.

A NOTE ON REUSING COMMERCIAL JARS

There have been several years when standard canning jars and/or lids have been scarce. This means that either garden produce was wasted or that alternative methods to preserve it—such as freezing—had to be used. It has also meant that *unsafe* methods of canning have been used in desperation by some people. This includes using jars with lids that didn't fit or were not self-sealing.

If you are the thrifty type who saves commercial jars and will use them for canning no matter what the experts say, for goodness sake do so *sensibly.* Here are some absolute rules you should follow:

1. Never use these jars under pressure. For low-acid foods that must be pressure canned use only good canning jars. Or use the freezer.

2. To be safe, never re-use commercial jar lids, especially those with cardboard liners.

3. The lids and jars must match.

4. When using a mason dome (self-sealing) lid on a non-canning jar, be sure it and the screw band fit exactly. Be sure there are no nicks or cracks in the rim of the jar.

5. Follow all directions for canning procedure exactly and the times to the letter. No shortcuts!

6. Use extra caution when subjecting these jars to heat. Be sure they are hot before filling

with hot food, or before placing in hot water for a boiling water bath. After processing, let the water stop boiling before removing the jars to a rack or towel. Don't bump. Avoid drafts and rapid temperature changes.

7. Most important of all: *Do not eat food canned in these jars unless you are positive there was an airtight, vacuum seal.* To test (after cooling and later before opening to use): Feel the top and look across it at eye level. It must be depressed (down) in the center. It should not give when pressed.

You are taking a big chance when using these jars for canning, so be prepared for some discouraging results. Better yet, don't do it. Save them for your jams and jellies.

THE EDITORS

Cans

We have not mentioned metal cans, since this method has become increasingly rare. During the Depression, extension agents traveled from community to community with tin can canning equipment. Equipment and cans are costly, cumbersome, and hard to find, although the cans themselves are much cheaper than jars. This may be the key to their present unpopularity. They can't be recycled, whereas the jars can be used year after year. For a thorough treatment of tin can canning, see the U.S. Department of Agriculture bulletins.

New Terms You'll Run Into

Nothing is more frustrating than starting something new only to encounter terminology that an author takes for granted you already know. To avoid this we have defined below the terms used in canning.

Raw or cold pack: These phrases are used interchangeably. They refer to clean, prepared but uncooked fruits or vegetables, packed in jars to which a hot liquid is added, and then processed.

Hot pack: Hot pack refers to foods that are precooked to some degree, then put into jars for processing. This makes for a more compact packing, particularly with greens. Hot pack sometimes requires less cooking time, since the food is already partially cooked. Sometimes it takes as long or longer because of the denser pack.

Which is best? The specific instructions for each vegetable and fruit will indicate whether hot or raw pack is best. Raw pack has the advantage of holding the shape of lower density foods. If you want tomatoes, for instance, to retain their shape, cold pack them. Take the precaution of packing tightly, since raw pack tends to shrink in processing.

Headroom or head space: Headroom refers to the space between the top of the food and the top of the jar. Generally ½ inch is allowed with the exception of starchy foods such as corn and peas which expand more. These require one inch or more. As bad as leaving too little headroom (which causes jars to overflow during processing and thereby ruins the seal) is leaving too much. Allowing too much headroom means too much air and the possibility of an improper seal. If you have only enough to fill half a jar, use it fresh or find a smaller jar.

Methods: Boiling Water Bath Canning

This is the cheapest and easiest form of canning for some foods. It involves a *kettle* deep enough to cover your jars with ½ inch of water and another inch for a *rolling* boil, which is necessary for canning and must never be turned down to a gentle boil or simmer. So you need a canner deep enough to avoid splashing over.

A *rack* on the bottom is necessary, too, to provide complete circulation of the boiling water under the jars. A lid on the kettle will help to maintain the rolling boil. Since most quart jars are 7 to 7½ inches tall, you will need a canner 11 to 12 inches deep.

Most people use a conventional black enamel canner with white spots, which is resistant to acids and salt solutions and so can double for processing pickles or brining vegetables. An aluminum kettle won't serve for this.

A lobster pot or large camping kettle or a large pressure canner may make a perfectly adequate water bath canner provided the lid is left unlocked and the vent open.

You can use old screw bands or bent coat hanger to improvise a bottom rack. It is important for maximum heat circulation that the jars don't touch each other.

If you purchase a boiling water bath canner, invest the extra money and buy the large model. It will accommodate quarts, which are the most practical size for the bulk of home canning. Don't do as one woman we heard about who processed her tomatoes in a too-small canner with the jar tops out of water. Then she turned them over to process the other halves! Jars *must* be covered with water to the proper depth.

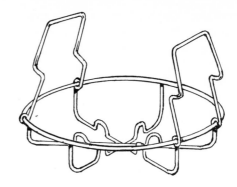

Wire basket for steaming. Use in a pot with a tightly fitting lid.

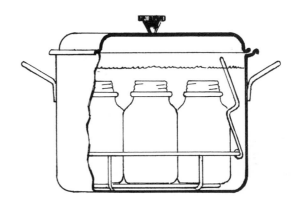

Boiling water bath. Cutaway shows jars in position.

STEP BY STEP

Put the kettle on the stove half full of water and begin simmering. Check the jar rims to be sure there are no nicks or cracks. Discard old screw bands that are rusty or warped. Use only new Mason jar lids and new rubber rings for bail jars. Wash your jars and screw bands in hot soapy water and rinse. It is not necessary to sterilize when using a boiling water bath. They will be heated to sterilizing temperatures in the canning process. Wash the dome lids or rubber rings in hot soapy water and rinse. Place them in a pan, cover with boiling water and leave them until needed.

Place your raw- or hot-packed food in the clean, hot jars, leaving the recommended headroom. You may add one teaspoon of salt to a quart of vegetables, although this isn't necessary for preservation — only for flavor.

Take a rubber spatula and run around the inside edge of the jars to release any air bubbles. Slice through densely-packed greens to aid heat penetration to the center of the jar. Wipe the top of the jar with a damp cloth if your syrup contains sugar, or with a dry towel if not. Do this thoroughly and carefully to prevent any small particles from interfering with the seal.

Place the lids and screw bands on and tighten them as firmly as possible. With bail jars, stretch the rubber rings over the mouths of the jars, pulling them down to the "shelf" just under the rim. Then set the glass lids in place and secure the longer clamp over the top. *Do not* press the second clamp down until after processing. One-piece lids (unless the manufacturer's directions say otherwise) should be tightened firmly, then backed off ¼ inch.

Lower the jars into the simmering water with a jar lifter, one of the indispensable small canning gadgets. Cold jars should be put into warm water and hot jars into hot water; they will crack from a sudden change in temperature. Make sure that they are not touching so you get good heat circulation. Add water to cover the jars by one or two inches. Put on the kettle lid, bring the water to a rolling boil, and then *(not before)* start keeping track of the processing time.

When the recommended time is up, remove the kettle from the heat and take out the jars with a lifter. Leaving them in longer will result in over-cooking. (But old jars should be treated with extra care, so leave them in the water until the boil has stopped.) Put the jars on a cake rack or towel in a draft-free area. Be careful not to knock them together, since they will shatter easily when hot. Don't cover the cooling jars unless there is a draft.

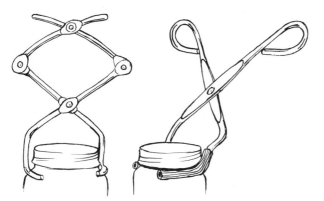

Jar lifter for removing jars from the canner.

Now clamp down the second wire on bail jars and complete the seal on one-piece lids by screwing them tight. Leave jars undisturbed for 12 hours to cool thoroughly.

Then test the seal. If it isn't good you can reprocess within 24 hours of the original processing. Try to find out *why* your jars didn't seal. The most frequent reasons are a bit of food caught between lid and jar rim, and cracks on the jar rim. Both of these can be avoided with care.

Now remove the screw bands from the Mason jars. Wipe the jars clean and label them with the product name, its origin and the date. This information will be helpful in deciding how and what to can next year.

Store the jars in a cool, dry, dark place. Dampness rusts the dome lids and causes the seals to deteriorate. Light tends to destroy vitamins and fade colors. Freezing and thawing will deteriorate the food's quality and possibly break the seals.

Process and store for no more than one year, since quality will deteriorate. The food may be safe to eat after a year, but why settle for old canned goods when next year's harvest will supply good fresh produce?

Now enjoy your garden's bounty, when the snow is four feet deep and summer is long past!

CANNING TOMATOES
(raw pack, with a boiling water bath)

1. Wash and sort tomatoes. Dip into boiling water for ½ minute.

2. Remove to cold water to cool for 1 minute.

3. Pull off skins. Cut off the stem as well as blemishes and green spots.

34

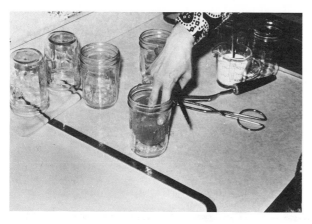

4. Cut into sections. Pack tightly into jars, pushing down so that the tomatoes are covered by their own juice, leaving headspace.

5. Optional: For seasoning you can add 1 tsp. salt to each quart of vegetable. See p. 99 for adding acid.

6. Run a knife around the inside of the jar to release trapped air bubbles.

7. Wipe the jar rims with a clean cloth. Adjust the lids.

8. Place jars in a boiling water bath canner. Cover with ½ inch of water. Cover. Start timing when you have a rolling boil—35 minutes for pints, 45 minutes for quarts. Remove jars. Complete seals if necessary.

WHAT CAN BE CANNED
IN A BOILING WATER BATH CANNER?

Boiling water bath canners are appropriate for all high acid foods. These include all fruits, pickles and those vegetables to which sufficient vinegar has been added to raise the acidity level high enough.

The principle of the pH scale used in measuring the acidity and alkalinity of your garden soil is the same employed here. To visualize high acidity, picture sucking on a lemon, nibbling raw rhubarb or sipping vinegar. It is this acidity that makes a boiling water bath possible for fruits (as they are high in acid) or for vegetables to which sufficient vinegar has been added. The heat achieved in a boiling water bath canner is that of boiling water (212°). This is not sufficient to kill heat-resistant bacteria that cause spoilage; they are inhibited from growing by heat and the presence of high acidity. See the accompanying table for pH values of common foods. A *low* number means *high* acidity, and a high number means low acidity. A food with a pH value of 4.5 or higher is considered low acid for canning purposes and *must* be processed in a pressure canner.

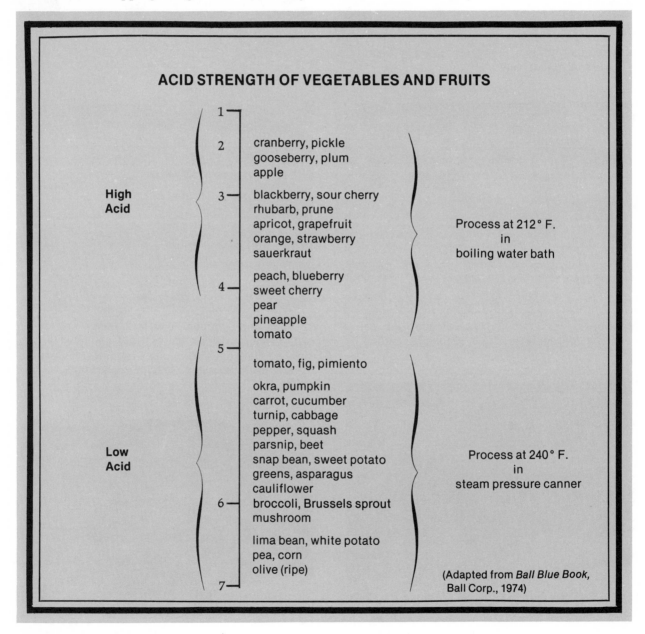

ACID STRENGTH OF VEGETABLES AND FRUITS

High Acid

1

2 — cranberry, pickle
gooseberry, plum
apple

3 — blackberry, sour cherry
rhubarb, prune
apricot, grapefruit
orange, strawberry
sauerkraut

peach, blueberry
sweet cherry
pear
pineapple
tomato

4

Process at 212° F.
in
boiling water bath

5

tomato, fig, pimiento

Low Acid

okra, pumpkin
carrot, cucumber
turnip, cabbage
pepper, squash
parsnip, beet
snap bean, sweet potato
greens, asparagus
cauliflower
broccoli, Brussels sprout
mushroom

6

lima bean, white potato
pea, corn
olive (ripe)

7

Process at 240° F.
in
steam pressure canner

(Adapted from *Ball Blue Book*,
Ball Corp., 1974)

ALTITUDE ADJUSTMENT CHART FOR BOILING WATER BATH CANNING		
Increase processing time if the time specified is:		
Altitude	20 minutes or less	More than 20 minutes
1,000	1 min.	2 min.
2,000	2 min.	4 min.
3,000	3 min.	6 min.
4,000	4 min.	8 min.
5,000	5 min.	10 min.
6,000	6 min.	12 min.
7,000	7 min.	14 min.
8,000	8 min.	16 min.
9,000	9 min.	18 min.
10,000	10 min.	20 min.

Vegetables are low in acid and, therefore, are *unsuitable for a boiling water bath canner* unless in a pickled form such as dilled beans or pickled beets. Your grandmother may have done it, but what you forget are the dozens of jars which were thrown away due to spoilage and the occasional case of food poisoning.

Hot Water Bath

A hot water bath is used *only* for sweet or acid fruit juices in jars. It involves a pasteurizing process (in which the jars are simmered at 180° to 190° F. in a water bath canner) and is *not* to be confused with a *boiling* water bath. In this method there is less loss in vitamins and flavor.

MORE RECIPES

Parade Magazine in 1975 put out a booklet on *Home Canning & Freezing* that contains more than 90 basic and unusual recipes, mostly in the area of preserves, jams and jellies. Copies still were available at this writing for $1.75 from *Parade* Magazine, Box 4, Department FF, Kensington Station, Brooklyn, N.Y.

Pressure-Canning Vegetables

All vegetables are low acid (except some tomatoes, sauerkraut and pickles) and must be processed in a steam-pressure canner.

There are old cookbooks still on our shelves that say that processing low acid foods for three hours in a boiling water bath is a substitute for using a pressure canner. Unfortunately, no matter how long you boil water the temperature will not go above 212° F., and you cannot be *sure* that the botulinum bacteria have been destroyed. We shudder when we talk with a homemaker who says she has "always canned vegetables without a pressure canner and hasn't had a problem yet."

It only takes one spoonful from one jar of poisoned food to cause serious illness or death. So *please*, for your family's sake, *always* use a pressure canner with low acid foods. If you cannot buy one, look into sharing the cost with a relative or friend, or borrow one. It may be the most important investment you ever make.

There are several types of pressure canners, but they all work according to the same principle. The pan has a tight-sealing lid with some type of regulator. When a small amount of water is heated in the canner (usually 1 to 2 inches of water), it is converted to steam which, as it builds up pressure, reaches temperatures substantially higher than boiling. At 10 pounds pressure the temperature is 240° F.; at 15 pounds it is 250° F. The pressure used for canning is 10 pounds, except at altitudes above sea level when higher pressure must be reached to achieve the right temperatures. (See Table A.)

The canner is fitted with safety features that are designed to maintain pressure at reasonable levels, and to "let go" if the pressure should become too high. It is essential that you become familiar with the directions for your type of canner, and follow directions exactly. The booklet that accompanies each new canner should be read thoroughly; if you have no booklet, read the following information carefully.

TABLE A
PRESSURE ADJUSTMENTS
FOR DIFFERENT ALTITUDES

Dial Gauge Canners

Altitude (Feet above sea level)	Pounds Pressure For Canning Low-Acid Vegetables
Up to 2,000	10
2,000	11
4,000	12
6,000	13
8,000	14
10,000	15

Weight Control Canners

2,000 and higher	15

(*Please note:* Use only Mason jars. Other glass jars in which you have bought mayonnaise or peanut butter, for example, are not suitable for home pressure canning. The shock of heat and pressure changes can cause them to shatter, with great danger to the people working with them. Controlled conditions in a commercial cannery make it possible for them to be used there.)

Different Types of Canners

There are two main types of canners: those with a *dial gauge* that visually shows the pressure; and those with a *weight-type control* that makes an audible noise when it reaches the required pressure. Another difference is in the type of seal of dial type canners: Some have a rubber gasket in the cover that seals it to the pan; others have a metal-to-metal closure with screw clamps. Before using any pressure canner, check each of its parts to be sure all are in good working order, and give all a thorough cleaning. Specific directions for each type of canner follow.

DIAL-TYPE CANNERS

1. Steam Gauge

Both rubber gasket and metal-to-metal seal canners may have a dial gauge that registers the pounds of steam pressure being maintained in the canner. *The gauge should be checked for accuracy each year before any canning is done.* Ask at your local extension service or a store where canners are sold where you can have it checked. If found to be off slightly, you can adjust for the error by adding or subtracting the necessary number of pounds on the dial reading. For example, if your gauge registers 10 pounds when it is only maintaining 8 pounds pressure, you should add 2 pounds so that the dial will read 12 pounds pressure when canning. If the gauge is off by more than a few pounds, it can be replaced with a new one. See the accompanying table of gauge adjustments, Table B.

The dial gauge is a delicate mechanism and should be handled with care. It must not be immersed in water, so the lid should never be washed in water. Use a wet cloth to wash the inside and outside of the lid, and wipe the gauge carefully.

TABLE B
PRESSURE CANNER: GAUGE ADJUSTMENTS

If the gauge reads high—
1 pound high—process at 11 pounds.
2 pounds high—process at 12 pounds.
3 pounds high—process at 13 pounds.
4 pounds high—process at 14 pounds.

If the gauge reads low—
1 pound low—process at 9 pounds.
2 pounds low—process at 8 pounds.
3 pounds low—process at 7 pounds.
4 pounds low—process at 6 pounds.

To protect the gauge, always store the cover placed upside down on the pan. This will also prevent the inside of the canner from becoming musty.

2. Automatic Air Vent–Rubber Gasket Canners

The air vent is both an air regulator and safety feature. It automatically vents air from the canner during the initial heating, and allows air to flow back in when pressure is reduced after processing, thus preventing the formation of a vacuum in the canner. It serves as an emergency pressure release, being designed to "blow out" if the vent pipe is clogged and pressure cannot be released normally. Check to see if the rubber part of the air vent is soft and pliable. If not, it should be replaced.

To clean it, remove by pushing down on it from the top. After cleaning, insert by pushing it up through the opening from the underside of the cover. When in place, the slightly rounded face of the automatic air vent will be exposed on the outside of the cover.

3. Pressure Regulator and Vent Pipe–Rubber Gasket Canners

The pressure regulator is placed on the vent pipe, and controls the amount of pressure that can be built up in the canner. The maximum pressure is 15 pounds, above which the regulator will rock to release excess pressure.

The regulator will not hold the pressure at 10 pounds, which is the pressure used for canning.

It is up to the operator to reduce the heat and watch the indicator closely to maintain 10 pounds. You can use 15 pounds when pressure cooking food for meals and 5 pounds when canning fruits and tomatoes. (Fruits and tomatoes may also be processed in a boiling water bath in your pressure canner with the pressure regulator removed and water filled up over the top of the jars.)

To clean, wipe out the interior of the regulator. The vent pipe should be cleaned regularly by drawing a pipe cleaner or tiny brush through it.

4. The Sealing Ring (Rubber Gasket)

The sealing ring fits into the canner cover and forms a pressure tight seal during cooking or processing. After the canner has been in use for a considerable period, the sealing ring may shrink. If there is an escape of steam around the edges of the cover because of this, replace the sealing ring.

The sealing ring should be washed after each use, and the groove in the lid into which it sets should be washed with a brush. Be sure it is thoroughly dry before replacing the ring.

5. Control Valve–Metal-To-Metal Canners

Some canners have a control valve rather than a pressure regulator and vent pipe. In the *open* (erect) position air and steam can escape from the canner during initial heating. It is closed (pushed down) to build up pressure for processing. When processing is over and the canner has cooled to zero pressure, the control valve is opened to allow air to flow back into the canner, breaking the vacuum that will form if cooled completely.

When cooking food for meals or canning in tin cans (but *not* when canning with glass jars), the control valve is opened soon after processing to release the steam, because liquid cannot escape from cans.

In the *closed* position (stem turned down) the control valve holds steam in the canner, allowing pressure to rise. The valve is designed to "blow off" at 20 pounds pressure, as a safety feature. The operator must watch the dial gauge and adjust the heat to prevent the pressure from building up past the 10 pounds needed for canning.

Clean the control valve by using a toothpick to keep the holes clear, so air and steam can escape through them.

6. Metal-To-Metal Closure

Canners with a metal-to-metal seal have knobs that screw down to lock the cover. Put a drop of oil on the threads of each of these before using. To close this type of canner, place the cover on the pan, evenly lined up with the knobs. Tighten all knobs slightly, doing two opposite ones at the same time to keep cover level. Then tighten all knobs firmly, using hand pressure only, and again always doing two opposite ones at a time.

When these pressure canners are used for canning *only*, the metal-to-metal seal must be lubricated with oil, paraffin or wax to prevent scratching and sticking of the seal.

To maintain a good sealing edge, the rim of the pan and sealing edge of the cover must not be banged against a sharp object (such as knocking a metal spoon on the rim of the cooker to clean it of food after stirring). Also do not clean with metal scouring pads.

A good vegetable scrub brush is handy and it safe-guards against spoilage. Small carrots can be scrubbed instead of peeled, which is a time saver. A brush is also a great asset with asparagus.

HOW TO OPERATE
A DIAL-GAUGE CANNER

1. Have basket or rack in place. For foods canned by the *hot pack* method, put boiling water, enough to be about 2 inches deep, into the canner. See accompanying table for exact amount to use. Set canner on low heat.

   For foods canned by the *raw pack* method (with cold food), pour the same amount of hot, but not boiling, water into the canner. Set on low heat but do not allow to reach simmering temperature.

2. Place each prepared jar upright into canner. Jars must not be touching each other or bottom of canner, so be sure rack or basket is in place.

3. Place cover on canner and lock securely. *Rubber gasket canners:* The lid may have arrows pointing to a closed position, or the handles must be centered over each other. Turn the lid until it reaches the locked position. Do *not* put pressure regulator on vent pipe.

   Metal-to-metal canners: Screw down the thumb-screws, always tightening two opposite knobs at the same time. Be sure control valve is in open (upright) position.

   Do not build up pressure in any canner until the cover is securely locked into closed position.

4. Set burner to highest heat. When steam flows freely from the vent pipe or control valve, reduce heat slightly to maintain a strong steam flow. Steam should flow freely from all four holes in the control valve on metal-to-metal canners. Allow steam to vent for seven (up to 8-qt.-size canner) to ten (16-qt. or larger) minutes to eliminate all air from canner and jars. If air is not vented in this way it will throw off the accuracy of your canning process.

5. Place pressure regulator on the vent pipe, or close control valve by turning down valve stem to horizontal position.

6. Steam will build up in the canner. *Rubber gasket canners:* Soon the automatic air vent will rise and seal the canner. If it does not, gently touch the metal plunger in it with something other than your hand (it is hot!)— perhaps something is stuck in the opening that is preventing the plunger from sealing.

7. Keep the heat on high, and the pressure will gradually rise to ten pounds. Watch the gauge closely and when the dial is almost at 10 pounds, turn the heat down to low on electric or gas ranges. When using a coal or wood stove, wait until the pressure reaches 10 pounds, then move the canner to a cooler spot on the stove. *Start counting the processing time as soon as the required pressure is reached.*

8. Make minor adjustments in the heat if necessary to keep the pressure at 10 pounds. It is important to keep the pressure steady; fluctuations in pressure can cause liquid to be lost from the jars. Do not touch or remove the pressure regulator during the processing period. Steam would be released, causing a sudden drop in pressure. If the pressure drops below 10 lbs. you must start over again, so watch the canner closely.

9. As soon as the processing time is up, turn off gas burner, or remove canner from electric burner or constant heat unit such as a wood stove.

TABLE C

AMOUNT OF WATER TO USE IN PRESSURE CANNERS*

Size of Canner	Amount of Water for Processing
4 Quart	1 Quart
6 Quart	1½ Quarts
8 Quart	1½ Quarts
16 Quart	2 Quarts
21 Quart	2 Quarts

*Increase the recommended amount of water by one pint if the canner is not filled to capacity with jars.

10. Allow pressure to return to zero naturally. Do *not* try to speed the cooling process by running cold water over the canner or removing the pressure regulator or opening the control valve. This could cause the jars to break or to lose liquid, spoiling the seal.

Rubber gasket canners: When the dial reaches zero and the automatic air vent has dropped, remove the pressure regulator from the vent pipe. Let canner cool another one or two minutes.

Metal-to-metal canners: When the dial reaches zero, open the control valve very slowly so that any pressure left will be released gradually.

11. Release the cover from locked position and remove carefully. To avoid getting a faceful of steam, lift up the far edge of the cover first and remove, shielding yourself with the cover.

12. Remove jars from canner and set on rack to cool. Complete seals if necessary.

13. If processing another batch of jars, be sure there is enough water in the canner before starting.

HOME STORAGE WITH A WOOD STOVE

The old kitchen range is ideal, because of its extended and variable heat, for cooking down tomatoes for ketchup, sauce and paste, and for jellies and jams, too. When it comes to drying herbs and some fruits and vegetables its warming shelves and oven are hard to beat.

It is another matter, though, if you're doing pressure canning, where it is critical that a *constant* steam pressure be held—sometimes for as long as 65 minutes. It can be done on a wood-fired range, but it takes constant attention and some quick shifting of the cooker to hotter or cooler parts of the stove top. Most people who cook with wood stoves, however, find they make the kitchen unbearably hot at the height of the freezing and canning season, and they resort to the less economical but more even and directed heat of a gas, electric or kerosene burner.

CANNERS WITH WEIGHT-TYPE PRESSURE CONTROL

1. Automatic Pressure Control

This type of canner has a one-piece, unbreakable metal weight-type control. It has three different settings, for 5, 10, and 15 pounds pressure. The control is placed on the vent pipe, and automatically releases pressure greater than the amount for which it is set. For example, to set the control for 10 pounds pressure, place the control with the hole marked "10" on the vent pipe. When the pressure builds up to 10 pounds, the control will begin to jiggle, releasing steam and preventing the pressure from rising further.

Rather than having to watch a dial, the operator listens for the jiggling sound that indicates the canner has reached the required pressure. The heat is then adjusted so that the control will jiggle only two or three times a minute. Low to medium-low temperature on a gas or electric range will usually be right; experiment until you find the right temperature. If the control jiggles less, too little pressure is being maintained, meaning the temperature is too low for proper processing; if it jiggles too much, a substantial amount of steam may escape which over a long period of time could cause the canner to run dry, overheating the cooker itself and possibly wrecking both it and your canned goods!

"Jiggling" is not the same as the slight shaking and sizzling the control makes as pressure is building up—there is a distinct change in sound

when it reaches the jiggling point which you will recognize as soon as you hear it.

Because this control is unbreakable, it does not have to be checked for accuracy each year as does the dial gauge. It is also self-cleaning by the action of the steam on it; but it may be washed in hot clean suds and rinsed thoroughly to insure that it is free of any obstructive particles that might hamper its operation.

The vent pipe that it fits on should be cleaned regularly by running a pipe cleaner or small brush back and forth through it. The whole cover may be washed along with the rest of the cooker.

2. Self-Sealing Gasket

This is similar to the sealing ring on dial gauge canners, and should be cared for in the same way.

3. Safety fuse

In the lid of these canners is a small round plug. It will release and drop into the cooker if the cooker becomes overheated due to lack of water, or it will "blow out" if the vent tube becomes clogged. If the proper amount of water and heat is used and if the vent tube is kept clear, the fuse should never blow. If it does, replacements can be purchased.

HOW TO OPERATE A WEIGHT-CONTROL PRESSURE CANNER

1. Set rack in canner and add enough water to be about 2 inches deep in canner. (See Table C.) For *hot pack canning,* add hot water and set on burner over low heat. For *raw pack canning* (with cold food): Use warm water, set on low heat but do not allow to simmer.

2. Set prepared jars on rack in cooker.

3. Close cooker, making sure the cover is locked in position with handles aligned over each other. Turn heat on high. Allow air to vent from the canner and jars for 7 to 10 minutes (see manufacturer's directions). Then put pressure control on vent pipe. Set at 10 pounds pressure (or 5 pounds for tomatoes or fruits).

4. It may take up to 45 minutes to bring a canner up to 10 pounds pressure when filled to capacity with raw packed quarts of vegetables. When the control begins to jiggle vigorously, start to count processing time. Reduce heat, but keep it high enough so that the control jiggles at least two or three times a minute. Avoid rapid temperature changes or drafts blowing on the canner, as this will cause uneven pressure which forces liquid from the jars.

5. When processing time is up, turn off heat. Remove canner from electric burners or constant heat units such as wood stoves. Move it carefully, as it is very hot and heavy. Do not dislodge the control.

6. Allow to cool normally. Do not rush cooling by running cold water over the cooker or by lifting the control. It will take at least 20 minutes (up to 45 minutes in larger canners) for the pressure to drop in a canner filled with jars.

7. When a reasonable length of time has passed, check to see if the pressure has returned to zero by lifting the control *slightly* with a fork. If you *see* steam spurt out, pressure is still up, so replace the control and wait a while longer. If you do *not see* steam, pressure is down and the control can be removed all the way. In either case you may *hear* a hissing sound, which indicates either steam coming out or air rushing in—so trust your sight rather than your ears!

8. After removing the pressure control, unlock the cover and lift off. Protect yourself from the steam by lifting the far edge off first and shielding your body with the cover as you remove it.

9. Remove jars from canner and carefully place them upright on a towel or rack, not touching, in a draft-free spot. Do not let them bump into each other as this may cause them to crack. Complete seals on bail-type jars and those with porcelain-lined zinc caps. Do not tighten screw bands on two-piece metal lids.

3. Pack loosely into hot jars and add salt. Add boiling water or cooking liquid, leaving ½ inch headroom.

PRESSURE-CANNING SPINACH

1. Wash spinach, lifting it to let dirt settle out. Remove tough stems and wilted leaves.

4. Run a knife or spatula around the inside of the jar to release air bubbles.

2. Steam about 2 pounds of spinach at a time until it is well wilted (8-10 minutes).

5. Wipe rim carefully with a damp cloth to remove pieces of food.

6. Put on Mason lids with sealing compound down against the glass. Put on the screw band and tighten firmly. See specific instructions for other types of lids.

7. Set jars in hot water (1-2 inches deep) on rack in pressure canner.

8. Tighten lid of pressure canner securely.

9. Follow manufacturer's directions for operating canner, or refer to page 38. All low-acid vegetables are pressure-canned at 10 lbs. pressure (240° F.). When pressure reaches 10 lbs., adjust heat to keep it steady. Time spinach 70 minutes for pints, 90 minutes for quarts. When time is up, remove canner from the heat and allow to cool slowly.

10. When pressure returns to zero, slowly remove weighted gauge or open petcock. Remove cover, tilting far side up so steam escapes away from you. Lift jars out and set upright on a cloth away from drafts. Do not tighten screwbands with dome lids. With other types of lids complete seals as necessary.

11. Allow jars to cool several hours. Test for a good seal (see page 30), remove screw bands, wash jars, label, and store in a cool dark place.

Hints for all Types of Pressure Canning

ALUMINUM CANNERS

The inside of a used aluminum canner may be discolored because of the action of acids, iron or various minerals in water and foods. These stains are harmless, but some may be removed if desired by using a solution of water and cream of tartar. (A strong vinegar solution also may be used.) Pour enough of the solution into the canner to cover the discoloration (do not fill over ⅔ full), then close cover securely. Place pressure regulator on vent pipe and heat until pressure regulator rocks gently. Remove canner from heat; allow to stand three to four hours.

Remove pressure regulator, open canner and empty contents. Scour thoroughly with a steel wool cleaning pad containing soap; wash, rinse and dry.

To prevent water stains in canner or on jars, add 1 tablespoon vinegar or 1 teaspoon cream of tartar to the water when processing.

STACKING JARS

In large canners half-pint and pint jars can be stacked in more than one layer. It is not essential to put a rack between the layers, but it is often recommended because it helps the steam to circulate more evenly.

PRESSURE SAUCEPANS

Small jars can sometimes be canned in small pressure cookers if: (1) the pressure can be regulated at 10 pounds (most saucepans can only be regulated at 15 pounds, so check this closely), and (2) there is adequate room for the jars to fit inside the cover when locked in place. It is generally recommended to add 5 percent to the processing time for the vegetables being canned when a pressure saucepan is used, because of the quicker heating and cooling times. Be sure to let it cool down normally, without putting it under running water or otherwise trying to speed up the cooling process.

WHAT CAUSES LIQUID TO BOIL OUT OF JARS DURING PROCESSING?

1. Jars packed too solidly with food.

2. Filling jars too full. Allow ½ inch headroom for most fruits and vegetables except shelled beans, corn, peas and sweet potatoes, which require 1 inch or more.

3. Too high a temperature or too high pressure.

4. Sudden fluctuations in temperature and pressure. When processing food in a pressure canner, the pressure regulator or control should not be removed or bumped, and pressure should be allowed to return to zero normally.

5. Failure to adjust lids and rings properly before processing.

WHAT CAUSES JARS TO BREAK?

1. Cracked or weakened jars, or using jars other than standard canning (Mason) jars.

2. Jars packed too tightly or too full.

3. Jars touching the bottom of the canner.

4. Improper tightening of lids before processing.

5. Sudden heat or pressure change, especially by cooling the canner too rapidly by unnatural means after processing.

CANNING CORN

1. Pick ripe corn and use it fresh. Husk, remove silk, then cut off kernels, leaving about ¼ of the kernel on the cob. Do not cut into the cob.

2. Pack corn loosely in clean jars, leaving 1 inch headroom. Do not shake or press down. Salt may be added: 1 tsp. for quarts, ½ tsp. for pints.

3. Add boiling water or cooking liquid, leaving 1 inch headroom. Fill pressure canner to within ½ inch of the top with boiling water. Adjust lids and process in canner at 10 lbs. pressure—pints for 55 minutes, quarts for 85 minutes. Remove jars. Complete seals if necessary.

6. Putting cold jars into boiling water; bumping together hot jars after removing them from the canner; or putting them in a cold, drafty place to cool.

WHY DON'T JARS SEAL?

1. The jar or lid may be defective.

2. Food may have been caught under sealing compound on rim, or may have been forced out of jar with liquid.

If a jar does not seal, either refrigerate and eat contents soon or re-process it. Remember it must be processed as long as the first time, and both flavor and food value will suffer.

To re-process, open the jar, inspect jar for defects and clean the rim carefully. Put on a *new* dome lid (the same screwband can be washed and re-used), and process for the full length of time specified in the directions.

The table on page 48 summarizes processing information for different vegetables. For complete details on harvesting, preparing and preserving each vegetable by different methods, refer to Chapter 4.

"Don't" Methods

Over the years, certain methods have developed and been passed on by word of mouth. These include *aspirin canning, oven canning* and *steam canning*. Rather than risk confusion, we have deleted any references to these methods. *None of them is safe or acceptable.* And there can be no compromise on this point.

Open kettle canning, once an acceptable method, now is recommended only for jellies and jams. This refers to cooking in a kettle and ladling them, boiling hot, into hot, sterilized jars and then sealing them without a finishing boiling water bath.

Open kettle canning is simple and easy, but variable quality, short shelf life, and spoilage have led researchers to endorse changes.

TIME TABLE
FOR PRESSURE CANNING VEGETABLES*

Vegetable	Method	Headroom in inches	Minutes to Pre-cook	Minutes in Pressure Canner at 10 lb. Pressure	
				Pints	Quarts
Asparagus	Raw Pack	½	—	25	30
	Hot Pack	½	2 – 3	25	30
Beans, Dry with Sauce		+		65	75
Beans, Fresh Lima	Raw Pack	+	—	40	50
	Hot Pack	1	bring to boil	40	50
Beans, Snap	Raw Pack	½	—	20	25
	Hot Pack	½	5	20	25
Beets	Hot Pack Only	½	15	30	35
	Pickled — Boiling Water Bath				
Broccoli	Hot Pack Only	1	3	30	35
Brussel Sprouts	Hot Pack Only	1	3	30	35
Cabbage	Hot Pack Only	1	3	45	55
Carrots	Raw Pack	1		25	30
Cauliflower	Hot Pack Only	1	3	30	35
	Hot Pack	½	1	25	30
Celery	Hot Pack Only	1	3	30	35
Corn, Cream Style	Raw Pack	1½	—	95	(pints only)
	Hot Pack	1	bring to boil	85	—
Corn, Whole Kernel	Raw Pack	1	—	55	85
	Hot Pack	1	bring to boil	55	85
Eggplant	Hot Pack Only	1	5	30	40
Mushrooms	Hot Pack Only	½	+	30	—
				(half-pints-30)	
Okra	Hot Pack Only	½	1	25	40
Parsnips	Hot Pack Only	1	3	30	35
Peas, Field	Raw Pack	+	—	35	40
	Hot Pack	+	bring to boil	35	40
Peas, Fresh Green	Raw Pack	1	—	40	40
	Hot Pack	1	bring to boil	40	40
Peppers	Hot Pack Only	1	3	35	45
Potatoes, White-Whole	Hot Pack Only	½	10	30	40
Potatoes, Cubed	Hot Pack Only	½	2	35	40
Pumpkin, Cubed	Hot Pack Only	½	bring to boil	55	90
Pumpkin, Strained	Hot Pack Only	½	+	65	80
Soybeans	Hot Pack Only	1	bring to boil	55	65
Spinach & Other Greens	Hot Pack Only	½	steam 10 min.	70	90
Squash, Summer	Raw Pack	1	—	25	30
	Hot Pack	½	bring to boil	30	40
Squash, Winter (See Pumpkin)					
Sweet Potatoes	Dry Pack	1	20 – 30	65	95
	Wet Pack	1	20	55	90
Tomatoes (See Chapter 4)					

*Only a pressure canner is recommended for processing low acid vegetables.
+For instructions see section which deals with the specific vegetable.

We often hear people say that if it was good enough for their grandmothers, it's good enough for them. This attitude is most often encountered when people are told that open kettle canning is no longer recommended. Resistance to the newer method of boiling water bath and pressure canning is not uncommon.

If you do wish to open kettle can, the following four conditions are required:

1. sterilized jars and lids.

2. boiling hot acid foods with a high level of sugar and/or vinegar.

3. hot jars filled and sealed immediately.

4. a vacuum formed by steam condensing as the jars cool.

Primarily because of this last condition, recommendations have changed. Jars do not always seal properly without the finishing boiling water bath. It makes sense to take the extra time and caution to insure a high quality product, particularly when you have already invested so much time, money and effort.

Also remember that getting a good seal won't prevent spoilage if the food should become contaminated between kettle and jar.

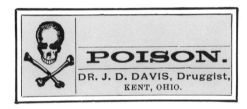

Honest Talk About Scare Factors in Canning

If the potential risks and dangers of home canning are honestly and simply weighed, people can make their own evaluations. Do try to keep the topic in perspective, however. In the past year there have been only a few deaths in the United States from botulism.

Remember that the keys to successful canning are careful handling and perfect seal *along with* proper processing times and temperatures. If you use faulty methods or equipment, you will have unsatisfactory results.

Beware of bulges, foam, odor, cloudy contents, and mold. If in doubt about your product, *don't* taste it. Throw it out so that children or animals won't have access to it. Better to be safe than sorry.

TYPES OF DETERIORATION YOU MIGHT ENCOUNTER

Flat sour is easy to recognize by its sour acid taste and offensive odor. It is caused by soil-borne bacteria which thrive at temperatures between 130° and 150° F. Hence, jars should be cooled quickly. Leaving plenty of space between the jars while they are cooling will hasten this process.

> Before trying to pressure can your vegetables, run through a practice session with your canner, getting used to the whole procedure. Use jars filled with water, or just 2 or 3 inches of water in the canner. You'll gain confidence and may avoid mistakes later if you do this.

Bacteria, molds and yeasts are everywhere—in the air, soil and water—and they must be destroyed by proper heat to prevent spoilage.

Molds are found on canned fruits, tomatoes and jellies and on non-canned foods.

Yeasts cause foods to ferment, and thrive on fruits, tomatoes, jams, jellies and pickles. Both yeasts and molds usually can be destroyed by being heated to the temperature of boiling water for several minutes.

Heat of the required degree and duration, proper sealing methods, plus cleanliness are the strongest weapons against yeasts and molds. Clean hands, clean counters, clean utensils and clean food are your best insurance against food spoilage.

Fermentation taking place in foods is caused primarily by yeasts. Bubbles are formed from a sour-smelling gas which generally breaks the seal. This is usually the result of under-processing the food.

Putrefaction spoilage is caused by bacteria and appears in meat or vegetables. Pickles, where it is often found, become soft and slimy with a very bad odor. Again, under-processing may be the reason.

ENZYMES

Enzymes are present in all foods and are beneficial. Enzymatic action is responsible for the maturing of color, flavor and texture. But, unless this action is stopped, the fruit or vegetable will continue to mature. When the optimum point is past, color, flavor and texture will begin to deteriorate.

The simple application of heat, as in blanching, is sufficient to retard enzyme growth. Some homemakers feel that blanching, especially before freezing, is a time-consuming process with dubious results. So far there has been no research advocating that blanching be abandoned, but use your own judgment. There is no danger of poisoning, just a lessening of quality.

BOTULISM

Clostridium botulinum are frightening words and they should be. While rare, an attack is usually fatal. The bacteria, *botulinum*, are found throughout the environment in water and soil and are harmless there. However, in an anerobic (airless) environment, such as a sealed canning jar, the spores divide and produce poisonous toxins and gas. The spores are extremely heat-resistant but can be destroyed in vegetables and fruits by processing at the temperatures and times called for in the instructions. The toxins can be killed by boiling the contaminated food for 15 minutes at 212°. If in doubt, however, *don't eat. Don't even taste.* Throw the food away so that no person or animal can get at it.

Salmonella, Perfringens and *Staphylococcus,* poisoning, are impossible for the homemaker to detect. Some forms of botulism also are impossible to detect while others can provide clues. Watch for bulging cans, an off-color, unusual odor, or suspect appearance. Deaths from commercially canned foods contaminated with botulism are rare, but there have been about 700 deaths from botulism since 1925 from home-canned products. Signs of botulism poisoning begin within 12 to 36 hours after eating the contaminated foods. Symptoms include double vision, inability to swallow, speech difficulty and progressive paralysis of the respiratory system. Obtain medical help rapidly, as there are antitoxins available that are effective if symptoms are identified soon enough.

The best insurance is to use only accepted methods and never take short cuts. Process at the temperatures and times called for. Use strictly sanitary conditions. And always boil home-canned food in an open pan for 15 minutes (20 minutes for greens and corn) before tasting!

CAPACITIES OF DIFFERENT SIZES OF CANNERS

Size of Canner	Half Pints		Capacity Pints		Quarts		Half Gallon*
4 Quart	4	or	4		—		—
6 Quart	7	or	7		—		—
8 Quart	14+	or	7	or	4		—
16 Quart	20+	or	9	or	7		—
21 Quart			18+	or	7	or	4*

*Because of the density of the food and length of time required to process them, it is not recommended that vegetables be canned in half-gallon containers.

+ If jars are stacked.

CANNING COLOR

Half the joy of canning foods is seeing the jars on the shelf, neat and vitamin-packed, and colorful. Something can be done to make the colors bright and appealing.

When canning fruits such as peaches, pears and apricots, which darken easily and unpleasantly, place the fruits in a quart of water to which a half tablespoon of salt and a half tablespoon of vinegar have been added. When ready to use them, drain, rinse fruit and pack in jars.

Cloudiness in canned peas and some other vegetables may be due to hard water being used in blanching or precooking. Find a soft water supply just for this. Rainwater is fine.

For the finest color in canned beets, add a tablespoon of vinegar to each quart.

Insure Safe, High-Quality Canned Foods

Scrupulously wash all produce. Soil-borne spores are the hardest to kill later, but will wash off before processing. Wash your produce several times, lifting the food out of the water rather than swishing it around. Change the water often and rinse the sink or pan repeatedly. This is especially important with leafy vegetables such as chard and spinach which are frequently sand-covered.

A CHECKLIST OF PRECAUTIONS

1. Prime, quality produce is good insurance. Bruises encourage the growth of bacteria.

2. Wash all produce carefully and completely.

3. Make sure of a good seal.

4. Most important, process for the correct time and at the correct temperature. This is the final key and the crucial factor which, along with the seal, cannot be over-stressed.

Don't, don't take short cuts. Follow directions carefully so that the end product will justify all your time and effort.

A common problem is *color change.* In fruit it is usually color fading which can be remedied by storing the food in a dark place. Occasionally pears, apples and peaches turn pink or blue, beets turn white and corn, brown. This is caused by oxidation, overprocessing, insufficient heat, chemical changes in the food, the use of iron or copper rather than enamel or stainless steel utensils. It is best to be safe, so don't eat any off-

When canning broccoli, select heads before yellow florets appear. Cut out any bad spots. If wormy, soak ½ hour in a solution of 4 tsp. salt to 1 gallon water. Rinse. Cut into serving-size pieces and process according to freezing or canning directions.

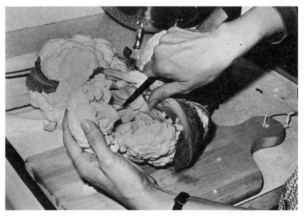

For cauliflower, choose firm, ripe heads. Break or cut into serving-size pieces and cut out the core. If wormy, soak for ½ hour in a solution of 4 tsp. salt to 1 gallon water. Rinse and process according to freezing or canning directions.

color foods. They may be harmless—but color change *is* one sign of possible food contamination.

On the question of preservatives, we are adamant. There are no directions available for the amateur, and preservatives, chemicals and powders may be harmful. In addition, it just doesn't make sense. Why go to all the trouble of growing and preserving your own food only to reproduce chemically treated, store-bought food?

Community Canning Centers

Just as community garden plots are filling the need for people who lack their own garden space, community canning centers are beginning to provide a matching aid. Mainly they serve the many gardeners who want to can their surplusses but don't want to invest in all the equipment that's called for.

During World War II the government promoted community canning centers as part of the effort to help families grow and store more of their own foods. And, in the past few years, these centers have begun to come back—for the same reasons. They now range across the nation from school kitchen setups using home-sized canners, to elaborate installations that use steam-fired equipment.

We — the authors — were fortunate to be a part of the operation of a canning center opened in 1975 as a pilot project of Gardens For All, Inc., a nonprofit organization that promoted community gardening. The equipment for the center was purchased from the Ball Corporation, which for several years has been marketing canning center-type equipment on a limited basis.

Operating the honey extractor.

Cutting beans at the Garden Way Harvest Center.

The Garden Way Harvest Center (located in a renovated barn workshop at Shelburne, Vermont) in its first 60 days of operation was used by 163 families for processing 49 different products. The basic equipment provided is two "tables," each including four 16-quart pressure canners, an atmospheric cooker (for boiling water bath canning), a blancher/sterilizer, and preparation spaces. A gas-fired boiler provides the steam to operate the equipment.

The center also includes two steam-jacketed kettles, two quick-cooling tanks, and this specialized equipment: two juicer-pulper machines (especially good for making large quantities of applesauce and tomato juice), a potato peeler (purchased from a restaurant and which works equally well with carrots and beets), a custom-built pea shucking machine, fruit pitters, apple peelers and a high-speed food chopper.

Making applesauce in a steam-fired kettle.

Packing pints of snap beans for canning.

53

Taking a peek into a whole bank of pressure canners.

Other related equipment available includes a dehydrator for drying foods, a honey extractor and a cider press. Grain-grinding equipment and facilities for baking bread may be added in the future.

When the center is operating one person always is on hand who is trained to operate all the equipment and is knowledgeable about the food-preserving processes. This helps the inexperienced and insures that all foods are preserved safely.

Patrons report that using the canning center is economical, timesaving, and fun. The use-fee charge usually is minimal to make it possible for everybody to benefit from the center's use. They find, too, that large quantities of fruits, vegetables and meats can be processed much more quickly here than in one's own kitchen because of the volume that can be run through these machines with little effort. Imagine doing 100 quarts of applesauce in three hours! The work is speeded up, too, by the use of cooling tanks, which surround the hot jars with a fine mist of cool water. Within 10 or 15 minutes jars are sealed and cooled enough to be packed in boxes and taken home.

Besides speed and efficiency, the center provides a congenial atmosphere where people can share ideas and recipes and keep each other company during what might otherwise seem like tedious work: peeling bushels of peaches, scrubbing beets, or husking dozens of ears of corn.

When many people with varying experience get together to put up food, everyone learns

Using the steam-fired jar sterilizer.

Checking on the juice extractor.

something, and new methods often are developed. We discovered, for example, that when cooking apples down for applesauce in a steam-jacketed kettle, excess cooking liquid could be run off and strained for use in jellies. And tomatoes run through the juicer-pulper machine could be separated with a fine sieve into thin juice and thick pulp. Both were reheated and canned—the juice for a beverage and the pulp, thick enough to need no further cooking, for sauce.

The center is particularly helpful for beginners at food preservation, because here they receive instruction and supervision (if they need it) at every step in the canning process, and they can watch more experienced people put up their own foods. Many beginners make several return visits, and each time go away with more confidence in their ability to process their garden produce either at the center or at home.

We suggest you look around your area for a canning center and try it. If there is none nearby

you might be interested in setting one up—for your own benefit and to help other gardeners in your community. Remember that people without gardens can take advantage of these centers, too—by buying fresh produce in season and processing it themselves at the center.

Organizations such as schools, churches, senior citizen groups, garden clubs and home demonstration groups sometimes sponsor canning centers, either on a small scale with volunteers working in an existing kitchen, or on a larger scale such as our Harvest Center. One successful setup uses school facilities after hours with home economics teachers and students as volunteer instructors.

For information on setting up a community canning center, write to Gardens For All, Inc., P.O. Box 371, Shelburne, Vermont 05482; to the Ball Corporation, Muncie, Indiana 47302; or check with the extension service at your state university if there is in your area an Expanded Food and Nutrition Education Program.

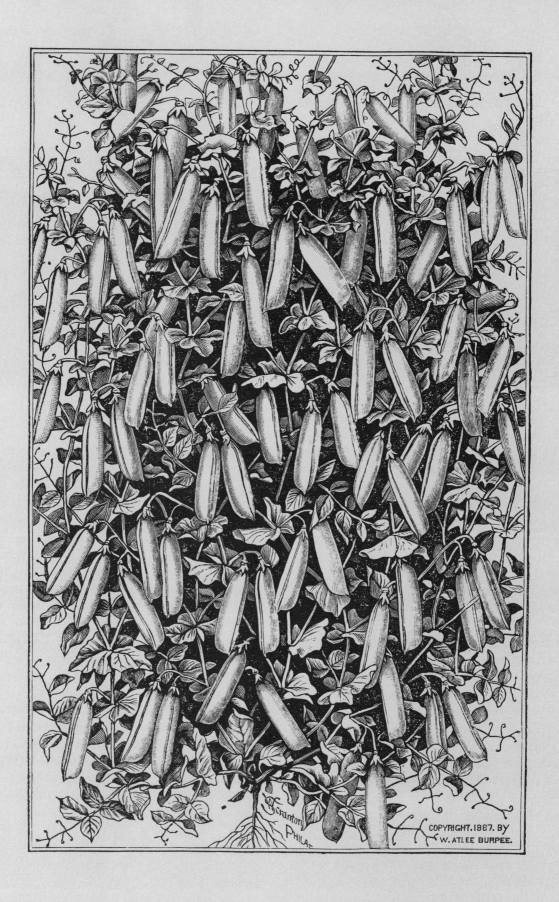

Scranton
Phila.

COPYRIGHT, 1887. BY
W. ATLEE BURPEE.

Chapter 4
Keeping Every Vegetable

This chapter, which is the real heart of our book, includes information on how to harvest, store and preserve all of the vegetables commonly grown in the home garden. Where appropriate we have suggested which preserving methods are most suitable for each vegetable. Cooking suggestions also are given where fitting.

Before going ahead with the preserving of any vegetable, please be sure to review the detailed how-to instructions in the chapters on canning, freezing, drying, pickling, curing with salt and common storage.

Asparagus

Harvesting. Asparagus should be picked when six to eight inches high and when larger than the size of a pencil. Thinner shoots should be allowed to grow and mature into ferns, as these will help replenish the roots, ensuring a good crop the following year. Harvesting can continue for six to ten weeks in an established bed.

The last stalks should be allowed to grow and go to seed.

Three Ways to Harvest

1. Cut the stalk at ground level with a sharp knife.

2. Cut just below the ground. Use caution so as not to injure any shoots that may be growing up beside the one you are cutting.

3. Snap off the stalk, holding it midway from the ground. This method automatically breaks off the tender part of the stem, leaving the tough end in the ground.

Preparation. Wash asparagus and scrub with a vegetable brush. Trim off a few scales. If sand is present behind them, trim off the rest and wash again. If you have cut your asparagus, hold the piece at each end and snap. It will break where the tender part ends. Otherwise trim off the tough ends. Sort for size or cut into pieces.

Pressure Canning. For spears, cut ¾ inch shorter than the jars.

Raw Pack: Pack whole spears, tips up, tightly into clean, hot jars. Pack cut pieces as tightly as possible without crushing them. Leave ½ inch headroom. Add salt if desired. Cover with boiling water, leaving ½ inch headroom. Adjust lids. Process in a pressure canner at 10 pounds pressure (240° F.).

       Pints . . . . 25 minutes
       Quarts . . . . 30 minutes

Remove jars from canner. Complete seals if necessary.

Hot Pack: Stand whole spears upright in boiling water, covering all but the tips, or cover cut up pieces with boiling water. Boil 2–3 minutes. Pack whole spears, tips up, in hot, clean jars, or pack hot pieces loosely to within ½ inch of top. The addition of salt is optional. Cover with boiling cooking liquid or fresh boiling water, leaving ½ inch headroom. Adjust lids. Process in a pressure canner at 10 pounds pressure (240°):

       Pints . . . . 25 minutes
       Quarts . . . . 30 minutes

Remove jars from canner. Complete seals if necessary.

Freezing. Blanch for 2–4 minutes depending on the thickness of the stalks. Cool immediately in cold water. Drain. Pack into containers, leaving no headroom (see page 20). For spears, pack tips up. Seal and freeze.

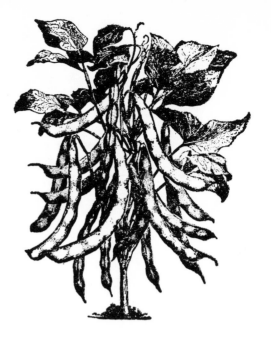

Beans, Dry

(Navy, Soldier, Kidney, etc.)

Dry beans contribute both vitamins and protein to our diet, and can be grown easily by anyone who has a little extra garden space. Being legumes, the bean plants have low fertilizer needs because, if inoculated when planted with nitrogen-fixing bacteria, they will supply much of their own nitrogen rather than taking it from the soil. Cooking beans with animal foods (meat, cheese, or milk) or with grains or nuts completes the protein mix so that they can supply the essential amino acids needed by the human body.

Harvesting. If planted early enough, the pods should be mostly dry on the vine by mid-fall. Harvest by pulling the entire plant (do not strain your back trying to pick each pod, as we did the first year!), then "stook" them by making piles of the plants around posts, and leave them for a week or so. Then spread them out or hang them up in an airy shed or garage, and leave them for several weeks until pods and vines are completely dry.

The next step is to thresh the beans, which can be done in several ways:

Before canning any vegetable, please read the instructions for operating your pressure canner. For a quick review, here are the key terms you will find used in the canning and freezing directions:

Headroom: The space between the top of the food and the top rim of the jar. For most vegetables this is ½ inch; however, for the starchy vegetables such as corn, shelled beans and peas it is as much as 1 inch or more.

"Adjust lids": The type of canning jar and lids you are using will determine what you do. For two-piece metal lids, put on the Mason lid with sealing compound down, and screw band on tightly. Do not tighten after processing. For bail type jars put on clean rubber, glass lid, and raise the upper wire over the top. Leave the lower wire in the up (looser) position. Press down immediately after processing. Porcelain lined zinc caps are adjusted differently. The rubber is placed on the ledge below the rim of the jar, and the lid screwed down tightly, then loosened about ¼ inch.

"Complete seals if necessary": This is not necessary for the two-piece metal lids. For bail type, snap down the lower wire. For porcelain lined zinc caps and other one-piece lids, screw them shut tightly.

Blanching: Boiling or steaming vegetables before freezing to halt enzyme action.

"Add salt": This is optional, depending on your taste. If you do add salt, it should be up to 1 teaspoon for quarts; ½ teaspoon for pints.

Raw Pack: This means putting the washed and prepared food raw into clean jars, usually adding boiling water to cover, and then processing.

Hot Pack: This means pre-cooking the food, primarily to allow for a denser pack. Sometimes the processing time will be longer for hot pack even though it is already partially cooked, because of the density.

After canning any vegetable, the jars must be allowed to cool in a draft-free place, and then checked for good seals. They should be washed, labeled and stored in a cool, dark dry place—ready to be enjoyed throughout the rest of the year.

BOILING WARNING

Note: For absolute safety, all low-acid foods canned at home should be boiled vigorously for 15 minutes in an open vessel before tasting! Greens and corn should be boiled for 20 minutes.

1. Hold the plant by the roots upside down in a can or barrel, and bang it from side to side. The beans will fall out of the brittle pods.

OR

2. Stuff the dry plants into sturdy burlap bags and close the tops securely. Then the fun begins! Invite as many children as you need to spend an afternoon jumping on the bags. Or, less joyfully, beat the bags with a stick. The pods will break with this treatment, and the beans will be freed. Turn the bag upside down and shake, then make a small opening and let the beans pour out.

Winnowing will remove the debris of broken vines and leaves that will be mixed with your beans. Pick a windy day, and using two buckets pour the beans from one to the other from about three feet above. The wind will carry away most of the chaff. The rest can be washed off just before using; but do not wash before storing.

Storage. The beans should be totally dry when stored. Use clean, dry containers that have tight-fitting lids, and seal them tightly to keep out worms and insects. Store filled containers in a cool, dry place. The best results, as with all dry foods, will be if you seal them up on a dry day. Check the containers occasionally and if moisture appears on the lid or sides, or if there is a musty smell, remove the beans, spread out in a warm dry place and re-dry, stirring occasionally. Repack in clean dry containers.

Canning

Dry beans with sauce: Shell and wash dry beans discarding discolored or withered ones. You can use the ordinary types (kidney, navy or yellow eye) or the beans from snap bean or pole bean varieties that may have gone un-picked. Cover beans with boiling water and boil 2 minutes. Remove from heat and soak 1 hour. Add more boiling water if there is not enough to keep the beans covered as they expand. Heat to boiling, drain, reserving the liquid for the sauce. Fill jars ¾ full with hot beans. Add a small piece of salt pork, ham or bacon. Cover with hot sauce, leaving 1 inch headroom. Adjust lids. Process in pressure canner at 10 pounds pressure (240° F.).

> Pints . . . . 65 minutes
> Quarts . . . . 75 minutes

Complete seals if necessary.

Tomato sauce: Heat to boiling a mixture of 1 quart tomato juice, 3 tablespoons sugar or molasses, 2 teaspoons salt, 1 tablespoon chopped onion, and ¼ teaspoon mixture of ground cloves, allspice, mace and cayenne. Or mix 1 cup tomato ketchup with 3 cups of liquid reserved from soaking beans and heat to boiling.

Molasses sauce: To one quart liquid from soaking beans add 3 tablespoons molasses, 1 tablespoon vinegar, 2 teaspoons salt, and ¾ tea-spoon powdered dry mustard. Heat to boiling.

Baked and Canned. Prepare and soak beans as above for *Beans with sauce.* Place beans in a pot or casserole. Cover with molasses sauce, and bury a piece of salt pork, ham, or bacon in the beans. Cover pot and bake 4 to 5 hours at 350° F. Add water as needed to prevent from drying out.

Hot pack: Pack hot beans into hot jars, leav-ing 1 inch of headroom. Adjust lids. Process in a pressure canner at 10 pounds pressure (240° F.).

> Pints . . . . 80 minutes
> Quarts . . . . 100 minutes

Complete seals if necessary as soon as jars are removed from canner.

Beans, Green and Wax Snap

Harvesting. The best quality will be achieved with young tender, crisp beans in which the bean seeds have only begun to form. Pick con-tinuously to prolong harvest. Remember to plant your beans at 2 week intervals in order to have fresh beans right up to the first frost and to spread the period of preserving.

Preparation. If you are preserving by the bushel, try doing them in a variety of ways to avoid the cry of "beans again." Straight young beans can be canned whole, packed vertically in pint jars. For canning or freezing, they can be French cut with a sharp paring knife or a "Frencher," such as is found on the end of some vegetable scrapers. Others can be cut into pieces, either straight across or on a slant, in varying lengths. More mature beans are best cut into ½ inch pieces, if you have the patience. The stem end should be removed from all beans; the blossom end can be left on or not, as you wish. On the older beans be sure to remove the strings down the side, if present.

Pressure canning

Raw pack: Pack washed, but raw beans tight-ly into clean jars leaving ½ inch headroom. Add salt (optional). Cover with boiling water, leaving ½ inch headroom. Adjust lids. Process in pressure canner at 10 pounds pressure (240° F.).

Pints................20 minutes
Quarts..............25 minutes

Complete seals if necessary as soon as jars are removed from canner.

Hot pack: Cover washed, cut beans with boiling water; boil 5 minutes. Pack hot beans loosely in hot jars, leaving ½ inch headroom. Add salt (optional). Cover with boiling cooking liquid, leaving ½ inch headroom. Adjust lids. Process in pressure canner at 10 pounds pressure (240° F.).

Pints................20 minutes
Quarts..............25 minutes

Complete seals if necessary.

Freezing. Blanch clean prepared beans in boiling water for 3 minutes. Cool immediately in cold water. Drain. Pack into containers, leaving headroom (see page 20). Seal and freeze.

Drying. Refer to Chapter 9.

Curing with salt. See sauer beans, Chapter 8.

TO FIGURE YIELD OF CANNED VEGETABLES FROM FRESH

The number of quarts of canned food you can get from a given amount of fresh vegetables depends on quality, condition, maturity, and variety of the vegetable, size of pieces, and on the way the vegetable is packed—raw or hot pack.

Generally, the following amounts of fresh vegetables (as purchased or picked) make 1 quart of canned food:

Vegetable	Pounds
Asparagus	2½ to 4½
Beans, lima, in pods	3 to 5
Beans, snap	1½ to 2½
Beets, without tops	2 to 3½
Carrots, without tops	2 to 3
Corn, sweet, in husks	3 to 6
Okra	1½
Peas, green, in pods	3 to 6
Pumpkin or winter squash	1½ to 3
Spinach and other greens	2 to 6
Squash, summer	2 to 4
Sweet potatoes	2 to 3

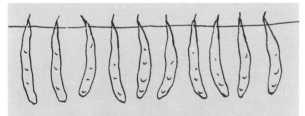

LEATHER BRITCHES

"Leather britches is a down-home name for dried green beans. String fresh green beans on white crochet thread, using a large-eyed needle. Hang on a clothesline in full sun for two or three days, taking them in at night. Once they're dry, slide them off the strings onto a cookie sheet. Warm up the oven, turn it off, and set the cookie sheet inside for five minutes. Store in glass jars. To cook, break beans, wash, and soak overnight in plenty of water. Pour off soaking water, add more, bring to a boil, and simmer all day."

Dick Raymond
Down-to-Earth Vegetable Gardening
A Garden Way publication

Beans, Lima

Harvesting. Pick pods when fat and bulging. Most prefer the beans before they turn from green to tan color.

Preparation. Shell, wash and sort beans by approximate size.

Pressure canning

Raw pack: Pack raw beans into clean jars. With small-type beans leave 1 inch headroom for pints and 1½ inch headroom for quarts; with large beans, leave ¾ inch headroom for pints and 1¼ inch headroom for quarts. Do not press or shake beans down. Add salt (optional). Cover with boiling water, leaving ½ inch headroom. Adjust lids. Process in pressure canner at 10 pounds pressure (240° F.).

    Pints . . . . 40 minutes
    Quarts . . . . 50 minutes

Complete seals if necessary.

Hot pack: Cover shelled beans with boiling water and boil 1 minute. Drain and save cooking liquid. Pack hot beans loosely in clean, hot jars, leaving 1 inch headroom. Add salt (optional). Cover with boiling cooking liquid, leaving 1 inch headroom. Adjust lids. Process in pressure canner at 10 pounds pressure (240° F.).

    Pints . . . . 40 minutes
    Quarts . . . . 50 minutes

Complete seals if necessary.

Freezing. Blanch beans in boiling water for 2–4 minutes depending on size (2 for small, 3 for medium, 4 for large). Cool immediately in cold water. Drain. Put into containers, leaving headroom (see page 20). Seal and freeze.

Drying. Refer to Chapter 9.

BURNS

The danger of contaminated food is well known, but one other danger exists in home food processing that is consistently overlooked—and it is one over which you have much control. That is burns. Every summer many people receive minor burns and some even need treatment in a hospital. Few other cooking procedures require such volumes of boiling water and/or steam.

So be careful! Keep small children from under foot when juggling large kettles of boiling water. Always wear shoes. A small spill on bare feet can be a forerunner of a much larger burn if you should then drop a kettle of water. Always open a pressure canner away from you to avoid a rush of steam in your face. Never use a damp towel or pot holder to lift a hot kettle as the dampness conducts heat rapidly.

If you **are** burned, immediately immerse the burned area in cold water. This will reduce the amount of blister.

SHELLING LIMA BEANS

Pods of mature beans will split fairly easily from thumb pressure applied edgeways on the outside curve. For under-mature or baby limas it helps first to pull off the string on the outside edge. Catch it, starting at stem end, with your thumbnail. Then thumb pressure will pop the pod.

Beans, Soy

See Soybeans.

Beets

Harvesting. No matter how far apart beets are planted they will still have to be thinned, because the "seed" is actually a pod containing several tiny seeds which will all germinate in the same spot. When thinning these plants, pull the largest and eat fresh or preserve them as greens. Leave the tiny beet on the greens for a surprise taste treat. These may be either frozen or canned. The small plants left several inches apart in the row can be further thinned (and eaten) to leave plants about eight inches apart to grow into full-sized beets.

The beets for storage should be harvested as late in the fall as possible before the ground freezes. For freezing or canning they can be picked whenever big enough. The best flavor is when they are small (1–3 inch diameter) and can be preserved whole.

For storage dig or pull the beets, and leave in the sun for two hours, so dirt falls free of the roots. Cut the stems about one inch from the beet. Do not cut the root. Beets will "bleed" away their color if cut into at all, except for the gold varieties. Do not wash before storing.

Storage. Beets are best packed in fresh-sawed sawdust; sand or leaves may also be used. (See the chapter on Common Storage for further information.) Store in a cold, moist place. In addition to being stored, pressure-canned and frozen, beets may also be pickled and used in relishes.

Preparation. Wash carefully, and leave on one or two inches of stems and the roots to prevent bleeding. Cover with boiling water and boil until the skins slip off easily, about 20 to 40 minutes depending on their size. Dip in cold water to cool enough to handle, and slip off the skins. Trim off roots and stems. Baby beets can be left whole; larger ones can be cut into cubes or slices.

Pressure canning

Hot pack only: Pack hot beets into hot jars, leaving ½ inch headroom. Add salt if desired, 1 teaspoon per quart; ½ teaspoon per pint. Cover with boiling water, leaving ½ inch headroom. Adjust lids, and process in a pressure canner at 10 pounds pressure (240° F.).

Pints . . . . 30 minutes
Quarts . . . . 35 minutes

Complete seals if necessary as soon as jars are removed from canner.

Pickled beets. Pickled beets should be processed in a boiling water bath rather than a pressure canner because of the acid in the vinegar. Prepare beets as for hot pack canning. Pack hot beets into hot jars, leaving ½ inch headroom. Add salt, 1 teaspoon per quart or ½ teaspoon per pint. Cover with boiling syrup (see below), leaving ½ inch headroom. Adjust lids and process in a Boiling Water Bath (212° F.).

      Pints. . . . . .30 minutes
      Quarts . . . . .30 minutes

Remove jars. Complete seals if necessary.

Pickling syrup: Mix and heat to boiling: 2 cups vinegar to 2 cups sugar.

Freezing. Freeze only very young, tender beets, as the texture and flavor of larger ones change during freezing. Pack prepared beets into freezing containers, leaving headroom (see page 20). Seal and freeze.

Broccoli

Broccoli, rich in vitamins A and C, is easy to prepare for eating and freezing. You can harvest it over a long period, well into frost. Early and late plantings of a few plants each will supply the average family with ample heads for eating fresh and preserving.

Harvesting. Broccoli will form a center cluster of green buds which should be harvested while the buds are shut and before any yellow flowers appear. These clusters should be cut with about 1½ inch of stem. Clusters may vary from the size of a small teacup to that of a large saucer. "Lateral" clusters of various sizes, but usually smaller than the center cluster, will start forming on the sides of the plants after the center cluster has been harvested. These should be harvested every few days to prevent them from flowering. If allowed to flower and set seeds, the plants will stop producing new clusters; if kept picked they will continue to produce through the fall until

frosts are severe. Late season broccoli is less likely to be infested with insects than during warm weather.

Preparation. Freezing is recommended. Broccoli, as well as Brussels sprouts, cabbage, cauliflower, rutabagas and turnips, becomes discolored and develops a strong flavor when canned.

Wash freshly picked broccoli and check closely for insects. Green cabbage worms are almost invisible in broccoli so you may have to pull apart a stalk or two to locate them. If insects are present (and they most likely will be), soak the broccoli in salt water (1 tbsp. per quart of water) for 15 minutes. Check again for worms. The salt water may not reveal them. However, with cooking they turn white and can easily be found. Rinse well.

Pressure canning

Hot pack only: Cut broccoli into serving-size pieces and boil for 3 minutes. Drain. Pack hot broccoli in hot, clean jars, leaving 1 inch headroom. Cover with boiling water, leaving 1 inch headroom. Adjust lids. Process in a pressure canner at 10 pounds pressure (240° F.).

Pints . . . . 30 minutes
Quarts . . . . 35 minutes

Remove jars from canner. Complete seals if necessary.

Freezing. Blanch 3 minutes in boiling water. Cool immediately in cold water. Drain. Pack into containers, leaving no headroom. Seal and freeze.

Brussels Sprouts

Harvesting. Brussels sprouts ripen from the bottom up and will appear all along the stem of the plant. They can be harvested as soon as they are about the size of a marble. Some may grow much larger. When the first sprouts on the bottom of the stem are harvested, break off the leaves around them and for 5–6 inches above them in order to encourage the stem to grow taller and to produce more sprouts. Repeat this process each time the sprouts are harvested. They can be cut off most easily if you follow the spiral formation in which they grow. The plants may grow as high as three feet and can be harvested throughout the winter in the South and, if covered, in the North.

WHY BROCCOLI?

"If you don't want to grow cabbage, then do grow broccoli. It is a handsome plant to have in the garden, and most rewarding, because it produces well into the fall after the first frost. Keep cutting and it will keep growing and, believe me, it is not the same thick-stalked vegetable that we are used to in the winter. *Italian Green Sprouting* to us is the best, and you can start your seeds inside and transplant after the last frost or start them directly in the ground in late May to produce a fall crop. Or you can buy eight plants from your local nursery and have broccoli in six weeks.

"... It is a very nutritious vegetable and makes delicious soup, salad, and soufflé, and it lends itself to both hot and cold service. When you pick your own broccoli, the stalks will be tender and not need peeling. If any stalks are over a half inch in diameter, you can split them. Like asparagus, the broccoli head and stalk must be cooked to the same degree of doneness. Be sure to soak the heads in salt water for half an hour, as there's bound to be at least one small green worm waving its antennae at you."

Marjorie Page Blanchard
Home Gardener's Cookbook
A Garden Way publication

RAISING BRUSSELS SPROUTS

"About the middle of September, pinch out the growing points in the top of each plant. The sprouts on the upper part of the plant promptly start to develop more rapidly and attain larger size."

Joseph Harris Co. catalog

Pressure canning. Brussels sprouts, like broccoli, are inferior as a canned vegetable. However, to can them, discard the loose outer leaves, wash, then follow the directions for broccoli.

Freezing. Sort, peel off the outer leaves, then wash. Blanch for 3–5 minutes depending on size. Cool immediately in cold water. Pack into containers, leaving no headroom (see page 20). Seal and freeze.

Cabbage

Harvesting. Early varieties for summer use: Cut off the head when needed. Leaving two or three leaves on the stem in the ground will usually grow several smaller heads later in the season as a bonus! Late varieties for storage: Wait until the cabbage has fully matured and the weather is cool. Cut the heads off the plants, discarding

loose outer leaves and any inner leaves that show signs of insect infestation. In wet weather you may find the cabbages are cracking. This is caused by the plant taking in water faster than it can be used. "Turn the water off" by twisting the cabbage one half turn, which breaks some of the plant's roots.

Storage. Wrap each head in three newspapers, securing them tightly with string or large rubber bands. Store in a root cellar or any cool part of the house. Cabbage may also be pulled up by the roots and hung in a garage or shed if safe from freezing and where the temperatures will remain fairly constant. They will, however, not keep as well as those wrapped in newspapers, especially if there is much fluctuation in temperature. Do not hang them in your cellar or in any other closed area, as the odor can become very strong.

Pressure canning. Cabbage presents the same canning problems as broccoli, but if you like New England boiled dinners a few jars of cabbage in the pantry will come in handy. Wash the cabbage, remove the loose outer leaves and, if there are insects, keep removing leaves until there is no sign of them. Cut into pieces that will fit into your jars, but leave on enough of the core to hold the cabbage together. Cover with boiling water and boil for 3 minutes. Pack hot cabbage into clean, hot jars, leaving 1 inch head-room. Salt is optional. Cover with boiling water, leaving 1 inch headroom. Adjust lids. Process in a pressure canner at 10 pounds pressure (240° F.).

Pints . . . . 45 minutes
Quarts . . . . 55 minutes

Remove from canner. Complete seals if necessary.

Freezing. Pick solid heads, cut off outer leaves. Cut heads as desired. Blanch for 1½ minutes in boiling water. Cool immediately in cold water. Pack into containers, leaving headroom (see page 20). Seal and freeze.

Curing with salt. See Sauerkraut in Chapter 8.

Cabbage, Chinese

Harvesting. Chinese cabbage is a late fall crop, growing best in cool weather. It can be harvested throughout the winter in mild climates and through several hard frosts in the North. The bugs that might be a problem in summer cannot survive the cold and so are no problem to late plantings.

Storage. Storage is not feasible except for short periods refrigerated in plastic bags.

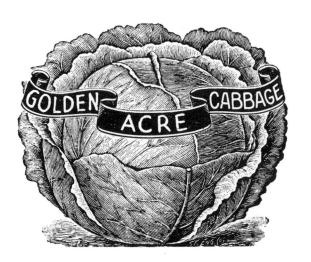

BAKED CHINESE CABBAGE

Wash the head, cut into small pieces and cook in enough salted water (1-1½ teaspoons to the quart of water) to barely cover the cabbage. Boil for about 7 minutes, or until tender. Drain and place 4 cups of cabbage in a greased baking dish, seasoning with a sprinkling of paprika. Combine two beaten eggs with two cups of milk and add ¼ teaspoon of salt. Pour this mixture over the cabbage, and place the baking dish in a pan of hot water. Bake at 350° for about ¾ hour, or until it is firm.

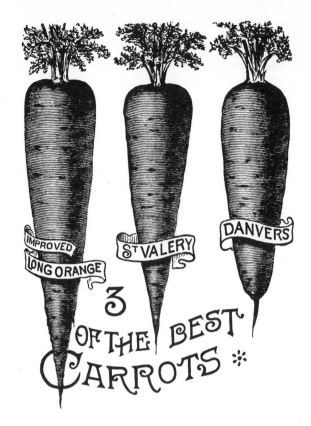

Carrots

Harvesting. Carrots can be eaten whenever big enough to be enjoyed; the size and shape when mature (long or short; thin or thick; blunt or tapered) will depend on the variety planted. Tiny whole carrots are delicious frozen; "table size"—up to 6 inches long and no more than 1 inch in diameter at the widest point—are good for all uses. Great big overgrown carrots tend to be tough and bitter, and are not desirable for eating.

Carrots planted early in the season should be harvested when ready for eating fresh, and any excess should be either frozen or canned. Always pull the largest carrots first; the smaller ones will fill in and catch up when given more space. The largest can be identified by looking for the tops that are darkest green; follow these down to the ground to pull the carrot.

Storage. For storage purposes plant carrots later in the season, allowing time for them to mature before frost. They will keep in the ground after frosts, but should be dug before the ground freezes if they are to be stored in the root cellar. If heavily mulched, they also can be kept in the ground through the winter and dug when needed. These will be sweet and delicious, but must be used immediately after digging.

After digging carrots for storage, leave them in the sun for two hours until the dirt dries enough to fall off them. Trim the stem close to the carrot, and pack in freshly-cut sawdust, or other packing material. (See the chapter on Common Storage for more information.) They

also may be kept in plastic bags, with a few holes for ventilation to prevent rot. Carrots do best stored in a cold, moist place.

Pressure canning. Carrots can better than they freeze, and they are very useful as a vegetable to be served alone, or to be used in stews, soups, and mixed vegetable dishes. Small ones can be canned whole; larger ones are either sliced or diced.

Wash thoroughly and scrape the skin; or parboil long enough for the skins to slip off.

Raw pack: Pack raw prepared carrots tightly into clean jars, leaving 1 inch headroom. Add salt if desired, 1 teaspoon per quart or ½ teaspoon per pint. Cover with boiling water, leaving ½ inch headroom. Adjust lids. Process in a pressure canner at 10 pounds pressure (240° F.).

Pints . . . . 25 minutes
Quarts . . . . 30 minutes

Complete seals if necessary as soon as jars are removed from the canner.

Hot pack: Cover washed, skinned and cut up carrots with boiling water and boil for 1 minute. Drain, reserving the cooking liquid. Pack hot

68

carrots into hot jars, leaving ½ inch headroom. Add salt if desired, 1 teaspoon per quart or ½ teaspoon per pint. Cover with boiling cooking liquid, leaving ½ inch headroom. Adjust lids, and process in a pressure canner at 10 pounds pressure (240° F.).

    Pints . . . . 25 minutes
    Quarts . . . . 30 minutes

Complete seals if necessary as soon as jars are removed from the canner.

Freezing. For freezing, use only very tender, tiny young carrots, as the texture of larger ones changes with freezing. Freeze whole little carrots for soups and stews.

Remove tops, wash and peel or scrub hard with a vegetable brush. Blanch whole carrots in boiling water for 5 minutes — 2 minutes for diced, slices or strips. Cool immediately in ice cold water. Drain. Pack into freezer containers, leaving headroom (see page 20). Seal and freeze.

Drying. Refer to Chapter 9.

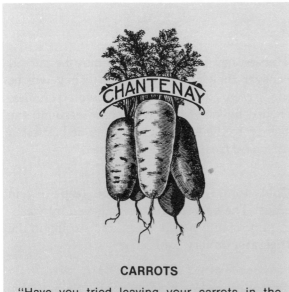

CARROTS

"Have you tried leaving your carrots in the ground during the early winter months to save storage space in the house? They can be kept there, covered with a heavy mulch of some kind. Many people prefer them to the frozen or shipped stuff you get at the supermarket."

Stu Campbell
The Mulch Book
A Garden Way publication

Cauliflower

Harvesting. Cauliflower is ready to harvest when the "curds" or flowerets are well formed, but before they shoot up and flower. The full-grown head may vary in size from several inches to a foot across. When the heads have begun to form (about 4 inches across) they must be blanched, or shaded from the sun, in order to be white and tender. This can be done by tying the leaves over the head (not too tightly or in damp weather they will rot). A better method is to partially break several of the large side leaves, pull them over the top and tuck them under the cauliflower head on the far side. The leaves will shed rain, lessening the chance of rot. The head should be ready to harvest about a week later.

To harvest, cut the head off above the leaves (no new head will form, so the space may be given up for lettuce or another quick-growing crop). The flowerets are delicious raw served with dips, or cooked. The best method of preserving is freezing; canning is a poor second best as cauliflower will develop a strong flavor and change color when canned. Cauliflower may be used in pickled mixed vegetables. (See Mustard Pickles, Chapter 7.)

Pressure canning. Cut the cauliflower up into the individual flower stalks and pressure can following the directions for broccoli.

Freezing. Choose firm, tender heads. Break or cut into flowerets. Soak for ½ hour in a solution of 1 tablespoon salt to 1 quart water if necessary to remove insects. Drain and rinse.

Blanch the cauliflower for 3 minutes in a boiling solution of either 4 teaspoons salt or the juice of one lemon to a gallon of water. This will help prevent it from darkening when frozen. Cool immediately in ice cold water. Drain and pack into freezer container, leaving no headroom. Seal and freeze.

RAISING CAULIFLOWER

"Too little is written about how to grow cauliflowers reliably well, and as a result it is probably the vegetable that fails to grow for more gardeners than any other type. The raising from seed is no stumbling block—place seed ½ in. deep in cold frame, flats or boxes some 4–6 weeks before last frost in your area (winter crops can be left until late May) in a temperature of 60°F (15°C). Transplant to their final quarters at 24 in. x 24 in. From now on it is imperative that they have no set-backs, so provide plenty of moisture, a rich humus soil with added lime. If the plants droop after transplantation for more than a few days, your crops will be affected. A well-grown crop of cauliflowers will not only show you a great saving over the grocery store but it is also the most satisfying of all vegetables to harvest."

Thompson & Morgan catalog

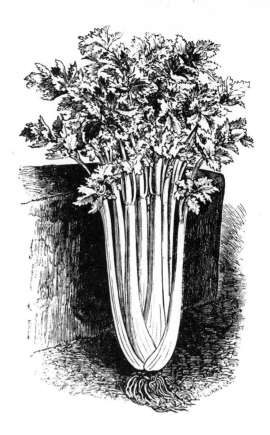

Celery

Harvesting. The outer stalks may be cut off whenever they are long enough. They will be dark green and strongly flavored unless bleached by placing soil or boards around the stalks up to the leaves. Celery can be harvested until a hard frost if heavily mulched.

Cold storage. Celery will not keep long in storage. The best results are achieved by washing, putting into plastic bags, and storing in the refrigerator or very cool cellar.

Preparation. Wash and cut off tough or discolored spots. Celery that has been blanched in the garden will make the most tender products. If necessary, remove tough strings and cut celery into strips or pieces.

Pressure canning. Celery that has been canned is convenient for use in soups and stews, as well as in vegetable combinations. It also may be canned with tomatoes or other vegetables. (See directions under Mixed Vegetables.)

Hot pack: Cover cut-up celery with boiling water and boil 3 minutes. Drain. Pack hot into clean, hot jars, leaving 1 inch headroom. Add salt. Cover with boiling water, leaving 1 inch headroom. Adjust lids. Process at 10 pounds pressure (240° F.).

Pints . . . . 30 minutes
Quarts . . . . 35 minutes

Remove from canner. Complete seals if necessary.

Freezing. Celery freezes best in combination dishes. Wash and cut. Blanch for three minutes in boiling water. Cool immediately in cold water. Drain. Pack into containers, leaving headroom (see page 20). Seal and freeze.

CELERY

"Celery I don't grow...."

Ruth Stout

"Some say celery should not be undertaken by the home gardener. Others say try it; you may be successful. Celery does like rich soil and a lot of moisture. It also needs coolish nights. If you can provide these necessities, then give it a whirl. The big question with this vegetable seems to be blanching. I say yes, it is necessary to blanch so that the stalks are not tough and stringy. But blanching is not that difficult a proposition. When your celery gets tall, just lay light boards along either side, on an angle of an inverted V. This will cover the stalks sufficiently and will save you the work of hilling. *Pascal* and *Fordhook* are good growers, and a ten-foot row should be sufficient unless you are avid celery eaters. You don't need to wait for full maturity to pick this plant; the stalks can be used from the time the plants are half grown."

Marjorie Page Blanchard
Home Gardener's Cookbook
A Garden Way publication

Corn cutters come in several varieties but after trying all of them, we feel nothing seems to improve on a sharp knife. The corn cutters are wasteful and have caused more than their share of gouged knuckles.

Sweet Corn

Harvesting. Check your sweet corn often as it approaches ripeness, so you can enjoy this garden favorite as early as possible — and before raccoons find it (if your garden is unfenced). We often find the first ripe ears in the center of the rows, so don't be mislead by immature ears at the ends.

There are several ways to tell when sweet corn is ripe. First look at the silk, which will darken and dry out as the ears mature. Then feel the top of the ear by pinching through the husk (without opening it). The end of the ear should be blunt rather than tapered as the kernels fill out near the top. When an ear looks and feels right the final test is to pull down part of the husk and press a kernel with your fingernail. If the corn is perfectly ripe the sweet juice will spurt out.

Pick as close to processing time as possible, since the sugars quickly turn to starch. Keep the ears cool. For preserving, plan to plant some corn that will mature two or three weeks before frost, so it will not stay in your freezer longer than necessary.

Pressure canning whole kernel corn. Cut off the kernels with a sharp knife. Avoid cutting the cob itself.

Raw pack: Pack corn in clean jars, leaving 1 inch headroom. Do not shake or press down. Add salt (optional). Cover with boiling water, leaving ½ inch headroom. Adjust lids. Process in a pressure canner at 10 pounds pressure (240° F.).

          Pints . . . . 55 minutes
          Quarts . . . . 85 minutes

Complete seals if necessary as soon as jars are removed from the canner.

Hot pack: To each quart of cut corn, add 1 pint of boiling water and heat to boiling. Drain, reserving liquid. Pack hot corn in hot jars, leaving 1 inch headroom, and cover with the boiling cooking liquid, leaving 1 inch headroom. Or fill to 1 inch of top with undrained corn and liquid. Add salt (optional). Adjust lids. Process in a pressure canner at 10 pounds pressure (240° F.).

          Pints . . . . 55 minutes
          Quarts . . . . 85 minutes

Complete seals if necessary as soon as jars are removed from the canner.

Freezing whole kernel corn. Heat ears in boiling water for 4 minutes. Cool immediately in cold water. Drain. Cut off the kernels, but avoid cutting the cob itself. Pack into containers, leaving headroom (see page 20). Seal and freeze.

CREAM-STYLE CORN

Use well-matured but still sweet ears, rather than the earliest ones that usually disappear at the picnic table.

Preparation. Husk and remove all silk. Wash. Cut down through the tops of the kernels with a sharp knife. Then turn the knife on its side and

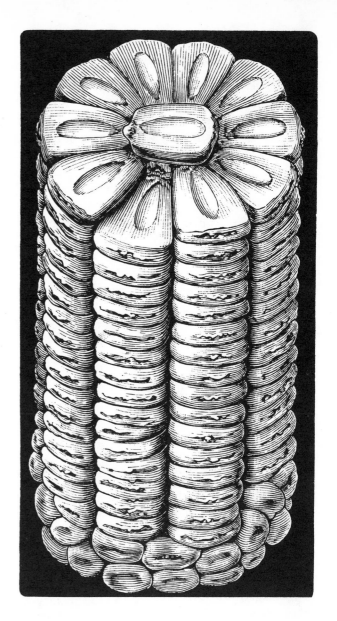

scrape down the sides of the cob to draw out the "cream" and insides of the kernels left on the cob. For canning, do not use quart jars for cream style, since the length of processing time would be so long that the flavor and food value would be destroyed.

Pressure canning cream-style corn

Raw pack: Pack corn and cream into clean jars, leaving 1½ inch headroom. Do not shake or press down. Add salt. Cover with boiling water, leaving ½ inch headroom. Adjust lids. Process in a pressure canner at 10 pounds pressure (240° F.).

          Pints . . . . 95 minutes

Complete seals if necessary as soon as jars are removed from the canner.

Freezing cream-style corn. Heat ears in boiling water for 4 minutes. Cool immediately in cool water and process as above. Pack into containers, leaving headroom (see page 20). Seal and freeze.

Freezing corn-on-the-cob. Many people feel that corn-on-the-cob is a doubtful use of freezer space unless you have lots of room to spare. The quality doesn't compare with whole kernel, but the treat of corn-on-the-cob in mid-winter is worth the space, and it's a special treat for children. Use freeze bags for packaging.

Blanch small ears 7 minutes, medium ears 9 minutes, large ears 11 minutes. Cool immediately in ice water. *Drain well* and pat dry with towels. Pack into containers, expelling as much air as possible. Seal and freeze. Optional: Use seal-and-freeze bags. Here corn doesn't come in

PARCHED CORN

"Be sure to let some of your large-eared yellow and white corns stand on the stalks until they dry. Remove them before frost and check for proper drying. The kernels of sweet corn shrivel up considerably with age. If you bite a drying kernel and feel it 'give' a little, it is good for parching. Remove the kernels, keep in a covered container in the refrigerator (for several months if you wish). Then to parch, proceed as with popping corn, using a small amount of cooking oil in the popping pan, and stirring until kernels turn light brown. They half-pop into a chewy but tasty treat to go with the Thanksgiving cider."

John Vivian
Growing Corn for Many Uses
Garden Way Bulletin O

Complete seals if necessary as soon as jars are removed from the canner.

Hot pack: To each quart of creamed corn, add 1 pint boiling water. Heat to boiling. Pack hot corn and juice in hot jars, leaving 1 inch headroom. Add salt. Adjust lids. Process in a pressure canner at 10 pounds pressure (240° F.).

Pints . . . . 85 minutes

contact with water during re-heating and stays crisper. Try including a little butter in the bags before sealing.

To cook: There are several schools of thought, but we have found that taking the corn straight from the freezer and putting it into cool water, then raising it to a boil until done, works best. A tablespoon of sugar added to the water will improve the flavor. Corn in seal-and-freeze bags should be placed frozen (bag and all) in boiling water and boiled for 15 to 25 minutes, depending on the size of the ears.

Drying. Refer to Chapter 9.

Eggplant

Harvesting. Pick when the eggplant has a glossy shine. The size will vary from several inches to a foot or more, depending on the variety, climate and soil conditions.

Preparation. Eggplant darkens in color as do potatoes when canned or frozen but is useful for Italian eggplant and tomato casseroles. Optional: treat with an anti-oxidant, (see under Chapter 5). Wash, pare, slice small or cube large eggplants.

Pressure canning

Hot pack only: To remove some of the moisture from the eggplant, sprinkle it with salt, cover with cool water and let stand for 45 minutes. Drain, cover with boiling water and boil for 5 minutes. Drain and Hot Pack into clean, hot jars, leaving 1 inch headroom. Cover with boiling water, leaving 1 inch headroom. Adjust lids. Process in pressure canner at 10 pounds pressure (240° F.).

Pints . . . . 30 minutes
Quarts . . . . 40 minutes

Complete seals if necessary as soon as jars are removed from canner.

Freezing. Freeze in an Italian or tomato casserole following your favorite recipe.

COPING WITH THE METRICS

To convert Fahrenheit degrees into Celsius or Centigrade, subtract 32, multiply by 5 and divide by 9. (212° Fahrenheit = 212 − 32 = 180 × 5 = 900 ÷ 9 = 100° Celsius.)

To convert Centigrade into Fahrenheit, multiply by 9, divide by 5 and add 32. (100° Centigrade = 100 × 9 = 900 ÷ 5 = 180 + 32 = 212° Fahrenheit.)

Garlic

Harvesting. Garlic requires a long growing season in well-aerated soil to achieve maximum size. It should be harvested late in the fall before the ground freezes, or when the tops have died completely if that is sooner. Like onions, bulbs must be dried in the sun for two or three weeks, or until the roots are completely dry and dead, before storing.

Storage. Garlic can be stored like onions. When thoroughly dry either braid the tops together or put the garlic in a mesh bag. Then hang them close to the ceiling in an airy, cool, dry, dark place.

GARLIC SPRAY

"Grow your own garlic and try this recipe. Take 3 to 4 ounces of chopped garlic bulbs and soak in 2 tablespoons of mineral oil for one day. Add a pint of water in which one teaspoon fish emulsion has been dissolved. Stir well. Strain the liquid and store in a glass or china container, as it reacts with metals. Dilute this, starting with 1 part to 20 parts of water and use as a spray against your worst insect pests. If sweet potatoes or other garden plants are attracting rabbits try this spray. Rabbits dislike the smell of fish, too. Garlic sprays are useful in controlling late blight on tomatoes and potatoes."

Louise Riotte
Secrets of Companion Planting
A Garden Way publication

TOO MUCH GARLIC?

For garlic breath, try eating a sprig or two of parsley.

Greens

(Spinach, Dandelions, Beet Greens, Collards, Kale, Chard, Mustard, Fiddleheads)

Harvesting

Kale is a hardy green that grows well in the fall and tastes better after the first frost. It can be harvested even under snow in the winter. Harvest the leaves when big enough to eat, discarding large, tough leaves and stems. Very young leaves are good raw in salads.

Collards are grown mainly in the South and have a mild cabbage-like flavor. They can be both frozen and canned successfully. In mild climates they can be harvested from the garden throughout most of the winter.

Harvest the outer, lower leaves as soon as they mature so that they don't have a chance to get too large and tough. For fresh eating, harvest when very green and small.

Swiss chard is a sturdy cousin of spinach, slower growing but much more durable. In fact, one or two rows of chard will provide all the cooked greens you can eat during the summer and fall up until severe freezing weather, plus supplying leaves for freezing or pressure canning.

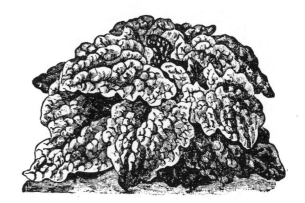

Whenever there is a lapse between other crops during the summer and after most others have gone by, Swiss chard appears on our table. The very tender center leaves are good in salad, but the larger ones are too tough. Swiss chard takes longer to cook than spinach, but it shrinks less, so not nearly as much need be picked for a meal.

When chard reaches 6–8 inches high (45–55 days from planting), it can be harvested like spinach. Cut off the whole plant about one inch above the ground which will give you a mix of large and small leaves. The plant will recover, and soon new leaves will be large enough to harvest. You also can cut just the larger outside leaves, leaving the inner ones to grow. Chard rarely bolts, so it does not make a lot of difference how you harvest it—our only problem is having more than we can use!

When allowed to grow extra large, the leaves develop a thick white (or red in Rhubarb Chard) stalk, which some people enjoy cooked and served like asparagus.

Swiss chard

Spinach

Spinach can be harvested as soon as the leaves are big enough to eat. For preserving, let them attain enough size so that you do not have to fuss with hundreds of tiny leaves. To harvest spinach, cut the entire plant off at about 1 inch above the ground, so that you will get the tender little leaves in the center of the plant as well as the more mature leaves on the outside. This will help prevent the seed stalk from growing, which causes the plant to "bolt" or go to seed. Unless the weather is hot there should be at least one more full growth of leaves on each plant, and often more than that before the plant bolts. If the seed stalks form, they are edible also, so they need not go to waste.

Since spinach grows poorly in hot weather, plant it very early in the season and also late in the summer for a fall crop. Be sure to allow enough time in planting for it to mature before the first expected frost. The plants can stand light frost, but will not grow much thereafter. Planting spinach in wide rows will save both time and space in the garden, as well as being easier to harvest.

New Zealand spinach, which is not a true spinach, is harvested differently. Just pick the leaves that are large enough, from the vines on which they grow.

Freezing and canning are both successful methods of preserving spinach.

Mustard can be grown and harvested year round in the South. As soon as the leaves are large enough to eat they can be harvested by cutting the entire plant off about 1 inch from the ground.

Preparation. The most important thing to remember is to use only fresh, tender, young greens that have been thoroughly washed in several rinse waters, lifting them from the rinse water each time, and picked over to remove wilted leaves, tough stems and weeds. Strong-flavored greens, such as wild dandelions, should be cooked in several changes of water before canning.

Pressure canning. Spinach and other mild greens may be steamed in a basket or cheese-cloth bag for about 10 minutes to wilt, or may be heated in a little water until wilted. Do small quantities at a time (1–2 pounds) so that the greens will be evenly cooked.

Hot pack only: Pack hot spinach or other greens loosely in hot jars, leaving ½ inch head-room. Cut through the greens at right angles with a sharp knife. Add salt. Cover with boiling water, leaving ½ inch headroom. Adjust lids. Process at 10 pounds pressure (240° F.).

Pints . . . . 70 minutes
Quarts . . . . 90 minutes

Remove from pressure canner. Complete seals if necessary.

Freezing. Blanch dandelion greens 1½ minutes. Blanch spinach, New Zealand spinach, kale, chard, mustard greens, turnip greens, and fiddleheads 2 minutes. Blanch collards 3 minutes.

Cool immediately in cold water. Drain. Pack into containers, leaving headroom (see page 20). Seal and freeze.

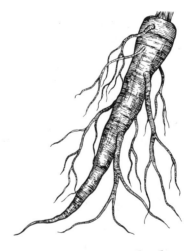

Horseradish

Horseradish grows like a weed, so plant only a few roots for your seasoning needs.

Harvesting. Horseradish roots can be dug as needed when the plants are dormant in the fall, winter or early spring, or they can be dug up in the fall and stored like other root crops. Leave enough root in the ground for the next year's crop.

DANDELIONS

"To avoid an unpleasant flavor to your dandelion greens, pick them young before the flowers blossom, and if possible get them from a field rather than your own lawn. If you are initiating your family into the practice of trying wild greens, start slowly with a few leaves or some tender roots, tossed with the usual lettuce salad. Or you may make the following dressing, an old Pennsylvania Dutch recipe which is delicious on any greens.

BIBS BROWN'S DRESSING
FOR DANDELIONS

"Cut 4 slices bacon into small pieces and fry. Pour off all but 3 tbsp. fat. When bacon is crisp, add 1 heaping tsp. flour and stir smooth. Brown this mixture. In a bowl crack 2 eggs and beat just enough to break yolks. Add about ½ tsp. salt and about ¾ cup brown sugar and ¾ cup vinegar. Add 2 tbsp. milk or cream. Mix all together and pour into bacon batter and cook. If you are using this on lettuce, add 1 heaping tsp. mustard. Add two chopped hard-cooked eggs. Pour over salad greens. Taste before adding mixture to bacon. Add more sugar or vinegar if necessary."

Marjorie Page Blanchard
Home Gardener's Cookbook
A Garden Way publication

Prepared horseradish. Wash and pare the horseradish root, and shred, or cut into small pieces. To each cup of horseradish add 3 to 4 tablespoons water, 1 to 2 tablespoons of vinegar and chop fine in an electric blender. For a color change add a few pieces of raw beet to the horseradish before chopping.

This spicy relish will keep a long time in the refrigerator, where it will always be on hand to pep up stews and clear your sinuses! It does lose its potency in time.

Kohlrabi

Harvesting. Kohlrabi is best eaten fresh. It may be harvested when the bulb-like stem just above the ground is two to three inches in diameter.

Storage. Kohlrabi can be stored under refrigeration for a brief time. It also may be used in soup, and frozen as a puree, tasting something like cabbage and turnip.

HORSERADISH

Gardeners find horseradish a crop that is easier to grow than to stop growing. The harvested part of the plant is the root, which consists of one main root and several smaller ones branching off from it. If any of these smaller roots are lost during the harvesting, they will produce yet another mighty horseradish plant the following summer. Horseradish is as strong as its flavor, and given the opportunity, will take over major portions of a garden.

"Horseradish and potatoes have a symbiotic effect on each other, causing the potatoes to be healthier and more resistant to disease. Plants should be set at the corners of the potato plot only and should be dug after each season to prevent spreading."

Louise Riotte
Secrets of Companion Planting
A Garden Way publication

KOHLRABI

"The best ones are those that have grown quickly; those that grow slowly are usually tough and woody. A side dressing of fertilizer will help to speed up growth."

Dick Raymond
Down-to-Earth Vegetable Gardening

"Although turnip shaped, it has a far more delicate and enjoyable flavour. Finely shredded over a salad it adds vitamins and variety or it can be cooked as fritters, puree, au gratin or boiled and finished off by sauté in butter."

Thompson & Morgan catalog

Mixed Vegetables

Pressure canning and freezing. Some vegetables go well together and may be preserved in the same canning jar or freezing container — such combinations as succotash (limas and corn), tomatoes and celery, or a mixed assortment of whatever is ripe and ready at the same time in the garden and that appeals.

Use your imagination and try a few combinations to spice up the winter menu. Prepare the vegetables by washing and cutting as you like them.

Mushrooms

Be sure to use only mushrooms that you know are edible!

Pressure canning. Cut bad spots and the tough ends off the stem of mushrooms. Soak in cold water for 10 minutes to remove dirt. Wash in clean water. If very badly soiled, they can be peeled.

Cut large mushrooms into pieces; small ones may be left whole. Do not boil; instead steam for 4 minutes or heat gently with little or no liquid, using fat, for 15 minutes in a covered pan.

Pressure canning. Hot pack and process in the pressure canner using the *longest* time required for any of the vegetables included. If there is a big time difference, one vegetable will be overdone, so you might prefer to can the vegetables separately and mix them at the time of eating.

Freezing. Blanch each vegetable separately if the recommended times are different. Then chill, drain and pack into freezer containers leaving headroom (see page 20). Seal and freeze.

Hot pack only: Pack hot mushrooms in hot ½ pint or pint jars, leaving ½ inch headroom. Add salt — ¼ teaspoon to half pints, ½ teaspoon to pints. Add boiling hot cooking liquid or water to cover mushrooms, leaving ½ inch headroom. Adjust lids and process in a pressure canner at 10 pounds pressure (240° F.).

Half-pints . . . . 30 minutes
Pints . . . . 30 minutes

Complete seals if necessary as soon as jars are removed from canner.

Freezing. Sort and wash mushrooms. Cut according to taste, trimming ends and bad spots. For "fresh" use, blanch in boiling water 5 minutes for whole, 3 minutes for sliced. Cool immediately in ice cold water. Drain. For use cooked: heat in a frying pan with butter or fat until done. Cool by placing pan in a bowl of ice cold water.

Wire baskets for blanching save time, insure against burns and prevent overcooking those pieces that might escape.

Pack into containers, leaving headroom (see page 20). Seal and freeze. Optional: treat with an anti-oxidant before freezing (see Chapter 5).

Drying. Refer to Chapter 9.

Okra

Harvesting. Pick pods when 2–3 inches long and harvest continuously. Plant in conditions suitable for sweet corn. Okra is good dried.

Preparation. Wash, cut off stem but don't cut into pod. Sort. For use in gumbo, cut the okra crosswise in slices after removing both stem and blossom ends.

Pressure canning

Hot pack only: Cook in boiling water for 1 minute. Pack hot okra in hot clean jars, leaving ½ inch headroom. Salt is optional. Cover with boiling water, leaving ½ inch headroom. Adjust lids. Process in pressure canner at 10 pounds pressure (240° F.).

Pints . . . . 25 minutes
Quarts . . . . 40 minutes
Complete seals if necessary.

Freezing. Blanch in boiling water for 3-4 minutes depending on size. Cool immediately in cold water. Drain. Pack into containers, leaving headroom (see page 20). Seal and freeze.

USING OKRA

In addition to storing okra for later use, usually in gumbos, it may be boiled and served dipped in a hollandaise sauce. It's a pleasing, nutritious—and slightly slippery—dish.

Onions

Harvesting. Onions for use fresh may be harvested green whenever needed, from the scallion or green-top stage right through the formation of a large bulb.

For winter storage onions should be harvested when 95 percent of the tops have turned brown and died, or late in the fall before the ground is frozen even if the tops have not died.

Bending the tops over in the early fall helps encourage the plant to funnel all its energy into enlarging the bulb rather than the top. Be sure all seed pods are picked off as soon as they appear so the onion will not wear itself out making seeds rather than a big bulb.

Curing. After pulling onions for storage, they must be cured. This means allowing them to dry out for about 2 weeks so the skins become paper crisp and roots completely dead, shrivelled and wiry. If the weather is dry and warm, the onions can be spread out on gravel or other dry area, turned occasionally and protected from animals and other hazards. An alternative is to spread them out on the floor or on newspapers in a dry well-ventilated garage or shed.

Storage. When the onions feel crisp and dry they can be put into mesh bags, or their tops may be braided or tied together, and then hung in a dry, cool, dark place, that is well-ventilated. This can be at the ceiling level of a cellar storage room, in an attic, a spare room or garage. As with all stored vegetables, one of the most important factors is consistency of temperature — when the temperature fluctuates between extremes, the onions may rot. Slight freezing of stored onions will not ruin the onions unless they are handled while frozen or are thawed out and refrozen, or there is a long delay after being frozen before being used.

Bermuda-type onions generally cannot be stored for any length of time.

Canning. Not recommended, except in pickle combinations. (See Chapter 7 on Pickling.)

LOOKING AHEAD WITH ONIONS

Storage of onions takes lots of planning. The right varieties must be planted, and must be planted at the right time.

The gardener who plants onion sets is limited to only a few varieties. Select one advertised as a "keeper," and plant it relatively late, so that it will be full-sized at the very end of the growing season.

The better method is to start onions from seeds, so that the best keepers can be selected. Three of these are *Yellow Globe, Southport* and *Ebenezer.* There's a relationship between the taste and the keeping qualities of onions, with the milder varieties, such as *Sweet Spanish,* not keeping well. And, no matter what variety, the thick-stemmed onions should be culled from the keeping crop and eaten early.

Freezing. Onions may be frozen in small quantities for a quick source of diced onion to put into sauces and casseroles. This is a good way to keep the Bermuda variety that does not store well. Peel, wash and dice onions. Pack into small freezer containers, leaving headroom (see page 20). Seal and freeze.

Freezing. Cut leaves with stems several inches long. Tie gently in bunches, shake in cold water to wash, drain. Place in freezer bags or containers (several bunches to the bag) and freeze. If in bags, store in the freezer where they will not be crushed by other packages. The parsley may be blanched before freezing which will help it retain its color, nutrients, and flavor over a longer storage period. To blanch, dip the washed bunches into boiling water for ½–1 minute, then cool rapidly in ice water, drain and freeze.

Drying. Refer to Herbs, Chapter 9.

Parsley

Parsnips

Although used mostly for decoration and flavoring, parsley is a powerhouse of vitamins and minerals. Ounce for ounce it contains more vitamin C than oranges, more iron than spinach, and nearly as much vitamin A as carrots!

Parsley can be harvested throughout the season whenever there are enough leaves to cut. For winter use, plants may be lifted and potted to grow inside on a sunny windowsill. It also can be preserved by freezing or drying.

Harvesting. Parsnips develop their distinctive sweet flavor after freezing in the ground, and are best left in the ground and harvested when the ground can be dug fall and spring. If mulched heavily, the ground should be soft enough to dig them throughout the winter.

Any parsnips left in the spring should be dug before top growth begins, because they become poisonous when they start growing again. This is the best time to harvest them for freezing or canning rather than during the busy fall harvest season.

PARSLEY

Parsley can be frozen or dried, for winter use, but why bother? Have it fresh all winter, and enjoy a friendly, perky plant in a sunny window in your kitchen.

In midsummer, soak parsley seed (it's extremely slow to germinate unless you do) and plant a short row in your garden. Well before frost, dig up several individual plants, and give each its own roomy pot. It will thrive in the kitchen if kept well watered, and doesn't resent being clipped for the many uses you will find for its tasty foliage.

Because parsley is a biennial, it turns to seed production the second year. Thus, for best parsley, start new plants each year.

If preferred, parsnips may be harvested in the late fall and stored in the root cellar, or canned or frozen.

Storage. Store as you would carrots. (Refer to Chapter 10 on Common Storage.)

Pressure canning. Thoroughly wash, scrape and wash again, then slice parsnips or leave whole if small. Cover with boiling water and boil 3 minutes.

Hot pack only: Pack hot into hot jars, leaving 1 inch headroom. Add salt, 1 teaspoon per quart, ½ teaspoon per pint. Cover with boiling water, leaving 1 inch headroom. Adjust lids. Process in a pressure canner at 10 pounds pressure (240° F.).

Pints . . . . 30 minutes
Quarts . . . . 35 minutes

Complete seals if necessary as soon as jars are removed from canner.

Freezing. Use only tender, smaller, top quality parsnips. Remove tops, wash and peel and cut into ½ inch cubes or slices. Heat in boiling water 2 minutes. Cool immediately in cold water. Drain. Pack into containers, leaving headroom (see page 20). Seal and freeze.

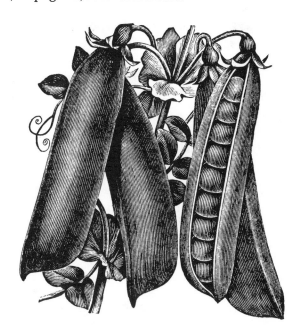

Peas, Field

(Southern and Cowpeas)

Harvesting. Harvest field peas for fresh use or preserving when the pods are well-filled with tender peas. For dry peas harvest as you would dry beans. The fresh field peas can be either pressure canned or frozen.

Pressure canning

Raw pack: Shell peas, discarding any that are hard. Wash and pack loosely into clean jars leaving 1½ inch headroom in pint jars and 2 inches in quart jars. Do not shake or press peas down.

Add salt if desired, 1 teaspoon per quart or ½ teaspoon per pint. Cover with boiling water, leaving ½ inch headroom. Adjust lids and process in a pressure canner at 10 pounds pressure (240° F.).

```
Pints................35 minutes
Quarts..............40 minutes
```

Complete seals if necessary as soon as jars are removed from the canner.

Hot pack: Cover shelled and washed field peas with boiling water, and bring to a rolling boil. Drain and pack hot peas in hot jars, leaving 1¼ inch headroom in pints and 1½ inch headroom in quarts. Do not shake or press peas down. Add salt if desired, 1 teaspoon per quart and ½ teaspoon per pint. Cover with boiling cooking liquid, leaving ½ inch headroom. Adjust lids and process in a pressure canner at 10 pounds pressure (240° F.).

```
Pints................35 minutes
Quarts..............40 minutes
```

Complete seals if necessary.

Freezing. Shell, sort and wash field peas. Blanch in boiling water for 2 minutes. Chill immediately in ice cold water. Drain. Pack into freezer containers, leaving headroom (see page 20). Seal and freeze.

SOUTHERN PEAS

Sometimes called **Field Peas** and also **Cow Peas,** Southern Peas often are raised for cattle forage and even as a green manure.

But there are tasty table varieties, too, which are a popular garden crop. While the "green" or "garden" peas of the North want cool weather, Southern peas demand warm soil. They resist drought very well, which the Northern types don't. Some but not all Southern-Field-Cow peas are blackeyed, like the more famous Blackeyed Beans.

Peas, Green

Harvesting. To eat or preserve, fresh peas should be picked when tender and sweet, before fully mature, when their sugars start to turn to starch. Watch the pods carefully as they ripen, and pick when enough are about ¾ full of ripe peas. Taste is the best, and most enjoyable, test!

Speed is essential to capture the sweet, fresh flavor, so peas should be picked and preserved within as short a time as possible. If it is necessary to hold them several hours before use, they should be refrigerated.

There are several different machines for shelling peas, some of which work best when the peas have been picked several hours before shelling. Considering the time-saving factor involved in doing a large quantity by machine, it may be worth it to you to sacrifice that first hour of freshness.

Sugar (or edible pod) peas are harvested before the peas form in the pod, and when the peas

84

are still tiny. They can be used fresh — raw in salads or as a quick-cooked vegetable — or frozen or canned like regular peas. The pods become tough and stringy when the peas mature, but they still can be harvested and shelled for the peas, if they get by you.

With all peas the freshest flavor is preserved by freezing; pressure canning is also a successful method. Fresh peas also may be dried (see Chapter 9 on Drying). Or dry the peas on the vine, and harvest as you would *dry beans*.

Pressure canning. Shell and wash fresh peas, and sort for size if there is much difference.

Raw pack: Pack peas loosely into clean, hot jars, leaving 1 inch headroom. Do not shake or press peas down. Add salt if desired, 1 teaspoon per quart or ½ teaspoon per pint. Cover with boiling water, leaving 1½ inch headroom. Adjust lids, and process in a pressure canner at 10 pounds pressure (240° F.).

Pints . . . . 40 minutes
Quarts . . . . 40 minutes
Complete seals if necessary.

Freezing. Shell and wash fresh peas, and sort for size. Large and small peas should not be mixed in freezing because they will cook unevenly when used.

Blanch peas in boiling water for 1½ minutes. Chill immediately in ice cold water and drain.

Pack peas into freezer containers, leaving headroom (see page 20). Seal and freeze.

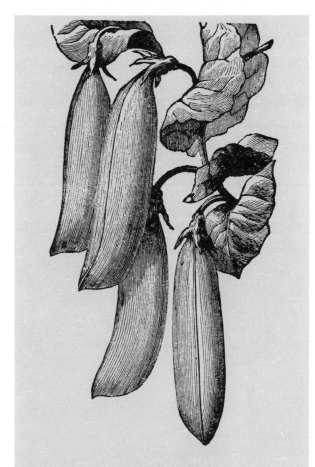

PLANTING PEAS

"Some years, I have planted peas in patches that were as large as 12 feet square. I am often asked, 'How do you get in to harvest them in a patch so large?' Easy. I take a stool, go out in the patch, sit down, reach out for the peas around me, and pick a peck. Then I move the stool, and do it again. You may raise so many peas you can't stay ahead of them!"

Dick Raymond
Down-to-Earth Vegetable Gardening
A Garden Way publication

ON SHELLING PEAS

"Children love to shell peas, especially if you make it a family project and don't regale them with too many stories about the old days on the farm. Start them off slowly, building gradually up to the night when the podding and freezing goes on into the wee hours."

Marjorie Page Blanchard
Home Gardener's Cookbook
A Garden Way publication

PICKING PEAS

"The last time you pick your peas, each season, pull up the whole vine before you remove the pods. This should help save your back. The vines should be stacked and saved too. Chopped or whole, they are a nitrogen-rich mulch which should be used anywhere on the garden, except on other peas."

Stu Campbell
The Mulch Book
A Garden Way publication

Peppers, Hot and Sweet

Harvesting. Pick at any size, but remember the more you pick, the more the plant will continue to set fruit. Any pepper, whether hot or sweet, will turn red if left on the plant long enough. Sweet red peppers make especially attractive additions to relishes. Grow sweet peppers far from hot varieties to avoid a mix-up.

Preparation. Wash, cut into desired pieces, removing seeds and stems.

Pressure canning

Hot pack only: Cut to preference and then boil for three minutes. To peel (if desired) dip hot in cold water and strip skins. Drain and pack into hot jars leaving 1 inch headroom. Add ½ teaspoon salt AND 1 tablespoon vinegar to each pint, or 1 teaspoon salt AND 2 tablespoons vinegar to each quart. The vinegar is necessary to increase the acidity and make the peppers safe for canning. Cover with boiling water, leaving ½ inch headroom. Adjust lids. Process in a pressure canner at 10 pounds pressure (240° F.).

Pints . . . . 35 minutes
Quarts . . . . 45 minutes
Remove jars. Complete seals if necessary.

Freezing. Although not quite like fresh, peppers freeze beautifully and don't need blanching. Peppers to be used in cooked dishes may be

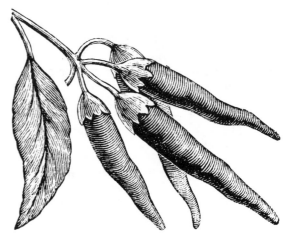

DRYING PEPPERS

"Small, hot peppers may be strung whole on twine by threading with a large-eyed needle. Large, sweet peppers may be washed, cut in half and seeded, then strung in the same way. Both may be hung on a clothesline or in any sunny, airy spot."

Phyllis Hobson
Home Drying Vegetables, Fruits and Herbs
A Garden Way publication

PLANTS OR PEPPERS?

Some gardeners believe that since a little nitrogen is good for their gardens, twice as much is twice as good. They shouldn't raise peppers.

For their pepper plants will be the best in town and with but a single fault—few peppers.

Give pepper plants a warm soil (they'll only sit and shiver in temperatures under 55°), a lot of moisture, a good compost base and a mulch only when the soil is well warmed, but go light on the lime—and hold the nitrogen.

blanched to get more into a container. If desired, blanch in boiling water for two minutes.

Pack into containers, leaving no headroom if unblanched, or leaving ½ inch headroom if blanched. Try flash-freezing diced peppers: spread out on a tray, put in containers when frozen. These can be used a little at a time, as they come apart easily.

Curing with salt. Refer to Chapter 8.

Drying. Refer to Chapter 9.

Pimientos

Use pimientos that are ripe, crisp and thick-walled.

Preparation. Wash, then to peel, roast in 400° oven for 3 to 4 minutes. Rinse off the charred skins in cold water. Remove seeds, stems and blossom ends. Flatten whole pimientos.

Pressure canning. Pack flattened pimientos in clean, hot jars, leaving ½ inch headroom. Add ¼ teaspoon salt and ½ tablespoon vinegar to ½ pints, or ½ teaspoon salt and 1 tablespoon vinegar to pints. Do not add water. Adjust lids and process in pressure canner at 10 pounds pressure (240 ° F.).

Half-pints . . . . 20 minutes
Pint . . . . 20 minutes

Remove from canner and complete seals if necessary.

Freezing. Pack prepared pimientos in containers, leaving ½ inch headroom. Seal and freeze.

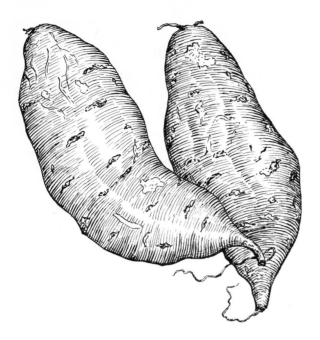

Potatoes, Sweet and Yams

Sweet potatoes are more delicate than white potatoes and are more difficult to store. Canning is the preferred method of keeping. There are two types of sweet potato—the dry meated and the moist or yam.

Harvesting. For summer eating, dig as needed when large enough. For storage, harvest when the plants are dead and the potatoes well matured. Avoid damaging with shovel or fork when digging, and handle gently. They should not be air-dried like white potatoes, so pack them directly into storage containers when harvesting.

Curing. Sweet potatoes will not keep well unless cured properly. Ideally they should be held for about 10 days under moist conditions at 80°–85° F. Cover the storage containers with paper or heavy cloth to keep up the humidity, and find a warm place (near a furnace or stove, for example) to cure them. If the temperature is below 75°, the curing should last 2–3 weeks.

Storage. After curing, the sweet potatoes like pumpkins and winter squash should be stored in a moderately warm (55°–60°) and dry place.

Avoid temperatures below 50°. A closet or under beds would make better storage places than a cold cellar. (See Chapter 10 on Common Storage.)

Pressure canning. Sweet potatoes are an exception to the usual canning techniques in that they can be packed and processsed dry in the jar, without adding boiling liquid to them.

Use freshly dug potatoes, and scrub. Boil or steam for 20 to 30 minutes, or until skins can be slipped off. Do not puncture with a fork. Remove skins and cut large potatoes into uniform pieces, or leave small ones whole.

Dry pack: Pack hot sweet potatoes tightly enough to fill air spaces in hot jars, without breaking up the pieces. Leave 1 inch headroom. Do not add salt or liquid. Adjust lids, and process in a pressure canner at 10 pounds pressure (240° F.).

> Pints . . . . 65 minutes
> Quarts . . . . 95 minutes

Complete seals if necessary.

Wet Pack: Pack hot sweet potatoes into hot jars, leaving 1 inch headroom. Add salt if desired, 1 teaspoon per quart, ½ teaspoon per pint. Cover with boiling water or light or medium syrup (see below), leaving 1 inch headroom. Adjust lids, and process in a pressure canner at 10 pounds pressure (240° F.).

> Pints . . . . 55 minutes
> Quarts . . . . 90 minutes

Complete seals if necessary as soon as jars are removed from canner.

SWEET POTATOES

"You can dig sweet potatoes as soon as there is anything big enough to eat. Storing them well is something of a problem—for me, at least. To keep really well, they should be put in a very warm and humid place for eight to ten days before they go into the root cellar. I find it easier to can or freeze them."

Dick Raymond
Down-to-Earth Vegetable Gardening
A Garden Way publication

88

Syrup: Light — 2 cups sugar and 4 cups water
  Medium — 3 cups sugar and 4 cups
  water
  Combine sugar and water and heat
  until dissolved.

Freezing. Use medium to large sweet potatoes that have been cured. Sort and wash. Cook until tender in water, steam or oven. Let cool at room temperature. Peel, cut into slices or mash, or use whole. Optional: to prevent darkening, dip whole or cut up sweet potatoes in a solution of ½ teaspoon lemon juice to 1 quart water for 5 seconds. Mix 2 tablespoons lemon or orange juice with each quart of mashed potatoes.

Pack into containers, leaving headroom (see page 20). Seal and freeze.

Syrup pack: Sweet potatoes may be covered with cold syrup made of equal parts of sugar and water before freezing. Leave ample headroom (see page 20), seal and freeze. Or simply roll pieces of sweet potato in sugar before packing and freezing.

Potatoes, White

Harvesting. Potatoes can be harvested anytime after they start to form around the roots of the plants—just dig down next to the plant and take as many as you need, then cover the roots back up and leave the plant to grow more. This is accomplished most easily when potatoes are planted on the ground under a thick covering of hay, rather than in the soil. Tiny new potatoes are a special treat in mid-summer.

For storage, potatoes are best harvested late in the fall when the tops are all dead and a skin has formed on potatoes that cannot be slipped or broken when you push your thumb across it. Late-maturing potatoes are the best for storage. Early varieties may begin to rot in the ground before digging if left until fall; and the weather may be too warm to store them if dug sooner.

To harvest potatoes for storage, dig them up in the late fall on a dry day, being sure to dig deeply around every plant to get all the potatoes. There may be no more than one or two potatoes, or as many as a dozen at each plant. The potatoes should be spread out on a dry surface until the dirt has dried and fallen off them. Do not leave them out in the sun for any length of time, however, because they will turn green when exposed to light. This indicates the presence of solanine, which is poisonous if eaten in any quantity.

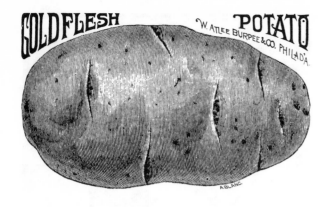

GOLDFLESH POTATO
W. ATLEE BURPEE & CO. PHILAD'A.

Storage. Potatoes will store moderately well under most conditions for the first few months when they are normally dormant anyway—as long as they are kept in the dark. For longer storage, and to prevent rotting, softening or early sprouting, try to achieve these more ideal conditions:

1. Use up potatoes damaged in harvesting, saving only the soundest for storage.

2. Store potatoes under moderately moist conditions in the dark, at 35°–40° F.

3. Store the potatoes in a slatted bin or big mesh bags, kept one or two inches off the floor. They need some air circulation, so pile them no more than 12–18 inches deep.

Pressure canning. If you common store the potatoes, it is more sensible than canning, but there are times when it is convenient to have some already clean and peeled in a canning jar to

be used at a moment's notice. Small ones may be canned whole; larger ones may be cubed.

Wash, peel and wash again. Cut up if desired. Cubes may be dipped into a brine made of 1 teaspoon salt to 1 quart water to prevent darkening. Drain. Cover with boiling water and cook 2 minutes for cubes and 10 for whole potatoes. Drain.

Hot pack only: Pack hot potatoes into hot jars leaving ½ inch headroom. Add salt if desired, 1 teaspoon per quart, ½ teaspoon per pint. Cover with boiling water, leaving ½ inch headroom. Adjust lids and process in a pressure canner at 10 pounds pressure (240° F.).

> Pints, whole . . . . 30 minutes
> Pints, cubed . . . . 35 minutes
> Quarts, whole or
>   cubed . . . . 40 minutes

Complete seals if necessary as soon as the jars are removed from the canner.

Drying. Refer to Chapter 9.

THE BEST POTATOES

If you are the industrious ant type, you will grow a bountiful crop of potatoes, wait until the tops are all dead, then store them by the bushel.

But, if you live more for today, you will sacrifice part of that crop, and enjoy far better eating.

When the tops are well up, run an inquisitive hand under the mulch or into the potato hill, depending on the method of growing you use, and seek out potatoes that have reached the size of golfballs. Pick enough of those for one meal, and plan on at least three or four per person. Sure, you'll be sacrificing what could be much larger potatoes if harvested later, but you'll also be enjoying the best potato eating of your life.

Pumpkin
and Winter Squash

Harvesting. Harvest before the first severe frost, leaving an inch or so of stem on. If your thumbnail can penetrate a winter squash, it isn't suitable for root cellaring. It should be eaten soon or processed.

For storage, pumpkins should be left in the sun to cure for a week before storing. They can be kept in a cool room where the temperature stays constant and the humidity is fairly dry for most of the winter.

Preparation. The best cooking varieties are the little round sugar pumpkins which have the thickest flesh. For making pies and puddings, it is very convenient to have the pumpkin already

partially cooked, either cubed or strained. For cubed squash or pumpkin, wash and cut open, removing seeds and stringy insides. Pare and cut into 1 inch cubes. Add just enough water to cover and bring to a boil. Drain and reserve cooking liquid.

Pressure canning

Hot pack only: Pack hot cubes into hot jars, leaving ½ inch headroom. Add salt (and be sure to label jar with how much so your recipe can be adjusted). Cover with boiling cooking liquid, leaving ½ inch headroom. Adjust lids. Process in a pressure canner at 10 pounds pressure (240° F.).

> Pints . . . . 55 minutes
> Quarts . . . . 90 minutes

Remove from canner and complete seals if necessary.

For strained pumpkin and squash: Wash pumpkin or squash and cut open. Remove seeds and stringy insides. Cut into large pieces and steam until soft, or cut in half if small enough and place face down in a shallow pan of water. Bake at 350° until soft. Scrape soft insides from rind and put through a food mill or strainer. Simmer over low heat until heated through, stirring often.

Hot pack only: Pack hot into hot clean jars, leaving ½ inch headroom. Add no salt or liquid. Adjust lids. Process in pressure canner at 10 pounds pressure (240° F.).

Pints . . . . 65 minutes
Quarts . . . . 80 minutes
Remove from canner and complete seals if necessary.

Freezing. Prepare as above. Put the fine, fiber-free pulp in a pan placed in a larger bowl of cold water to cool. Stir occasionally. Pack into containers, leaving headroom (see page 20). Seal and freeze.

ANOTHER REASON FOR PUMPKINS

Most of us raise pumpkins for eating or for jack-o'-lanterns. But there's another reason for them, and that's for the nutritious seeds they contain.

Many people don't like to eat them because of the bother of shelling them. And here science has come forward with a hand. The new *Lady Godiva* pumpkin is fat with seeds, and they can be eaten just as they come from the pumpkin, since they are naked (or without hulls). These seeds can be eaten raw or roasted, and they're high in protein. But don't count on using the pumpkin as well, since it ranks low for table use.

TRY A NEW ONE

One of the newer and more appealing Winter Squashes is the bush-type **Golden Nugget** (available from Jung Seed Company). These delicious little squashes have fairly low germination rate but one hill will produce in early fall a dozen or more grapefruit sized squashes that look like miniature pumpkins. Their outer shell is very hard but they aren't the best keepers since they mature early.

Rutabagas

Harvesting. Rutabagas, like turnips, are harvested for fresh use as soon as the roots are large enough; for storage they should be harvested as late in the fall as possible before the ground freezes. In areas without severe winter weather they can be mulched and left in the garden for winter use.

Dig or pull the rutabagas, and leave them in the sun for a couple of hours until the soil dries and falls off. Trim off the stems to within about 1 inch of the top; do not cut the roots off.

Storage. To store the rutabagas, pack them in freshly-cut sawdust or sand. They should be

BAKED RUTABAGAS

"Bake the rutabagas whole for about an hour or a little more in a 375° oven and serve them right in their skins with lots of butter, salt and pepper."

Marjorie Page Blanchard
Home Gardener's Cookbook
A Garden Way publication

kept in a cold place. (See Chapter 10 on Common Storage.)

Rutabagas can be frozen satisfactorily, but canning is undesirable because they discolor like turnips and develop a strong taste.

Freezing. Cut off the tops of young tender rutabagas. Wash and peel. Cut into cubes. Blanch for 2 minutes in boiling water. Cool immediately in ice cold water. Drain. Pack into containers, leaving headroom (see page 20). Seal and freeze.

STORING RUTABAGAS

The best crops for storing are those grown late in the season, so the harvesting time is late and the length of storage time is kept to a minimum.

This is true of rutabagas, and the reason for starting the storage crop in mid-summer, about the last week in July in New England and similar latitudes.

Those purchasing these Swedish turnips in grocery stores will find they are often waxed, to increase their durability. The home gardener can do this also. But most persons have found this hearty vegetable will keep if well insulated in boxes of dry sawdust.

VIRTUOUS SALSIFY

Salsify is the unsung hero of the vegetable garden, and it's difficult to explain the silence. Here's a plant that is easy to grow (you can almost plant and forget it), easy to harvest and store (leave it in the garden until you want it) and delicious (much like oysters in flavor, which accounts for its other name, *oyster plant*).

Here's a Vermont recipe that's guaranteed to make you sing for salsify. It's good for lunch.

Salsify Cakes

6 salsify roots
1 teaspoon vinegar
½ teaspoon salt
⅛ teaspoon pepper
4 tablespoons butter
⅛ teaspoon garlic powder

Wash and peel roots and cut them in 1 inch lengths. Drop them in water in which vinegar and salt have been added, to halt browning of roots. Bring to boil, then cook, covered, for 20 minutes. Drain and mash, adding 1 tablespoon of butter and garlic powder. Form into small cakes, dredge in flour and cook in remaining butter.

For mashed rutabagas, continue cooking until tender, then mash. Cool by placing the pan in a bowl of cold water. Stir occasionally to speed up the cooling. Pack into containers, leaving ½ inch headroom. Seal and freeze.

Salsify

Harvesting. Salsify can be used anytime after it is half grown.

Storage. Treat like other root crops. At least an inch of stem should be left when the tops are cut off to help prevent the root from shriveling. Storage works well in an outdoor pit or where it grew in the garden.

Soybeans

Soybean is the one vegetable food that is a complete protein; that is, it contains all the essential amino acids needed by man. It is, however, low in one of them (methionine), so for completely balanced meals some animal protein (for example, milk or cheese) should be cooked or served with it.

Shallots

Harvesting. Shallots taste like a delicate cross between onions and garlic. They grow in clusters of many separate cloves attached at the roots. For use in summer salads the clusters can be pulled as needed.

Storage. For winter storage treat like onions. We usually plant, harvest and store them right along with the onion crop.

Harvesting. Soybeans can be picked while green and the beans eaten as a fresh vegetable, or they can be allowed to mature completely until most of the pods are dry. In the fall when the plants are dying pull the entire plant and stack them to dry out completely, as you would *dry beans.* Some varieties of soybeans are harder to remove from the shell than most other beans, and you may have to shell many of them by hand. This is done when completely dry and brittle, and it makes a good occupation for cold evenings in front of the fire. It will go quickly if many hands help.

Other varieties open readily and can be harvested and threshed like other dry beans. Be sure to harvest before they open naturally and spill your beans in the garden!

MEET THE SHALLOTS

The shallot is a mild-breathed member of the onion family, widely used in French *haute cuisine,* but certainly not a familiar figure in the American kitchen.

This is a pity, considering its flavor, which is milder than onions, and has a hint, but not the muscle, of garlic.

Expensive in grocery stores, shallots are as easy to grow as others of its relatives. They are started from either seeds or the cloves themselves, as with garlic. The most troublesome part may be finding the cloves or seeds for starting. Excellent "keepers," shallots will, like garlic, be in perfect condition for a year or more.

Those for storage are pulled up only when the tops have turned brown, and the bulbs are then dried and separated. But they can be used, too, while still green. In this case, don't throw away the tops. Cut them up for a delicious addition to salads.

Pressure canning. Use green soybeans. Prepare as for hot pack lima beans. Process in a pressure canner at 10 pounds pressure (240° F.).

Pints................55 minutes
Quarts..............65 minutes

Complete seals if necessary as soon as jars are removed from canner.

Soy flour. Soy flour is a protein- and vitamin-rich supplement that can be added to other flour when making bread, cookies and other baked goods. Use in small quantities because it will affect the flavor and rising qualities. To make soy flour, freeze the dried beans, then run them through a hand or electric grain grinder. Their oil content may cause them to glaze the stones of a grinder if milled unfrozen.

Storage. Store soybeans as you would other dry beans.

Cooking. To use the dried soybeans, wash and sort, then cover them with plenty of boiling water and let them soak for several hours. Use them sparingly, as one cup dry will make about three cups when soaked. Drain and cover with fresh water (or use soaking water), add salt (½ teaspoon/cup) and simmer for 2 to 3 hours, adding more water if they start to dry out.

A pressure cooker can be used to speed up the cooking of soybeans. Rinse the dry beans in cold water. Put 3 to 4 times as much water as dry beans in the pressure cooker and bring to a boil. Add the beans, lock cover and bring to 10 pounds pressure. Cook for 20 to 25 minutes. Cool cooker under running water.

Other vegetables, seasonings or salt pork or bacon may be added the last hour of conventional cooking to overcome the uninteresting, "raw" flavor of the beans, or the plain cooked beans may be used in mixed casseroles or loaf dishes. Soybeans are delicious baked like other dry beans.

Spinach

See **Greens,** *above.*

Squash

(Summer, Zucchini, Cocozelle, Yellow Crookneck, etc.)

Harvesting. Pick when very young with tender skins and immature seeds. These should not be peeled but should be sliced. If necessary, the slices can be halved or quartered so that they are all of uniform size. Older squash also can be used but only the firm flesh. These must be peeled, seeded and the soft core removed, before cutting the flesh into cubes.

The blossoms, when they are about 2 inches long and before they open, can be sauteed for use in casseroles or in soups.

Zucchini also can be pickled if you have an overabundance. (See Chapter 7 on Pickling.)

Pressure canning

Raw pack: Pack washed and cut-up squash tightly into clean jars, leaving 1 inch headroom. Add salt if desired, 1 teaspoon per quart, ½ teaspoon per pint. Cover with boiling water, leaving ½ inch headroom. Adjust lids and process in a pressure canner at 10 pounds pressure (240° F.).

Pints. . . . . .25 minutes
Quarts . . . . .30 minutes

Complete seals if necessary.

Hot pack: Cover washed and cut up squash with boiling water and bring to a boil. Drain and reserve cooking liquid. Pack hot squash loosely into hot jars, leaving ½ inch headroom. Add salt. Cover with boiling cooking liquid, leaving

½ inch headroom. Adjust lids and process in a pressure canner at 10 pounds pressure (240° F.).

Pints. . . . . .30 minutes
Quarts . . . . .40 minutes

Complete seals if necessary as soon as jars are removed from the canner.

Freezing. Prepare squash as for canning. Blanch in boiling water for 3 minutes. Cool immediately in cold water and drain. Pack into freezer containers, leaving ½ inch headroom. Seal and freeze.

Summer squash tends to be pretty rubbery when frozen this way. Also try cooking and mashing it before freezing; or cook and put through a food mill or blender to puree. The squash puree can be used as the base for thick soups or combined with tomatoes for a thickened tomato sauce. Freeze in appropriate containers, leaving ample headroom (see page 20) as for wet pack (see *Potatoes, Sweet).*

Drying. Refer to Chapter 9.

SQUASH TIPS

Most family gardeners find one hill of each of their favorite summer squash varieties is about right. Plant one perhaps to *Yellow Crookneck* or the *Smooth Straightneck*, another to *Patty Pan* or *Zucchini.* Allow the bushes ample air and sunlight. Check the plants every day, and pick the little squashes when they are small—just before you'll serve them.

Squash, Winter

(*See* **Pumpkins and Winter Squash.**)

Tomatoes

Almost everyone who has a garden grows tomatoes, our most versatile fruit. Even a few plants placed in flower borders or in buckets on an apartment patio can produce enough tomatoes to preserve. During the season large quantities can be bought fresh at a farmers' market or picked yourself at a truck farm for reasonable prices to be put up at home.

The tomato has come a long way since the time when it was called the "love apple," and was grown for its shiny appearance, while being considered unfit to eat. Fortunately someone realized its potential as a food, and its many uses were developed: sliced, stuffed, stewed, juiced and made into sauces.

Tomatoes are important as a source of vitamins A and C, having approximately one-tenth the vitamin A as an equal amount of carrots, and the juice having about one-third as much vitamin C as an equal amount of orange juice.

Tomatoes actually are fruits, and as such have traditionally been considered high enough in acid to be canned by the boiling water bath method. Unfortunately for homemakers — though happily for those suffering from stomach ailments—there are new varieties of tomatoes being developed that are low-acid. These may include yellow tomatoes, Italian-style paste tomatoes and some commercial varieties of reds. Meaty tomatoes tend to be lower in acid than juicy, seedy varieties, and overripe tomatoes are less acid.

Low-acid tomatoes must be pressure canned at 10 pounds pressure like other low-acid vegetables. Even tomatoes of a high-acid type may be lower in acid when grown in certain soils. Check with your seed supplier or extension service if you wonder about the acidity of your tomatoes.

97

Many extension service people are now recommending the addition of citric acid or white distilled vinegar to all tomatoes when canning to increase their acidity. This is a simple, sensible precaution, and we likewise recommend doing it.

Tomatoes may be both canned and frozen. We think the canned product has superior flavor, texture and versatility. Once processed and stored on a shelf it is ready to be used at a moment's notice for stewed tomatoes or the base of a sauce. Frozen tomatoes tend to separate, making them less attractive for stewing. But if you are putting up small quantities, have space in your freezer and prefer not to can them, then frozen tomato sauces and juice are fine. Also, you may prefer freezing mixtures of tomatoes and low-acid vegetables or meats to canning them, because they must be processed in a pressure canner.

Harvesting. Tomatoes are ripe and ready to harvest when a uniform red color (except, obviously, the yellow varieties). For best flavor and texture be sure they are ripe but still firm before canning. If not, there will be tough spots that will end up as waste, and the skins will be more difficult to peel. Tomatoes may also be used in an unripe, green state for pickles, relishes, mincemeat, marmalade, and as "green tomato

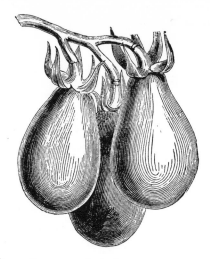

pie" filling. Some recipes for green tomatoes are included in Chapters 7 and 8 on Pickling and Curing with Salt.

Canning. Ripe tomatoes are canned whole or cut up (usually peeled) for use as stewed tomatoes or sauce, or they are cooked briefly and strained for juice, or cooked more for sauce and a lot more for paste. There may be no seasoning added, or some salt, or a variety of spices and herbs. If a low-acid vegetable is added, such as onion, green pepper or celery, it is necessary to pressure-can your sauce (see *Mixed Vegetables*). Ketchup and chili sauces are exceptions, because the large amount of vinegar used increases the acidity enough to allow safe processing in a boiling water bath.

Ripe tomatoes bruise easily, which spoils their flavor. So be careful when you pick, pack and carry them. Ideally they should be stacked not more than two layers deep in box or basket, unless they are to be removed immediately.

Extra care. Because of the borderline nature of tomato acidity, we urge you to use extra care when canning them. Many bacteria harbored in the soil are carried into the kitchen. So wash tomatoes, utensils, canning jars, work areas and hands thoroughly with detergent immediately before canning. Cut away any hint of decay from the fruit; do not use any that is more than slightly cracked or otherwise damaged or diseased. Use only firm, just-ripe tomatoes. Take no shortcuts. And before tasting or eating tomatoes, boil vigorously in an open pan for 15 minutes.

Added acid. Adding acid will help ensure that the acidity of your tomatoes is high enough for processing by the *boiling water bath* method. Two kinds are recommended: pure crystalline citric acid (USP) and white distilled vinegar. Buy citric acid from a drugstore, and have it on hand before your tomatoes are ready. It is easy to use and will not affect the flavor of the tomatoes (while vinegar will).

Amounts to use, as recommended by USDA Extension Service experts:

Citric Acid (USP)
¼ teaspoon per pint of tomatoes
½ teaspoon per quart
White distilled vinegar
1 tablespoon per pint of tomatoes
2 tablespoons per quart.

To add, place either citric acid or vinegar on top of the tomatoes in the canning jar at the time salt is added. Then adjust lids and process.

Peeling. These directions call for peeling the tomatoes, but this can be omitted if you expect to cook them further and put them through a food mill. Some people use them in stews, skins and all, and say that by the time you are ready to serve you hardly know the skins are there.

Tomatoes peel easily if scalded for about ½ minute in boiling water, then chilled in ice water. We use a blanching kettle to scald the tomatoes, keeping them in the steaming basket for chilling and draining.

Remove the tomatoes from the cold water after a minute. Do not allow them to soak much longer or they will become soggy and lose nutrients. Pull off the skins with a paring knife, cut out the stem and core, removing any blemishes, green spots or bruises.

Raw pack canning. Raw pack tomatoes either whole or quartered. This is the method most used in the past, since it is the quickest and easiest. If you are sure your tomatoes are high acid this method is acceptable. Otherwise increase acidity or pressure-can only.

Wash the tomatoes thoroughly with lots of water and a vegetable brush to remove soil and any pesticide residues. Peel.

If the tomatoes are too large to fit into your jars easily, cut them into quarters. The time required for processing them is so long that even if you leave them whole they will not retain a firm round shape anyway. Pack the tomatoes tightly into clean canning jars, pushing down on them to force their juice to run out and cover them. Leave ½ inch headroom over juice and tomatoes.

A frequent mistake made with tomatoes is to plop too few into the jar, press gently and seal, only to find after processing a small concentration of tomatoes floating near the top of the jar and a lot of juice below. So do not hesitate to squeeze in as many tomatoes as you can, and if they are very juicy you may find there is enough extra juice from several quarts to pour off to either drink fresh or can separately!

Salt (optional): If desired, add one teaspoon salt per quart; one-half teaspoon per pint.

Acid: Add per directions above. Adjust lids and process in a boiling water bath.
Pints . . . . 35 minutes
Quarts . . . . 45 minutes
Remove when done; complete seals if necessary; and cool on a rack or towel. Check for a good seal, remove bands, wash jars, label and store in a cool, dark place. Tomatoes will darken if stored in the light.

Preferred method — hot pack: Tomatoes may also be packed by the hot pack method to reduce processing time and to make a more solid pack.

Wash, peel, and quarter tomatoes, put them in a kettle and bring to a boil, stirring to prevent sticking. Ladle them boiling hot into clean, hot jars, leaving ½ inch headroom. Add salt (1 teaspoon per quart) if desired. Add acid per instructions above. Adjust lids and process in boiling water bath:

       Pints . . . . 15 minutes
       Quarts . . . . 30 minutes

Adjust seals, cool and store as for raw pack tomatoes.

Pressure canning. Prepare tomatoes as for *raw pack.* Process in pressure canner at 10 pounds pressure (240° F.).

       Pints . . . . 15 minutes
       Quarts . . . . 20 minutes

All canned tomatoes should be boiled 15 minutes in an open pan before tasting or using. They can be used for stewed tomatoes, adding a favorite seasoning with croutons, or used as a base for chili con carne and other tomato dishes. For a smooth sauce put the tomatoes through a food mill to remove seeds and skins, if they were not peeled. You also can put them through a blender, which breaks all parts down, making a good base for soups and spaghetti sauce. For a different breakfast or lunch dish, try canned tomatoes served on waffles, topped with grated cheese.

Canned salad tomatoes. Try canning a few perfect tomatoes whole for use in salads. Prepare them whole as for raw pack. Pack in jars without pressing down so their shape is retained. Cover with boiling hot *tomato juice,* leaving ½ inch headroom. Add acid and salt as for raw pack. Adjust lids and process in boiling water bath:

       Pints . . . . 35 minutes
       Quarts . . . . 45 minutes

Adjust seals. Cool and store as for raw pack tomatoes.

TOMATO JUICE

This is a healthful drink, high in vitamins A and C, which those who live in the North can produce and preserve at home. It can be chilled and drunk as it is, or doctored to taste like tomato juice cocktail. It also can be used as a base for soups, or cooked down for sauce when needed. It is quick and easy to make, requiring little cooking time before canning. In fact, the less time the better to preserve the most vitamin C, which is destroyed by overcooking and by exposure to air. (See also pp. 126-27.)

Ripe, juicy tomatoes fresh from the garden make the best juice. Pick tomatoes in their prime (firm and not overripe), and wash thoroughly. Cut into quarters and remove every blemish, hint of rot, green or white spots, and blossom and stem ends. We go so far as to taste each one because one with an off-flavor will spoil a whole batch.

Put the tomatoes in a kettle (enamel ware or stainless steel, preferably) and simmer over medium heat, stirring occasionally to prevent sticking. Do not boil. Cook just long enough for the tomatoes to be soft and juicy. Put them through a food mill, food press or sieve. The finer the sieve, the finer the pulp of the juice will be and the less it will settle out after processing. There should be very little waste, mostly seeds and skins, if the tomatoes are ripe enough.

Pour the juice back into the kettle and reheat just to boiling. Ladle the hot juice into clean hot jars, leaving ½ inch headroom. Add salt if desired, one teaspoon per quart, and acid, per instructions above. Adjust lids and process in a boiling water bath.

   Pints and quarts ..... 15 minutes
Remove from hot water as soon as time is up in order not to overcook, and complete seals if necessary. Cool and store as for canned tomatoes.

TOMATO SAUCES

You may can tomato sauce with no seasoning or just salt, waiting until you are ready to use it to add appropriate seasonings. Or you may add spices and sugar before canning. Chili sauce and ketchup are, of course, seasoned first.

   One advantage of canning sauce rather than juice or whole tomatoes is that you cook out much of the water and thus reduce the number of jars and space needed to store the same amount of tomatoes.

   To make a plain tomato sauce, follow the directions for juice, except the tomatoes must be cooked (either before or after being strained) for 1 to 2 hours, or as long as it takes to reduce the water, and thicken them as much as desired. Then proceed to can the sauce as you would juice. To reduce the cooking time, turn the juice into a fine strainer to drain off the watery liquid, saving it to drink or for soups. The remaining thicker pulp will cook down quickly.

   For ketchups and other seasoned sauces, add onions and peppers when cooking begins and

---

BASIC TOMATO KETCHUP

8-10 pounds very ripe tomatoes (35-45 medium)
  1-2 ripe sweet red peppers (use all green if red are unavailable)
  1-2 sweet green peppers
  4-5 onions
    3 cups cider vinegar
  1-3 cups sugar or honey
    3 tablespoons salt

Tie in cheesecloth bag:
½-1½ teaspoons whole allspice
½-1½ teaspoons whole cloves
½-1½ teaspoons broken stick cinnamon

Quarter tomatoes, removing blossom and stem ends and blemishes. Seed and cut up peppers; dice onions. Mix all vegetables and cook until tender (15 minutes to ½ hour). Put through a food mill. (Or raw vegetables may be put through an electric blender, ¾ full at a time, and then cooked down.) Add all remaining ingredients, except vinegar. Simmer uncovered, stirring often, until thick. Add vinegar and cook additional 15 minutes. Remove bag of spices; ladle into clean, hot pint jars. Adjust lids and process in a *boiling water bath* for 10 minutes.
           Yield: 4-5 pints

---

before putting through the food mill. Then add other seasonings. For a chunkier chili sauce, peel and cut vegetables up finely before cooking but do not put through food mill.

TOMATO PASTE

Traditionally tomato paste was a dried product, cooked until thick and then spread on boards or paper to dry in the sun. It then was rolled into balls, dipped in oil and stored.

   Nowadays we cook it down over low heat to a very thick paste, stirring frequently to prevent scorching. A large, heavy skillet will give the best results by providing more surface area for heating and evaporating the fluid. Avoid using iron, since the acid in tomatoes causes a chemical reaction with the metal.

   Prepare tomatoes as for tomato juice. Cook one hour and put through food mill or sieve.

Measure and add ½ teaspoon citric acid (or 1 tablespoon distilled white vinegar) for every four cups of sauce. Continue cooking until thick.

When the paste is the desired consistency, pack it hot into small (½ pint) jars, leaving ½ inch headroom. Adjust lids and process in boiling water bath for 35 minutes. Remove jars and complete seals if necessary.

Freezing. Frozen tomatoes are particularly good for casseroles, but they are not as convenient to use as canned, since they must be defrosted before using.

Wash fresh ripe tomatoes. Blanch for ½ minute in boiling water, chill in cold water, peel and quarter. Cool in a pan set in cold water. Stir occasionally. Or cook further, then cool. Pack into containers, leaving ample headroom for liquid pack (see page 20), seal and freeze.

Freezing stewed tomatoes. Cook peeled tomatoes with peppers, celery, onions to taste. Simmer for 10 to 20 minutes. Place cooled container in ice water and stir occasionally. Pack into containers, leaving ample headroom for wet pack (see Potatoes, Sweet), seal and freeze.

Salad tomatoes. You can try freezing a few small tomatoes whole or cut into wedges for use in salads. Success will depend on careful handling, very fast freezing, and storage for only a few months. These should be thawed only partially before being used, leaving some ice crystals in the tomatoes for good texture. Using small, firm ripe tomatoes, scald briefly, ¼–½ minute, dip briefly in cold water, peel and core. Quarter or leave whole, pack loosely in freezer

---

CHILI SAUCE

Follow the basic ketchup recipe, adding one or two hot chili peppers, or ½ teaspoon ground red peppers. Peel tomatoes and cut the vegetables up finely. Cook down without putting through a food mill.

VARIATIONS TO BASIC CHILI SAUCES

For a different flavor try adding any of the following seasonings to your chili sauce: celery or celery seed, basil, bay leaf, apples or apple sauce; mustard seeds or dry mustard, peppercorns.

---

containers, leaving no headroom, seal and freeze in the coldest part of the freezer (turned down to –19° to –20° F. if possible). Use within two or three months in salads.

Storage. Green tomatoes can be stored for one or two months, depending on their ripeness when brought in and the storage temperature. Our last one is usually ripened and gone by the end of November, and it always amazes us how good they taste compared to "fresh" ones bought in the stores at that time of year!

We cover our tomato plants in the garden with heavy cloths when the first light frosts come, but when a severe frost is warned we bring in all the tomatoes left on the vines, except those that are diseased or very small. Tomatoes will ripen, but not grow any larger in storage than they were when picked, so only sound full-sized fruit need be brought in. Tomatoes planted late, or varieties that require longer growing time, will provide the best green tomatoes.

Sort the tomatoes according to ripeness, and store spread out on newspapers on shelves or floor. Cover with more newspaper to keep them dark, and the air around them moist; otherwise they will shrivel up. Do not put them in the sunlight to ripen; it tends to rot them instead. The tomatoes may be washed before storing, or not; but do not try to wipe off soil because it will cause sand scarring, which can cause decay.

The warmer tomatoes are, the quicker they will ripen. At 65°–70°F. the mature green tomatoes (ones that have started to turn red or are whitish at the blossom end) will ripen in about two weeks. At 55° it will take up to four weeks. The less-mature tomatoes will take longer to ripen; if too moist they may rot first, if too dry they may shrivel up and never ripen. Check the tomatoes every week or so to remove ripe ones and those that have spoiled.

Tomatoes also may be brought in on the vine. The plants are pulled, roots and all, and hung up in a warmish shed or cellar. The tomatoes will gradually ripen right on the vine. Some are bound to get bruised between garden and cellar, and the debris that drops to the floor makes a mess. However, if in a hurry to beat Jack Frost, this method is worth a try.

Curing with salt. For *Green Tomatoes with Beans* refer to Chapter 8.

Turnips

Harvesting. Turnips are used for both the roots and the greens. For greens choose a variety that is especially good for that purpose.

The greens are ready about 30 days after planting, when the leaves are big enough to cook. Harvest them then, by cutting off all but a few of the littlest ones which should be left on the plant to support the growth of the root. As the plant matures the leaves become tough and bitter and not good for eating. Turnip greens can be preserved like spinach and other greens. (Refer to the section on *Greens* above.)

The turnip root should be harvested as late in

the fall as possible before the ground freezes. Pull or dig up the roots, and leave them in the sun for several hours until the soil dries and falls off them.

Storage. Trim the stems to within about 1 inch of the turnip; do *not* cut off the roots. Pack in fresh-sawed sawdust or sand and store in a cold, dark place. The ideal storage temperature is as close to 32° as possible with a moist atmosphere. Turnips also can be waxed. (For further details on root crops see Chapter 10 on Common Storage.)

Canning. Pressure canning turnips is possible but undesirable because they develop a strong flavor and off-color when canned.

Freezing. Turnips may be prepared as for serving and frozen. Cut off tops of young, tender turnips. Wash and peel. Cut into cubes. Blanch for 2 minutes in boiling water. Cool immediately in ice cold water. Drain. Pack into containers, leaving headroom (see page 20). Seal and freeze.

For mashed turnips, continue cooking until tender, then mash. Cool by placing the pan in a bowl of cold water. Stir occasionally to hasten cooling. Pack into containers, leaving ½ inch headroom. Seal and freeze.

Curing with salt. Refer to *Sauerruben*, Chapter 8.

TURNIPS

There's a cycle of unpopularity surrounding the turnip, and you can break it by not ignoring this blue-collar member of the gardening family.

Turnips get planted and weeded—and then ignored until they have grown big and strong. Then someone remembers the turnips should be picked, and they are harvested and cooked, and there's general agreement not to grow turnips again because they are too woody and too bitter, no matter how they are cooked.

Break this chain of events by harvesting the turnips **before** they are full grown, while they are small and tender—and edible.

Chapter 5
Fruit: Preserving Sunshine

Since the Northeast is great apple country, canning apples comes as a natural fall activity, and when the orchards open their gates to the public in September, you know the season has arrived. Families make yearly outings to their favorite orchards on mild, sunny weekends.

Everyone has his favorite variety—MacIntosh for all-purpose use, Northern Spies for keepers, Cortlands for salads, Greenings for pies, Delicious for eating. For older favorites you have to go to an old orchard, as the newer orchards are usually limited to a few of the well-known varieties.

Apples store well and dry beautifully. We've had late Cortlands last until February in the cellar, but applesauce is a mainstay of our cooking twelve months of the year. And commercial applesauce just doesn't make it. It should taste just one way, and that's homemade. We use it as a side dish, in cakes and in cookies. We can our applesauce in a *boiling water bath*. It's easy and it saves room in the freezer for things which freeze better than can.

Although the preparation of the applesauce itself is particular to apples, the canning procedure is the same for all fruits, since they are high in acid. There are, however, some specifics that set fruit apart, both in the growing or purchasing and the processing.

Fewer people grow their own fruit than their own vegetables. Fruit trees take time to care for and often they take years to bear. Many berry fruit crops require more space than the average home gardener has available. But this need not discourage the home canner.

Co-ops offer excellent buys on fruit by the bushel. Local farms often have public picking of strawberries, apples, cherries, tomatoes and even raspberries. Pick with care and according to directions. Abuse of carefully nurtured trees and plants is one reason more growers don't let the public pick. Roadside stands often have high-quality fresh fruit at reasonable prices. Also, foraging for wild berries can provide a pleasant family expedition.

As with other produce, pick or buy only the best. Unripened fruit is lower in flavor and sugar content. Cherries, plums, and berries especially, should be firm, never overripe or bruised.

Wash the fruit carefully, tenderly and gently after chilling them. This can't be overemphasized, unless you've seen valuable raspberries go to pieces under a heavy stream of water. Don't let small fruits sit in water. Softer, large fruits can be saved for jams.

Discoloration is common with some fruits—especially apples and peaches. Work quickly and in small batches. Use any of the following three anti-oxidants:

1. A commercial preparation such as "Fruit-Fresh," according to label directions.
2. One teaspoon ascorbic acid (vitamin C) to a cup of water. Dip the fruit in as you go along. Or add ¼ teaspoon ascorbic acid as you pack the fruit into jars *if* you didn't soak them beforehand. Ascorbic acid in a crystalline form can be obtained at drug stores.
3. A solution of 2 tablespoons salt and 2 tablespoons vinegar to 1 gallon cold water to soak fruit in before packing. Rinse thoroughly before canning since food values will deteriorate after 20 minutes in salt water.

If a firm product that is to retain its shape is desired, *raw packing* is a necessity. Hot packing is necessary with applesauce.

With most hot packs and all raw packs, a syrup will be needed. Directions will call for thin, medium or heavy syrup made of sugar and water or sugar and fruit juice, heated. The sugar will help the fruit retain its color and flavor.

Honey or corn syrup may be substituted for half the sugar in a recipe, or more if you like the flavor. If the honey is strong, be cautious, since if can have an overpowering flavor. Cover the fruit completely to avoid darkening. Also a tight pack will avoid shrinkage that causes floating fruit. However, the floating doesn't affect the storing qualities.

In general, aim for good natural color with no fading or floating and good shape retention, with uniform, unbroken pieces.

After packing and adjusting the lids, process all fruit in a *boiling water bath* for the time called for in the specific directions. Remember to begin timing only when the water has reached a rolling boil.

Store all your jars in a cold, dry, dark place. Store red berries, especially, in the dark, as they will fade when exposed to light.

Many fruits, with the exception of applesauce, and peaches, freeze easier than they can and retain a better color and shape. But by following the canning directions carefully, you can store summer flavor for winter use. And nothing brightens a winter meal more than colorful, out-of-season fruits.

Apples

Wash, pare, core and cut into pieces. Use of anti-oxidant is optional but recommended.

Boiling water bath

Hot pack: Prepare as above. Boil 5 minutes in thin syrup or water. Pack hot fruit into hot clean jars. Cover with hot, thin syrup leaving ½ inch headroom. Adjust lids. Process in a boiling water bath.

> Pints . . . . 15 minutes
> Quarts . . . . 20 minutes

Remove jars. Complete seals if necessary. (If you like apple jelly, save the cores and peels to boil down for jelly.)

Freezing. A tip: Freeze unsweetened or pre-sweetened apple slices treated with an anti-oxidant in a pie shell until solid. Then wrap in

The old-fashioned apple parer that screws onto a table will quickly peel the apples with a few turns of the hand crank. A simple coring knife also is helpful at apple harvest time, as are gadgets that section and core an apple in one push.

For making applesauce and tomato and other purees and juices there are hand-cranked food mills (our favorite), food presses in a cone shape with wooden handles, plus hand-cranked juicers that screw down to a table. All are helpful when doing large quantities.

freezer paper without the pie tin. The pie-shaped apples are ready to slip into a pie crust later.

Wash, peel, core, and slice apples.

Syrup pack: Put into a rigid container and cover with medium syrup, allowing ½ inch headroom for pints and 1 inch for quarts. Seal and freeze.

Sugar pack: To each quart of prepared apples, add ½ cup sugar and stir. Optional: To prevent darkening, soak apples in a solution of 2 tablespoons salt to 1 gallon water after slicing. Leave in no longer than 15 minutes. Rinse well. Pack into containers, leaving headroom (see page 20). Seal and freeze.

Drying. Refer to Chapter 9.

Applesauce

Wash and quarter sound apples. Don't remove skins, as they provide color. Put in a kettle with two inches of water. Cover and let cook until soft, stirring occasionally to prevent scorching. Put through a food mill or press, adding sugar and cinnamon to taste (these can be added later).

BOILING WATER BATH TIME CHART FOR CANNING FRUIT

Fruit	Pints	Quarts
Apples	15 min.	20 min.
Applesauce	10 min.	10 min.
Berries (except		
strawberries)	10 min.	15 min.
Cherries, raw pack	20 min.	25 min.
hot pack	10 min.	15 min.
Peaches, raw pack	25 min.	30 min.
hot pack	20 min.	25 min.
Pears, (same as peaches)		
Plums, raw pack	20 min.	25 min.
Rhubarb	10 min.	10 min.

Boiling water bath

Hot pack: Pack hot applesauce into hot clean jars, leaving ½ inch headroom. Adjust lids and process in a boiling water bath. (See page 108.)

Pints . . . . 10 minutes
Quarts . . . . 10 minutes

Remove jars. Complete seals if necessary.

Freezing. Cool prepared applesauce and pack into rigid containers, leaving headroom (see page 20). Seal and freeze.

Remember, thawing applesauce takes some time. If you will be using it often at the last minute, can it.

Apricots

Boiling water bath canning. Ripened apricots may be canned whole or the pits removed from fruit harvested before it is completely ripe.

Raw pack: Wash, sort and cut into halves. Peel if desired. Pit. (Optional: treat with antioxidant.) Pack into hot, clean jars, leaving ½ inch headroom. Cover with hot, medium or thin syrup, leaving ½ inch headroom. Adjust lids. Process in boiling water bath:

Pints . . . . 25 minutes
Quarts . . . . 30 minutes

Hot pack: Wash and scald apricots. Slip skins and remove pits. (Optional: treat with antioxidant.) Cook apricots, a few at a time, in a thin or medium syrup, until heated through. Pack hot into hot, clean jars, leaving ½ inch headroom. Cover with boiling syrup, leaving ½

MAKING APPLESAUCE

1. Cut up apples and place in a kettle with enough water to prevent burning. Cover. Stir often. Add a stick of cinnamon if desired.

4. Heat applesauce just to boiling, stirring often.

2. When apples are soft, put them through a food mill or press.

5. Pour into hot, clean jars, leaving ½ inch headroom.

3. Add sugar or other sweetener to taste, about 1 cup per dozen apples.

6. Wipe rims with a damp cloth. Adjust lids and process in a boiling water bath for 20 minutes for both pints and quarts. Remove jars. Complete seals if necessary.

inch headroom. Adjust lids. Process in a boiling water bath:

     Pints . . . . 20 minutes
     Quarts . . . . 25 minutes
Remove jars. Complete seals if necessary.

Freezing. Wash, halve or slice. Pit. If not peeled, place in boiling water for ½ minute to keep skins tender. Cool immediately.

Syrup pack: Pack apricots in containers. Optional but recommended: Add ¾ teaspoon crystalline ascorbic acid to each quart of medium syrup. Cover with syrup leaving headroom (see page 20). Seal and freeze.

Sugar pack: Add ½ cup sugar to one quart prepared fruit. Stir to dissolve. Pack into containers, leaving headroom (see page 20). Seal freeze. (Optional: anti-oxidant.)

Puree or crushed: Peel fully ripe apricots by dunking them in boiling water and cooling them immediately in cold water. Peel, slice and pit. Crush with a masher for crushed, or use a food mill or blender for puree. Add 1 cup sugar to 1

APRICOT NECTAR LEMON SUPREME CAKE

1 package Lemon Supreme Cake Mix
1 cup apricot nectar
¾ cup cooking oil
½ cup sugar
4 eggs

Preheat oven to 350°, and oil a tube pan. Mix cake mix, nectar, oil and sugar. Add eggs one at a time, beating thoroughly after each one. Pour into oiled tube pan and bake at 350° for 1 hour or more, until cake springs back at a touch. Cool 10 minutes, turn out upside down on a plate and glaze with one cup sifted confectioners' sugar, mixed (most easily in an electric blender) with the juice of one lemon.

For variation, try substituting other flavor nectars or juices and a different type cake mix. Orange juice and chocolate cake topped with sifted confectioners' sugar is great!

---

quart fruit. Optional: add ¼ tsp. crystalline ascorbic acid dissolved in ¼ cup water to fruit before adding sugar. Pack into containers, leaving headroom (see page 20). Seal and freeze.

Avocados

Few of us are lucky enough to grow our own or live where they are grown, but they are on special occasionally. Some like them pureed for milk shakes and ice cream, but we love guacamole.

Peel the avocado. Then mash soft but not mushy. Optional: Add ⅛ teaspoon crystalline ascorbic acid to one quart of puree. Pack into containers, leaving headroom (see page 20). Seal and freeze. Season for guacamole when thawed.

TO FIGURE YIELD OF CANNED FRUIT FROM FRESH

The number of quarts of canned food you can get from a given quantity of fresh fruit depends upon the quality, variety, maturity, and size of the fruit, whether it is whole, in halves, or in slices, and whether it is packed raw or hot.

Generally, the following amounts of fresh fruit or tomatoes (as purchased or picked) make 1 quart of canned food:

Fruit	Pounds
Apples	2½ to 3
Berries, except	1½ to 3
strawberries	(1 to 2 qt. boxes)
Cherries	
(canned unpitted)	2 to 2½
Peaches	2 to 3
Pears	2 to 3
Plums	1½ to 2½
Tomatoes	2½ to 3½

In 1 pound there are about 3 medium apples and pears; 4 medium peaches or tomatoes; 8 medium plums.

Pints. . . . . 10 minutes
Quarts . . . . 15 minutes
Remove jars. Complete seals if necessary.

Freezing. It is possible to freeze berries to be used for making jellies or jams at your leisure. Be sure to label with how much sugar has been added, and adjust your jelly or jam recipe accordingly.

Firm berries (listed above): Wash, sort, drain. Optional: Steam one minute to tenderize skins, cooling immediately.

Syrup pack: Pack berries into containers, covering with medium syrup, leaving headroom (see page 20). Seal and freeze.

Sugar pack: Not recommended.

Unsweetened pack: Pack berries into containers, leaving headroom (see page 20), seal and freeze.

Crushed or pureed: Prepare as above, then crush by using blender or food mill. Stir in 1 cup sugar to 1 quart fruit. Pack into containers, leaving headroom (see page 20). Seal and freeze.

Drying. Refer to Chapter 9.

Berries

(Firm Berries: Blueberries, cranberries, elderberries, currants, gooseberries, huckleberries)

(Soft Berries: Blackberries, dewberries, loganberries, raspberries, youngberries)

Many of these berries are unknown to many of us unless they happen to be a local or family favorite. Fresh raspberries are almost a vanishing fruit for most families, so if you can buy, pick or grow them, appreciate them.

Don't overlook picking from the wild. Elderberries for wine, blackberries and black raspberries, small blueberries, and even cranberries from bogs are often found growing wild, and the picking makes a memorable event for most families. Be sure of your identification with a good field guide before tasting, however, if you are unsure.

Boiling water bath. The firm berries listed above make a better canned fruit when hot packed.

Hot pack: Wash and sort. For each quart of berries, add ½ cup sugar to a kettle. Slowly bring to a boil, treating the fruit as carefully as possible. Shake the kettle rather than stir the berries to prevent sticking.

Fill hot clean jars with berries and a thin syrup to cover, leaving ½ inch headroom. Adjust lids. Process in a boiling water bath.

Cherries

Use tree-ripened cherries. Stem, sort and wash. Drain and pit. Pitting can be done with a commercial cherry pitter or a sharp paring knife (but with some loss of shape).

SOUR CHERRIES

Boiling water bath

Raw pack: Prepare as above. Fill jars compactly with cherries. Cover with thin syrup, leaving ½ inch headroom. Adjust lids. Process in a boiling water bath.

Pints. . . . . 20 minutes
Quarts . . . . 25 minutes
Remove jars. Complete seals if necessary.

Hot pack: Prepare as above. Add ½ cup sugar for each quart of berries in a kettle. Slowly bring to a boil, adding water if it sticks. Boil covered. Pack hot into hot clean jars. Shake down, cover with syrup leaving ½ inch headroom. Adjust lids. Process in a boiling water bath.

Pints . . . . 10 minutes
Quarts . . . . 15 minutes

Remove jars. Complete seals if necessary.

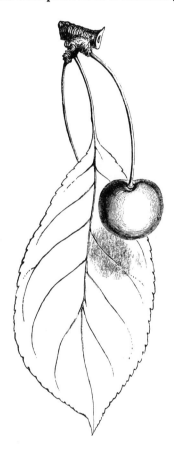

Freezing

Sugar pack: Prepare as above. Add ¾ cup sugar to 1 quart fruit. Mix well until dissolved. Pack into containers, leaving headroom (see page 20). Seal and freeze.

Syrup pack: Prepare as above. Pack into containers, covering with heavy syrup, leaving no headroom. Seal and freeze.

Pureed: Crush prepared cherries. Heat to boiling, cool and press through food mill or blender. Add ¾ cup sugar to 1 quart fruit. Pack into containers, leaving ½ inch headroom for pints and 1 inch for quarts. Seal and freeze.

Crushed: Prepare as above. Crush, adding 1½ cups sugar to 1 quart fruit. Mix well. Pack into containers, leaving headroom (see page 20). Seal and freeze.

SWEET CHERRIES

Red are usually best. Process quickly. Some people find freezing with the pit in gives an off-flavor, but we haven't found this so. If you have picked quarts, pitting can be very tedious, so think about freezing some with pits in, to be pitted when used. If pitted when still semi-frozen, they do nicely.

Freezing

Syrup pack: Prepare as above. Pack into containers, covering with medium syrup, leaving ½ inch headroom for pints and 1 inch for quarts. Seal and freeze. Optional: Add ½ teaspoon crystalline ascorbic acid to 1 quart fruit.

Crushed: Prepare as above. Add 1½ cups sugar to 1 quart of crushed cherries. Optional: Add ¼ teaspoon crystalline ascorbic acid to each quart of fruit.

Mix well. Pack into containers, leaving headroom (see page 20). Seal and freeze.

Drying. Refer to Chapter 9.

Cranberries

Buy cranberries when on sale and save for sauce or breads.

Boiling water bath canning. For cranberry sauce, prepare as follows:

1 quart cranberries
1 cup water
2 cups sugar

Wash and sort berries, adding water and cooking until berries are soft and pop. Press through

Melons

Few of us in the North raise enough melons to freeze, but occasionally they are on special and are excellent frozen. Serve plain or in a mixed fruit or salad dish.

Cut ripe melons in half, scooping out seeds, peel and slice or dice. Pack into containers, covering with thin syrup. Leave headroom (see page 20), seal and freeze.

a sieve, adding sugar and boil for 3 minutes. Pour into hot sterilized jars, leaving ½ inch headroom. Adjust lids. Process in a boiling water bath.

Pints . . . . 10 minutes
Quarts . . . . 10 minutes

Remove jars. Complete seals if necessary.

Yield: 2 pints

Freezing. Freeze directly in the box or bag from the store. After thawing for use, wash and sort.

Grapefruit and Oranges

Grapefruit and oranges, in season, are often good buys and can be purchased by the bushel through a co-op. Their season, late winter, is when the freezer is getting low.

Use extra-meaty fruits. Wash, peel, cutting out membrane and seeds. Save juice.

Syrup pack: Pack in containers. Cover with medium syrup using fruit juice or water. Leave headroom (see page 20), seal and freeze.

Mixed Fruits for Fruit Salad or Compote

Combine any combination of fruits except oranges and bananas. Remember, color makes a dish, so let your imagination loose. Mixed fruits are just right for those odd lots of fruit not large enough to freeze separately.

Boiling water bath

Raw pack: Prepare as in specific directions for each fruit. Pack into hot clean pint jars and cover with hot medium syrup, leaving ½ inch headroom. Adjust lids. Process in a boiling water bath for the time required by the fruit having the longest processing time.

Freezing. Prepare each fruit according to specific directions. Cover with medium syrup after packing into containers. Leave headroom (see page 20). Seal and freeze.

Peaches

Nothing is more satisfying than peaches, so if you are wondering where to start with fruit, look no further. However, check your local quality. Shipped peaches are picked unripened and are often sadly lacking in flavor and texture.

To peel, scald briefly by dipping into boiling water. Cool quickly in cold water and the skins will slip off easily.

For canning: wash, peel and section. Peach halves may retain air bubbles in the packing. Optional but recommended: Treat with an anti-oxidant (see under *Apples*).

HOT SPICED FRUIT COMPOTE

Combine: 4 pounds dried prunes
1 orange, diced
1 lemon, diced
1 package (about 8 sticks)
    stick cinnamon
½ pound dark brown sugar
½ pound granulated sugar
1 pint maple syrup

Bring to boil and simmer until prunes are plump and tender (approximately ¾ hour).

Add: 1 No. 2 can chunk pineapple
1 No. 2 can sour cherries

Let simmer for another half-hour. Pull and cool. Reheat as needed. This will keep in the refrigerator.

Boiling water bath canning

Raw pack: Pack sections into hot clean jars. Fill with medium syrup, leaving ½ inch headroom. Adjust lids. Process in a boiling water bath.

Pints . . . . 25 minutes
Quarts . . . . 30 minutes
Remove jars. Complete seals if necessary.

Hot pack: Treat sections with an anti-oxidant (optional but recommended). Boil for three minutes in a medium syrup. Pack into hot clean jars, leaving ½ inch headroom. Add additional hot syrup if necessary to cover, leaving ½ inch headroom. Adjust lids. Process in a boiling water bath.

Pints . . . . 20 minutes
Quarts . . . . 25 minutes
Remove jars. Complete seals if necessary.

Nectarines

Freezing. Freeze as you would peaches. Over-ripe fruit may have a disagreeable flavor if frozen.

Freezing

Syrup pack: Process as above. Pack into containers and cover with medium syrup. Optional but recommended: ½ teaspoon crystalline ascorbic acid to 1 quart syrup. Press fruit down, using a crumpled wad of wax paper to keep fruit below surface of syrup. Leave headroom (see page 20). Seal and freeze.

Sugar pack: Add ⅔ cup sugar to 1 quart fruit. Mix well. Pack into containers, leaving ½ inch headroom for pints and 1 inch for quarts. Seal and freeze. Optional: Sprinkle ¼ teaspoon crystalline ascorbic acid mixed with ¼ cup water over fruit.

Puree or crushed: Prepare as above. Crush coarsely. For puree, heat for 4 minutes in just enough water to prevent scorching. Mix 1 cup sugar to 1 quart fruit. Pack into containers, leaving headroom (see page 20). Seal and freeze. Optional: Add ⅛ teaspoon crystalline ascorbic acid to 1 quart puree.

Drying. Refer to Chapter 9.

Hot pack: Prepare as above. Boil briefly in syrup. Drain, saving syrup. Pack hot into hot clean jars, leaving ½ inch headroom. Add hot syrup, leaving ½ inch headroom. Adjust lids. Process in a boiling water bath.

Pints . . . . 20 minutes
Quarts . . . . 25 minutes
Remove jars. Complete seals if necessary.

Pears

Firm pears are necessary. *Bartletts* are best but try *Seckel* for spicing. Pears are best when picked slightly underripe and just turning yellow. Wrap each one in paper and store at room temperature for two or three weeks. Check them often. They will ripen evenly and be delicious. Wash, peel, cut and core. Anti-oxidants are optional but recommended, (see under *Apples*).

Boiling water bath

Raw pack: Prepare as above. Pack into hot clean jars, leaving ½ inch headroom. Add boiling thin or medium syrup, leaving ½ inch headroom. Adjust lids. Process in a boiling water bath.

Pints . . . . 25 minutes
Quarts . . . . 30 minutes
Remove jars. Complete seals if necessary.

CINNAMON PEARS

14 pounds pears
1 teaspoon stick cinnamon
1 teaspoon whole cloves
1 qt. cider vinegar
6 pounds honey

Peel pears. Put spices in cheesecloth bag. Heat honey and vinegar to boiling, adding spice bag and pears. Cook until pears are tender. Remove pears and spices. Boil syrup until thick. Pack pears into hot clean jars, leaving ½ inch headroom. Cover with hot syrup, leaving ½ inch headroom. Adjust lids. Process in boiling water bath.

Pints . . . . 20 minutes
Quarts . . . . 20 minutes
Remove jars. Complete seals if necessary. Makes 6 quarts.

Pineapples

Few of us live where pineapple is native, but it is a good buy from time to time and worth putting up.

Boiling water bath

Hot pack: Wash, slice and peel pineapple, removing eyes and core. Slice into rings or wedges. Boil in medium syrup for 5–10 minutes. Pack into hot clean jars, leaving ½ inch headroom. Adjust lids. Process in a boiling water bath.

Pints . . . . 15 minutes
Quarts . . . . 20 minutes

Remove jars. Complete seals if necessary.

Pineapple (and other juicy fruits) may be canned in their own unsweetened juice rather than in a sugar syrup. Cut up and crush the ripest parts of the pineapple. Simmer (185 – 210° F.) until the juice runs freely. Strain through a jelly bag or several layers of damp cheesecloth. Use this juice in place of the sugar syrup called for in the canning recipe. You may want to try using pineapple juice as a substitute for the syrup used with other fruits too, or make unsweetened juice from those fruits.

Freezing. Wash, slice and pare ripe pineapples and cut according to preference.

Syrup pack: Pack tightly into containers, covering with thin syrup made with juice or water. Leave headroom (see page 20). Seal and freeze.

Unsweetened pack: Pack into containers, leaving headroom (see page 20), seal and freeze. Remember that uncooked pineapple cannot be used in gelatin-type salads or desserts.

Plums and Prunes

Use ripe, firm fruit. Sort, wash, pit and cut according to preference. If you are canning plums whole, prick the skins with a needle to prevent bursting.

Boiling water bath

Raw pack: Prepare as above. Pack into hot clean jars, leaving ½ inch headroom. Add boiling medium or heavy syrup, leaving ½ inch headroom. Adjust lids. Process in a boiling water bath.

Pints . . . . 20 minutes
Quarts . . . . 25 minutes

Remove jars. Complete seals if necessary.

Hot pack: Heat prepared plums in medium syrup. Measure the juice from sectioned plums. For each cup of juice, add ¾ cup sugar. Reheat

to dissolve sugar. Drain the fruit but save the syrup. Pack the fruit into hot clean jars, leaving ½ inch headroom. Add boiling syrup (you have to add more than you obtain from the boiling, so have extra syrup ready) leaving ½ inch headroom. Adjust lids. Process in a boiling water bath.

Pints................20 minutes
Quarts.............25 minutes

Remove jars. Complete seals if necessary.

Freezing

Syrup pack: Prepare as above. Pack into containers, covering with medium syrup. Optional: Add ½ teaspoon crystalline ascorbic acid to 1 quart syrup. Leave headroom (see page 20). Seal and freeze.

Unsweetened pack: Prepare as above. Pack into containers, leaving headroom (see page 20). Seal and freeze.

Rhubarb

Harvesting. As soon as the stalks are as thick as your thumb, they can be harvested. There are both red and green varieties, so the color is not important. To pick, pull off (don't cut) the outside stalks. Be sure to cut out the seed pods as they form in the center of the plant, in order to keep the plant producing stalks.

Preparation. Whether rhubarb is technically a fruit or vegetable is for the horticulturists to decide. Low on the pH scale, it is processed as a fruit. Wash and cut off both ends, then cut into pie-sized pieces. The leaves contain oxalic acid which is poisonous, so warn children. Consider putting up rhubarb as a dessert sauce or stretching strawberries by making strawberry-rhubarb pie or jam.

Boiling water bath canning. Add ½ cup sugar to each quart. Let the fruit stand for several hours to draw out the juice. Boil for 1 min-

ute. Pack into hot, clean jars, leaving ½ inch headroom. Cover with hot juice, leaving ½ inch headroom. Adjust lids. Process in a boiling water bath.

Pints and quarts ..... 10 minutes

Freezing

Unsweetened: Pack tightly into containers, leaving headroom (see page 20). Seal and freeze.

Syrup pack: Optional: put rhubarb into boiling water for 1 minute, cooling it quickly in cold water. Pack into containers and cover with medium syrup, leaving headroom (see page 20). Seal and freeze.

GROWING RHUBARB IN THE WINTER

If you're fortunate enough to have an excess of rhubarb crowns, dig up a few (2-year-olds are best) any time after the first heavy frosts of the fall. They will provide a taste of summer in the winter.

With each crown, dig up as much of the roots as possible in one clump, and pot each crown in a roomy container with rich soil or compost. Store in a cold, dark place. A month before rhubarb is wanted, move the pot into a warm, dark location. (Temperature of 60 degrees is ideal.) Soil should be kept moist for maximum growth. As much as 2 pounds of rhubarb will be produced by each crown.

Strawberries

Harvesting. Strawberries should be picked as soon as they are ripe, red and juicy. Keep them picked every couple of days, so the plant will put its energy into ripening more fruit, rather than maturing the first berries.

Strawberries have the best quality when frozen; they tend to lose color and texture when canned. In both cases be sure to cut off any green or spoiled spots before preserving, and process as soon after harvest as possible. Do not wash until ready to use, as strawberries spoil rapidly after washing.

Boiling water bath canning. The boiling water bath is not advisable for strawberries, so better freeze them or make jelly. Canned, strawberries tend to fade and float. However, to can them, follow these directions:

Hot pack only: Wash, hull and sort berries. Use ½–1 cup sugar for four cups of berries. Alternate layers of berries and sugar in pans, and let stand covered for 2–4 hours. Simmer in a kettle for 5 minutes. Pack into hot, clean jars, leav-

ing ½ inch headroom. Cover with a thin syrup, leaving ½ inch headroom. Adjust lids. Process in a boiling water bath:

Pints . . . . 10 minutes
Quarts . . . . 15 minutes

Remove jars. Complete seals if necessary.

Freezing. Sort, wash ripe, red strawberries, remove hulls and wash again.

Syrup pack: Put berries into containers and cover with cold heavy syrup leaving headroom (see page 20). Seal and freeze.

Sugar pack: Add ¾ cup sugar to one quart fruit and mix thoroughly. Pack into containers, leaving headroom (see page 20). Seal and freeze. Strawberries frozen this way may be whole, sliced or crushed.

Unsweetened: Pack into containers, leaving headroom. Seal and freeze. *Optional:* Add 1 tsp. crystalline ascorbic acid to 1 quart water and pour over berries. Pack into containers, leaving headroom (see page 20). Seal and freeze.

Flash freezing: Using only perfect, large berries, place them on a metal sheet and freeze until solid. Then transfer them to freezer containers. Seal and freeze. These are ideal for decoration on cheesecakes or strawberry shortcakes, especially when used semi-thawed so as to retain their shape.

Puree: Prepare strawberries, then press through a food mill or run through an electric blender. Add ⅔ cup sugar to 1 quart berries. Mix well and pack into containers, leaving appropriate headroom (see page 20). Seal and freeze.

117

No-Sugar Canning and Freezing of Fruit

If you are looking for sugar-free directions for either dieting or diabetic reasons, Kerr Glass Manufacturing Corp. has some good guidelines.

Fruit can be canned safely without sugar. For hot pack, preheat fruit over low heat in a small amount of water. Then pack fruit into jars, covering with juice from the kettle, and process according to the specified directions. For raw pack, pack the fruit into jars raw. Add fruit juice obtained by crushing completely ripe fruit and boiling it over low heat. Then strain the juice through a clean cloth and fill to within 1½ inches of the top of the jars. Process according to specific directions.

For using artificial sweeteners, check the directions for each and consult with your doctor before using. More information can be had by writing to American Diabetic Association, Inc., 18 East 48th St., New York, N.Y., 10017.

To freeze without sugar, prepare according to individual instructions. Use either 3 tablespoons of lemon juice to one gallon of water as an antioxidant or ascorbic acid per earlier instructions. Process quickly and freeze, leaving appropriate headroom.

CANNING AND FREEZING FRUIT JUICES

Fruit juices are quick and easy to make. They are a practical use for extra fruit and for misshapen or slightly bruised fruit which would be unattractive preserved whole. Good quality juice requires fruit with a full, ripe flavor and from which all signs of rot or blemish have been carefully cut.

If storage or freezer space is limited, you may hesitate to fill it with juice which is, after all, largely water. But weigh against this the many ways home-canned juices can be used. They may be iced for a healthful beverage; used for leisurely jelly-making when the crush of the harvest season has passed; or made into syrups to brighten breakfast pancakes or dinner desserts. Fruit juices can provide the liquid base for homemade gelatin desserts and salads. Several varieties can be blended for a special Christmas punch. Or serve them steaming hot on a cold winter afternoon with a stick of cinnamon. In summer children love popsicles made of sweetened berry juice frozen in molds made for that purpose or improvised from ice trays or paper cups into which a stick is put; or "snow cones" in winter made from sweetened juice poured over fresh snow and served in a paper cup with or without benefit of a spoon!

HONEY

In recent years honey has become increasingly popular as a sugar substitute. It is more healthful than sugar but should be used in moderation when substituted for sugar in canning recipes. Substituting half the sugar in a recipe with honey seems to achieve satisfactory results—if it is mild-flavored, such as Clover honey. Buckwheat honeys are typically stronger and will overpower the subtle flavors of fruits in jams and jellies or fruits. Old-fashioned recipes, some of which come down from the eighteenth century when honey was more readily available than sugar, call for pure honey and no sugar.

118

Fruit juices will retain their fresh flavor if heated as little as possible during preparation, and for freezing they should be chilled as rapidly as possible. Processing in a 5-minute boiling water bath is recommended for most of the fruit juices to ensure safe storage. The traditional method was to pasteurize the hot-packed fruit juices (except tomato juice and fruit nectars) in a *hot water bath* at simmering temperature (180° – 190° F.) for 30 minutes. Open Kettle Canning is not recommended for fruit juices.

EQUIPMENT NEEDED

Kettles and *bowls* should be made of stainless steel, glass, plastic or unchipped enamelware. Aluminum pans are safe to use, but the acid in the fruit juice will cause unattractive pitting in the pan, and aluminum salts dissolved in the juice may cause unpleasant color or flavor changes. A *double boiler* is used for gentle heat-ing of the juice to simmering for hot pack canning, or an *asbestos pad* can be used under a pan if the juice is heated directly over the flame. The *jelly bag* should be made of tightly woven muslin or canvas for the clearest juice. You will need *cheesecloth* for straining pressed juice. It should be washed and rinsed before use to avoid imparting off-flavors to the juice. To be sure the temperature of the juice does not exceed that recommended, a *thermometer* is helpful but optional.

For canning: *Standard canning jars* should be thoroughly washed and sterilized. Leave them in simmering water (or hot in dishwasher with sterilizing cycle) until ready to use. *Lids* or *rubber rings* are prepared according to manufacturers' directions, or wash and cover with boiling water. Leave in water until ready to use. *Water bath canner* or *large kettle with rack* is needed for boiling water bath. Water should be

hot but not boiling when hot jars of juice are placed in it.

For freezing: The best containers to use are rigid plastic freezer containers. *Freezing jars* with wide mouths and tapered sides with no shoulders may also be used. Other standard canning jars may be used only if recommended by the manufacturer for both freezing and canning. Be sure enough headroom is left (see chart following) so that the glass will not break when the juice expands during freezing. Containers should be thoroughly washed in hot soapy water, rinsed and scalded with boiling water.

ASCORBIC ACID

Crystalline ascorbic acid may be added to juices to help preserve color and flavor, as well as adding supplementary vitamin C. See the earlier section on freezing fruits for information on sources. To citrus juices, ¾ teaspoon may be added per gallon of juice; add 1 teaspoon to a gallon of other types of juice.

SWEETENING

Natural, unsweetened fruit juices are delicious and healthy for you, but sugar does enhance the flavor and may be added if desired. One cup of sugar to a gallon of the sweeter juices is usually enough. About half as much mild-flavored honey may be used instead. If the juice is to be used for jelly, omit the sugar; or label the jar with the amount of sugar used and adjust the jelly recipe accordingly. For people on sugar-restricted diets, a sugar substitute that is recommended by your doctor may be used as the sweetener. The use of sugar depends on personal preference and is not necessary for preserving the juice.

PREPARATION OF THE FRUIT

Use ripe, fresh, flavorful fruit for the best juice. Juice for jelly-making should be made up of the type of fruit recommended in the jelly recipe. Generally, jelly cooked the *long way* requires

APPROXIMATE YIELD OF FROZEN FRUITS FROM FRESH

Fruit	Fresh, as Purchased or Picked	Frozen
Apples	1 bu. (48 lb.)	32 to 40 pt.
	1 box (44 lb.)	29 to 35 pt.
	1¼ to 1½ lb.	1 pt.
Apricots	1 bu. (48 lb.)	60 to 72 pt.
	1 crate (22 lb.)	28 to 33 pt.
	⅔ to ⅘ lb.	1 pt.
Berries	1 crate (24 qt.)	32 to 36 pt.
	1⅓ to 1½ pt.	1 pt.
Cantaloups	1 dozen (28 lb.)	22 pt.
	1 to 1¼ lb.	1 pt.
Cherries, sweet or sour	1 bu. (56 lb.)	36 to 44 pt.
	1¼ to 1½ lb.	1 pt.
Cranberries	1 box (25 lb.)	50 pt.
	1 peck (8 lb.)	16 pt.
	½ lb.	1 pt.
Currants	2 qt. (3 lb.)	4 pt.
	¾ lb.	1 pt.
Peaches	1 bu. (48 lb.)	32 to 48 pt.
	1 lug box (20 lb.)	13 to 20 pt.
	1 to 1½ lb.	1 pt.
Pears	1 bu. (50 lb.)	40 to 50 pt.
	1 western box (46 lb.)	37 to 46 pt.
	1 to 1¼ lb.	1 pt.
Pineapple	5 lb.	4 pt.
Plums and prunes	1 bu. (56 lb.)	38 to 56 pt.
	1 crate (20 lb.)	13 to 20 pt.
	1 to 1½ lb.	1 pt.
Raspberries	1 crate (24 pt.)	24 pt.
	1 pt.	1 pt.
Rhubarb	15 lb.	15 to 22 pt.
	⅔ to 1 lb.	1 pt.
Strawberries	1 crate (24 qt.)	38 pt.
	⅔ qt.	1 pt.

¼ under-ripe and ¾ ripe fruit; and jellies made with added pectin require fully ripe fruit.

Sort and wash the fruit, and remove blemishes, stems, pits or what have you. Some fruits are cut up and heated slightly (in enough water to prevent sticking, if necessary) to start the juice flowing. Juicy fruits are cut up, crushed and the juice squeezed from them without heating. Apples for cider are crushed and pressed without heating; for apple juice, water is added to cut-up apples and they are simmered until soft. Orange, grapefruit and lemon juice is squeezed from the fresh fruit, and heated only enough to be hot packed into canning jars; for freezing no heat is applied. Light cherries and white grapes also are not heated except enough to hot-pack for canning.

A blender may be used to break down the fruit without heat, and the resulting emulsion can be pressed through a jelly bag to extract the juice. An electric juicer will quickly separate juice from the pulp of most fruits.

EXTRACTING THE JUICE

The juicy pulp prepared from the fruit can be squeezed through a jelly bag, and for a clearer juice re-strained through 4 layers of damp, washed cheesecloth. Sugar and ascorbic acid are added if desired, and the juice is ready for processing.

FREEZING

The prepared juice is poured into clean containers, cooled rapidly (if hot) in the refrigerator or packed in ice, labeled and put into the coldest part of the freezer to freeze. Be sure to leave adequate headroom in standard canning jars.

After the juice has been frozen in the coldest part of the freezer, it can be moved for storage to any part of the freezer where the temperature is 0° F. or less. Under these conditions frozen citrus juices should be good for 3–4 months; other juices for up to 8 months.

HEADROOM REQUIRED IN CONTAINERS FOR FREEZING JUICES

Type of Jar	Amount of Headroom Needed
Wide mouth, no shoulder (Also plastic containers)	
Pints	1 inch
Quarts	1½ inches
Wide mouth, with shoulder	
Pints and Quarts	1½ inches
Regular mouth, with shoulder	
Pints	1½ inches
Quarts	2 inches

Canning Fruit Juices

Reheat the prepared juice to simmering (185°–190° F. for most juices; 165° F. for citrus juices), and pour immediately into hot sterilized canning jars, leaving ½ inch headroom. Adjust lids, and process in a boiling water bath for 5 to 10 minutes according to the specific instructions (both pints and quarts).

Have the water below boiling when the jars are placed in the kettle to keep the total heating time of the juice to a minimum. Start timing as soon as the water reaches a full boil, and as soon as the time is up, remove the jars.

Complete seals if necessary, set on a rack or towel in a draft-free spot, and allow to cool completely. Check for a good seal, remove screw bands, label, and store in a *dark*, cool place. The jars can be wrapped in paper or cloth to exclude the light if the storage area is not dark. Color and certain vitamins may be lost by exposure to light.

When the directions call for a *hot water bath* instead of a *boiling water bath*, follow the directions above *except* do not allow the water to exceed the recommended simmering temperature—a maximum of 175° F. for citrus juices, 190° F. for other juices. In a hot water bath the juice is pasteurized and the jar sealed, without imparting a cooked flavor to the juice.

SHORT-CUT JUICE

A quicker way to make canned juice is to can whole or cut-up fruit in boiling water. The juice will make itself when processed and stored—all you need to do is strain and chill it before serving.

Use fully ripe fruit. Wash, stem, pit, cut up as necessary, depending on the type of fruit. Put from 1–1½ cups fruit into a hot sterilized quart jar. Add up to one cup of sugar and ¼ teaspoon crystalline ascorbic acid to the less tart fruits. Fill with boiling water, leaving ½ inch headroom. Adjust lids, and process for 10 minutes in a *boiling water bath*. This method is particularly successful with grapes and berries.

With all juices, if you want them crystal clear, especially for jelly, do not squeeze them through the jelly bag. They should just be allowed to drip for several hours or overnight. For greater quantity and a thicker juice, squeeze the bag and re-strain the juice through 4 layers of damp, washed cheesecloth.

Apple Juice

Wash and quarter apples that have good flavor. Remove stem and blossom ends, and blemishes and bruises. Leave on skins and core. Cover with water and simmer until soft (25-30 minutes). Press through jelly bag and re-strain through cheesecloth. Reheat juice to simmering and pour into hot sterilized jars, leaving ½ inch headroom. Process in boiling water bath for 5 minutes.

Apple Cider

Wash, crush and press tart, ripe, juicy apples. Large quantities are most easily done in a cider press, outside on a sunny Fall day. Presses can sometimes be borrowed or rented or improvised. Small quantities of apples can be chopped up in a food grinder or juicer, and the cider squeezed through a jelly bag or pressed out with a rolling pin, a messy process!

A cider press may have an attached grinder that chops or grinds up the apples, which go into a cloth bag made of clean muslin, bleached burlap, a sheet or pillowcase. The ground apples are then pressed and the cider flows out, leaving the apple residue or "pomace," in the bag. Water can be added to the pomace in order to extract a greater quantity of cider.

Cider-making is a big occasion at our house, attracting lots of kids (and their parents) all wanting to help grind apples and taste the cider. The grinder on the press we use is exposed at the bottom and a great hazard to little fingers, so it

SAVING CIDER

"If you bottle and refrigerate cider you can expect it to hold its flavor for about one to two weeks. But there are other ways of preserving cider for longer periods. Freezing is easily accomplished and is a reliable method if you have the space. Or you can pasteurize the juice and keep it just about indefinitely. The traditional method is to store the cider in oak barrels; it is a more complicated procedure, but the time and effort are worthwhile because the result—delicious natural hard cider—is so satisfying."

Judy Raven
Making Apple Cider
Garden Way Bulletin N

is important to supervise the operation closely. Yellow jackets never fail to show up, too, presenting another hazard. Our pony is equally interested in the fragrant apples, and he shares the pomace with the pigs and chickens.

Cider that you make or buy fresh from a cider mill can be canned like apple juice, and since it is pasteurized in the process it will not ferment into "hard" cider. However, if you want the taste of cider and not apple juice, we suggest you freeze it.

Freezing. Pour fresh cider into containers, leaving ample headroom (see preceeding chart), seal and freeze.

BOTTLING ROOT BEER

1. Rinse bottles. Put yeast in 1 cup of lukewarm water. Let stand for 5 minutes and then stir to mix.

4. Add 4 gallons of water and yeast mixture. Stir well.

2. Measure 4-5 pounds of sugar, depending on taste.

5. Bottle immediately, leaving ½ inch headroom.

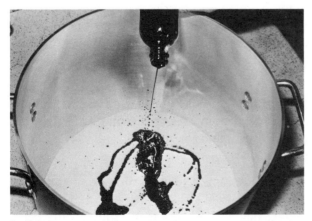

3. Pour contents of 1 bottle of Hire's extract over the sugar.

6. Cap bottles. Don't use screw cap bottles or Mason jars. Store in a warm, draft-free place for at least 5 days. Serve ice cold.

Apricot Nectar

Nectarines, pears and peaches also can be made into nectars, which are thick pulpy juices to which ice water can be added before drinking. Apricot nectar is the important ingredient of an easily made cake that is a favorite with our family, so we have included the recipe at the end of this section.

To make nectar, use fully ripe fruit. Wash thoroughly, pit and quarter. With pears remove stems and blossom ends and quarter. It is not necessary to peel the fruit unless pureeing in a blender. Press raw through a sieve or food mill, or heat for several minutes to the boiling point with a little water to prevent scorching, and then press.

To each quart of nectar, add 1 cup sugar. To help preserve the color and flavor, ¼ teaspoon crystalline ascorbic acid dissolved in ¼ cup water may be added to the nectar just before adding the sugar.

Freezing. Pack the nectar into containers, leaving ample headroom (see preceeding chart), seal, chill and freeze.

Canning. Heat the nectar to simmering (185°–210° F.), pour hot into hot sterilized jars, leaving ½ inch headroom. Adjust lids and process in a boiling water bath (212° F.).
Pints and quarts . . . . . 10 minutes

Berry Juices

Wash (if necessary) in cold water and crush fully ripe berries. Simmer briefly until juicy; do not add water. Press through jelly bag, then re-strain juice without squeezing through damp cheesecloth. Add sugar if desired, about 1 cup to 9 cups of juice; or for strawberry juice, ⅔–1 cup to 4 cups juice.

Freezing. Pour juice into containers, leaving ample headroom (see preceeding chart), seal, chill and freeze.

Canning. Reheat juice to simmering; pour into hot sterilized jars, leaving ½ inch headroom. Adjust lids and process in a boiling water bath (212° F.).
Pints and quarts . . . . . . 5 minutes

Berry Purees

Wash, sort, and crush fully ripe berries, and press through a sieve or food mill. Then proceed as for *Apricot Nectar.*

Cherries, Red
(Sweet and Sour)

Use bright red, tree-ripened cherries. Stem, sort and wash thoroughly. Drain, pit and crush, heat slightly to start juice flowing, then press through a jelly bag. Let stand overnight or for several hours in refrigerator, and then pour off clear juice. Or else process as is and strain when ready to use. Sweeten sour cherry juice with 1½ to 2 cups sugar to each quart of juice; sweet cherry juice with 1 cup sugar to 9 cups of juice. Juice made from sweet cherries hasn't much zing, so you may want to mix some sour cherry juice with it, either before processing or when ready to use.

Freezing. Pour juice into containers, leaving ample headroom (see preceeding chart), seal, chill if warm, and freeze.

Canning. Reheat juice to simmering and pour into hot sterilized jars, leaving ½ inch headroom. Adjust lids and process in a boiling water bath (212° F.).
Pints and quarts . . . . . . 5 minutes

Cherries, White

Use tree-ripened fruit with good color and flavor. Sort, stem, wash and drain. Remove pits and crush. Do not heat. Press through a jelly bag. Warm juice to 165° F. in a double boiler or over low heat. Let juice stand overnight in the refrigerator and then pour off clear juice, or process as is and strain before using. Crystalline ascorbic acid may be added, ¼ teaspoon per quart of juice. Sweeten to taste.

Freezing. Pack juice into containers, leaving ample headroom (see preceeding chart), seal, chill if warm, and freeze.

Canning. Heat juice to simmering and pour into hot sterilized jars, leaving ½ inch headroom. Adjust lids and process in a boiling water bath (212° F.).
    Pints and quarts . . . . . . 5 minutes

Citrus Fruits

(Grapefruit, Orange and Lemon)

Work quickly with small batches of citrus fruits to preserve the natural vitamin C that can be lost both from exposure to air and by heating. Use firm, tree-ripened fruit heavy for their size and free from soft spots. The fruit should be at room temperature. Squeeze or ream juice from the fruit using a squeezer that does not press oil from the rind. Strain out seeds and pieces of fruit. Add ¾ teaspoon crystalline ascorbic acid to each gallon of juice.

Freezing. Pour juice into containers, leave headroom (see preceeding chart), seal and freeze immediately.

Canning. Heat juice barely to simmering

(165° F.). Immediately pour into hot sterilized canning jars, leaving ½ inch headroom. Adjust lids and process in a boiling water bath (212° F.).
    Pints and quarts . . . . . . 5 minutes

Cranberry Juice

Sort and wash ripe cranberries. Add an equal amount of water and boil for 15 minutes, or until berries burst. Press through a jelly bag and re-strain through damp cheesecloth. Sweeten to taste.

Freezing. Pour juice into containers, leaving ample headroom (see preceeding chart), seal, chill and freeze.

Canning. Reheat juice to simmering and pour into hot sterilized jars, leaving ½ inch headroom. Adjust lids and process in a boiling water bath (212° F.).
    Pints and quarts . . . . . . 5 minutes

Cherry pitters are really a matter of taste. The large crank type which is screwed onto a counter is expensive and takes storage space but if you do quarts of cherries, it might be worthwhile. A small hand pitter is handy and retains the shape of cherries. But a pointed paring knife is adequate.

Grape Juice
(Concord Grapes and White Grapes)

Use fully ripe grapes with good flavor and color. Wash, stem and crush. *Concord grapes:* Add just enough water to cover and simmer gently until soft, about 10 minutes. *White grapes:* Do not heat after crushing. Squeeze through a jelly bag, then let juice stand overnight in refrigerator. Pour off clear juice, being careful not to disturb the sediment that has settled to the bottom. This should remove the crystals of tartaric acid that are a nuisance in grape juice. If crystals are present after processing, re-strain the juice before using.

Freezing. Pour juice into containers, leaving ample headroom (see preceeding chart), seal and freeze.

Canning. Heat juice to simmering, and pour into hot sterilized jars, leaving ½ inch headroom. Adjust lids and process in a boiling water bath (212° F.).

    Pints and quarts . . . . . . 5 minutes

Pineapple Juice

For juice use firm ripe pineapples with full flavor and aroma. Pare and remove eyes. Chop or grind the pineapple, add enough water just to cover and boil for 10 minutes. Press juice through a jelly bag and sweeten to taste.

Freezing. Pour juice into containers, leaving ample headroom (see preceeding chart), seal, chill, and freeze.

Canning. Reheat juice to simmering and pour into hot sterilized jars, leaving ½ inch headroom. Adjust lids and process in a boiling water bath (212° F.).

    Pints and quarts . . . . . 10 minutes

1. Sort, wash, and cut red, ripe tomatoes. Put in a kettle and simmer over medium heat, stirring often. Cook until soft and juicy.

2. Put hot tomatoes through a food mill, press or sieve.

3. Put juice back into kettle and reheat just to boiling.

126

4. Ladle hot juice into clean, hot jars. (Optional: Add 1 tsp. salt to each quart.) Adjust lids. Process in a boiling water bath for 20 min. for pints and 30 min. for quarts. Remove jars. Complete seals if necessary.

Plums and Prunes

Use firm tree-ripened fruit with good color. Wash plums and fresh prunes, and simmer for 15 minutes in enough water just to cover. Dried prunes may also be used. They should be soaked overnight in cold water, using 1 quart of water to ½ pound prunes, then simmered in the same water until plump and tender. Turn prepared fruit into a jelly bag and press out juice. Sweeten if desired with ½-1 cup sugar to a quart of juice, or to taste.

Freezing. Pour juice into containers, leaving ample headroom (see preceeding chart), seal, chill and freeze.

Canning. Reheat juice to simmering and pour into hot sterilized jars, leaving ½ inch headroom. Process in a boiling water bath (212° F.).
Pints and quarts . . . . . . 5 minutes

Rhubarb Juice

Rhubarb comes so early in the season you can use it to practice putting up juice before the real fruits arrive. It can be used all summer as a tart cooler, mixed with other juices or ginger ale.

Use tender, red stalks with few fibers for the most colorful juice. Wash, trim and cut into pieces up to 4 inches long. Add one quart water to 4 quarts (5 pounds) rhubarb, and bring just to boiling. Press through a jelly bag, then re-strain through damp cheesecloth. Sweeten to taste or with ½ cup sugar to a quart of juice.

Freezing. Pour juice into containers, leaving ample headroom (see preceeding chart), seal, chill and freeze.

Canning. Reheat juice to simmering and pour into hot sterilized jars, leaving ½ inch headroom. Process in a boiling water bath (212° F.).
Pints and quarts . . . . . . 5 minutes

SYRUPS

Try making syrup from any of the flavorful fruit juices that you make. The process is similar to making jelly except that the cooking time is long enough to thicken the syrup but not long enough to make it jell. This recipe is particularly adapted to berries and grapes, and it makes one pint of syrup.

Basic Syrup

1¼ cup juice
1¾ cups sugar (or 1½ cups sugar and ¼ cup
  light corn syrup for thicker syrup)
1 tablespoon lemon juice (optional)

Heat juice in a large kettle, add sugar and stir to dissolve. Bring to a full rolling boil and boil hard for one minute. Remove from heat and skim off foam. Pour in containers and store in refrigerator for immediate use.

Canning. Pour hot into hot sterilized ½ pint jars, leaving ½ inch headroom. Adjust lids and process in a boiling water bath (212° F.) for 10 minutes.

Freezing. Let syrup cool, pour into containers, leaving ample headroom (see preceeding chart), seal and freeze.

W.C. Scranton Des. - Phila -
COPYRIGHT. 1887.

Chapter 6
Jams and Jellies

Jams and jellies are a special treat for children and grownups alike. They can be made from any fruit or berry, and also from such things as tomatoes, wine, and herbs, particularly mint. This is an area of preserving where your imagination and taste can take full rein to suit your family's tastes and for gifts with a homemade, personal touch.

Our family joins in the fun of picking berries and fruits from early summer to fall, and after we have sated ourselves on fresh fruit, the rest is frozen or made into preserves. In our own garden we pick rhubarb in May, strawberries in June, and raspberries in July. Later in the summer and fall there are wild black caps in the woods nearby, tart grapes growing along the fence, and bright red crab apples down the road. Many area orchards provide an abundance of apples in the fall. The mint that grows around our house can be made into jelly either with apples as the base or with store-bought fruit pectin.

Jams and jellies can be made in season when the fruit is freshly picked, or you can use canned or frozen (your own or bought) fruits and fruit juices during other times of the year.

In addition to jams and jellies there are preserves, conserves, marmalades, fruit butters, and chutneys. The methods for making these are similar. Traditionally all were preserved by the *open kettle method* of canning. However, unless your storage facilities are cold (below 50° F.), it is now recommended that all jellies and conserves be sealed in canning jars and processed in a *boiling water bath* for 5 minutes.

Jellies are made from fruit juices or other flavored juices, jelled enough to be shimmeringly firm. *Jams* are made from ground or crushed fruit and have enough jell to hold their shape. *Preserves* are whole or large pieces of fruit in a slightly jelled syrup; the word "preserves" is often used to mean all of these different types. *Conserves* usually consist of mixed fruits and citrus, with raisins and nuts. *Marmalades* are clear jellies in which pieces of citrus or other fruit are mixed. Fruit pulp cooked with sugar until thick is called a *butter*; and chutneys are a spicier mixture of fruits and spices cooked with sugar and vinegar.

All of these preserves contain fruit and sugar, with pectin and some form of acid, either naturally present or added. The fruit provides the distinctive flavor and nutrient base for the jelly. In some cases it also provides the pectin and acid which make it jell. Apples and quinces are especially high in pectin, while most other fruits require the addition of more pectin. Apples can be used as the pectin source for other types of fruit, or you can buy commercially prepared fruit pectin in either a powder or liquid form. Most fruits have some natural pectin, more when underripe than ripe. If you make preserves *without* adding pectin, use all slightly underripe or ¼ underripe with ¾ ripe fruit to provide enough natural pectin.

Most fruits have plenty of natural acid, especially when underripe. For the milder fruits, like peaches, recipes may call for the addition of acid, usually in the form of lemon juice, to aid the jelling process. You can substitute ⅛ teaspoon crystalline citric acid (which can be purchased at a drug store) for one tablespoon lemon juice.

Sugar is most important as a preservative in these products. It also helps the jelling process and of course adds to the flavor. It is possible to make diet jellies and other preserves with the non-sugar substitute recommended by your doctor. However, these must be refrigerated or frozen unless they are cooked the long way and processed in a boiling water bath, since they lack the preserving qualities of sugar. You can also replace part of the sugar with honey or corn syrup. For jelly ¼ of the sugar can be replaced with honey or corn syrup and in jams and other preserves ½ of the sugar. Using all honey will affect the color and texture of the product, as well as giving it a distinctive honey flavor. You may find you like the difference, so go ahead and experiment using honey for all the sugar called for in both the long cook and pectin-added recipes. You will have difficulty getting jellies to jell sufficiently when using all honey, but jams and preserves will present less of a problem as they do not need to jell as much to be satisfactory.

Hints for Successful Preserving

Always work with small batches when making preserves. Cook only four to eight cups of juice or fruit at a time. When you have a large quantity to do, divide it up. It will not take much longer to boil several small batches than to boil one large one, and the results will be superior. Large batches require a longer time to cook, are harder to handle, may refuse to jell, or may have a poor flavor.

Use a kettle that seems three times too big (8 quarts or larger) and which preferably is stainless steel with a wide, flat bottom. It is amazing how high the juice and foam will rise when boiling, especially if you are using honey, and boiled-over jelly is no fun to clean off the top of your stove. One-half to one teaspoon of butter added before boiling will reduce the amount of foam and help prevent the juice from boiling over.

Use a candy, jelly, or deep-fry thermometer when making jellies and jams; it takes the guesswork out of deciding when you have reached the jellying stage. The jellying point for jelly is 220° F. (8° F. over the boiling point of water), and for jams it is 221° F. (9° F. over the boiling point of water). If you live at an altitude above sea level, measure the temperature of boiling water with your thermometer, and add 8° F. to that for jelly and 9° F. for jams to reach the jellying point. Since changes in atmospheric pressure can affect this temperature from day to day, test your

thermometer on the day you are planning to make jelly or jam.

If you are using commercial pectin, follow the directions provided by the manufacturer, or use only the recipes which specifically refer to the kind of pectin you have. Never substitute the liquid type for the powdered or vice versa, since the fruits are cooked differently, and the pectins are added at different points in the cooking process. More sugar is usually required with the liquid than the powder type. In other respects—cost, cooking times, and quality of the final product—they are similar.

Also do *not* use a commercial pectin recipe if you are not adding any pectin. It just won't work! Jellies and jams made without added pectin must be boiled much longer for them to jell. Besides, less sugar is used than with store-bought pectin. You will end up with smaller quantities and the jelly will have a darker color because it has cooked longer.

STORAGE

All preserved foods should be stored in a cold, dark, dry place. Ideally temperatures should be between 32° and 50° F. to preserve flavor, color and the nutrients which light will destroy, and to prevent the growth of molds and bacteria. This is especially true of jars sealed with paraffin, a common method of sealing *firm* jams and jellies. If your storage facilities are too warm, you should use standard canning jars for your preserves which can be processed in a boiling water bath for 5 minutes to help preserve them longer.

JELLY GLASSES AND JARS

Manufacturers of canning jars also produce very attractive jelly glasses with colorful, decorated lids and decorations embossed in the glass. These serve as a mold for the jelly and can easily be turned over onto a serving dish, leaving a pretty pattern in the jelly. There are less expensive, plain glasses, which make for an attractive, smoother surfaced, molded jelly. All jelly glasses must be sealed with paraffin.

There also are canning jars with decorated lids made especially for preserves and relishes, which make lovely gifts. Don't forget, however, that unless they have straight or flared sides, they cannot be used as a mold for the jelly. These and regular small canning jars are self-sealing and can be put through a boiling water bath. In warmer climates they should be used in preference to paraffin, and they should be used for soft jams and preserves on which the paraffin tends to weep.

If you are preserving by the open kettle method (without using a boiling water bath) and plan to seal with paraffin, you can use any type of jar or glass that is strong enough to resist cracking when the hot jelly is poured in. If you use jars with shoulders, be sure to fill them with

jelly beyond the shoulder so that the paraffin will not be caught under the edge, making it difficult to remove.

PARAFFIN

Paraffin, or household wax, can be bought in grocery or hardware stores where other canning supplies are available. It is highly flammable, so should be melted with great care. Do not let it come in contact with an open flame or hot burner. Before starting to make your preserves, cut the paraffin into small pieces and put it over hot water in the top of the double boiler, or into a can or pitcher that can be set into the hot water. Simmer the water slowly, and it should be melted by the time you need it. Paraffin can be reused. After opening a jar of jelly rinse all traces of jelly from the paraffin under hot running water and store for melting down next year.

OTHER EQUIPMENT NEEDED

In addition to glasses or jars, lids, paraffin, a large kettle and thermometer, you will need:

- jelly bag or cheesecloth for jellies
- a stand or colander to set it on
- measuring cups
- dishes for holding fruit
- vegetable brush for washing hard fruits such as apples
- potato or other masher
- paring knife
- wooden spoons for stirring
- a timer to measure exactly one minute when using added pectin
- a damp cloth for wiping jar rims
- a slotted spoon to skim off foam
- a rack or towel to cool hot jars on.

An asbestos pad to separate the pot from the burner will help prevent scorching your fruits. If you can find one, a "jelmeter" is a help in measuring the pectin content of a fruit juice.

Jelly bags can be bought, or you can make your own from a piece of unbleached muslin or flannel (napped side in), or several layers of cheesecloth. Sew the material together around a

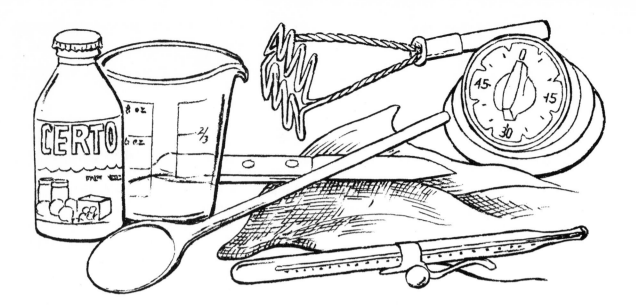

hoop made from a coat hanger, or tie the corners together and suspend it over the bowl from a handy hook or cupboard door. You may want to try the old trick of turning a chair upside down on a table, and suspending the bag by tying the corners with string to the chair legs. Place a bowl underneath on the upturned chair seat. (This is a great conversation piece if the neighbors drop by!)

Or if you have a food press (the cone-shaped type that fits into a frame), you can use the frame to hold the bag, attaching it with clothespins. The simplest method is to put four layers of damp cheesecloth inside a colander and set it in a bowl.

Preparation of Equipment— Sterilizing

Unless you are going to process your preserves in a boiling water bath for at least 10 minutes (and only 5 minutes is recommended), you *must* sterilize your jars. To do this, wash them in hot soapy water, and rinse thoroughly. Put them in a kettle, cover with hot water and boil rapidly for 10 minutes. Leave the jars in the hot water until you are almost ready to use them. Remove the jars, drain, and invert them on a cloth, while the jelly is in its last minutes of cooking. Some dishwashers have a sterilizing cycle, which may be used to sterilize your jars. Leave them hot in dishwasher until needed. If you are using canning jars, follow the manufacturers' directions on how to prepare the self-sealing Mason lids. These and the rubber rings used with bail-type and procelain-lined zinc lids should be washed with hot soapy water, rinsed, put in a bowl or pan and covered with boiling water. Do not actually boil the lids on the stove, as this can spoil the sealing compound. Leave the lids or rings in the hot water until ready to use.

Fruits to Use

Fruits that usually contain enough pectin to jell by themselves include sour apples, crab apples, currants, underripe Concord grapes, quinces, lemons, blueberries, raspberries, blackberries, cranberries, wild cherries, and green gooseberries.

Fruits usually too low in pectin and acid include apricots, peaches, pears, strawberries, elderberries, cherries and oranges. They can be cooked with cut-up apples or with fruit pectin, and often lemon juice or citric acid is added. Since the pectin content decreases as the fruit ripens, even the high pectin fruits may need to be treated in this way if fully ripe when used. If you intend to add commercial fruit pectin, fully ripe fruit generally is specified.

TESTING FRUIT
FOR PECTIN AND ACID

It is possible to make a simple test to see if your fruit juice has enough pectin and acid for it to jell properly.

Pectin test: After making your fruit juice (see below), put 1 teaspoon of the juice into a glass and add one tablespoon of rubbing alcohol (70 percent alcohol). *Do Not Taste!* Stir it gently. If there is enough pectin in the juice, a gelatinous mass will form that you can pick up with a fork. If there is not enough pectin, a few pieces of jelly-like material will form. You can add 1 tablespoon liquid pectin for each cup of juice to increase the pectin content, testing again to see if this is enough. When the pectin content is high enough, you can proceed to cook the juice for jelly by the Long Cook Method. (See also "too stiff" jelly, further on.)

Acid test: This is a *taste* test. Compare the acid flavor of the fruit juice with that of a mixture containing 1 teaspoon lemon juice, 3 tablespoons water and 2 teaspoons sugar. If the fruit juice is not as tart, add 1 tablespoon of lemon juice for each cup of fruit juice.

AMOUNT OF SUGAR TO USE

If the fruit juice contains an adequate amount of pectin, use ¾ to 1 cup sugar per cup of juice; if slightly less pectin, use ⅔ to ¾ cup sugar. Too much sugar will make a syrupy jelly. These directions apply only if you are going to cook the jelly by the long method rather than following directions for a commercial pectin.

HOMEMADE FRUIT PECTIN

You can make and can your own "pectin" to use with strawberries, peaches and other low pectin fruits. Choose hard, tart ripe apples. Weigh, wash and cut up fine, leaving on stems and cores. Add one pint water and one tablespoon lemon juice for each pound of apples. Cover and boil rapidly for 30 minutes, stirring occasionally to prevent scorching. Press through a jelly

APPLE JELLY

    4 cups apple juice made from about
      3 pounds apples and 3 cups water
    2 tablespoons strained lemon juice
      (if apples are very sweet)
    3 cups sugar

Use tart apples, about ¼ of them underripe and ¾ ripe. Wash thoroughly, cut off blossom and stem ends and bad spots. Leave on skins and core. Cut the apples into small pieces, add water, cover and bring to a boil. Lower heat and simmer until soft (about 25 minutes). Turn into jelly bag and let drip for clearest jelly; for more, less-clear jelly squeeze bag and re-strain through two layers of damp cheesecloth. Measure 4 cups juice into kettle. Add lemon juice and sugar and stir well. Rapidly bring mixture to a full boil over high heat, and continue to boil until it reaches the jelly point (8° F. over the boiling point of water on candy thermometer, or use the sheet or refrigerator test, p. 134).

Remove from heat and quickly skim off all the foam. Pour boiling hot into hot, sterilized containers, leaving ½ inch headroom in jelly glasses for paraffin or ⅛ inch headroom in canning jars, and seal. (See "Sealing Jelly," page 136.)

Yield: 4 or 5 eight-ounce glasses

APPLE JELLY WITH HONEY

    7 pounds apples
    juice of lemon
    2½ cups honey
    4 cloves
    1 stick cinnamon
    ¼ teaspoon allspice

Wash and quarter apples. Cover with water, adding lemon juice, and simmer until soft. Drain through a jelly bag. Measure 4 cups juice into kettle and boil 5 minutes. Add honey and spices tied in a cheesecloth bag. Boil for 8 more minutes.

Pour into sterilized jelly glasses and seal with paraffin (see p. 136).

Makes four 8 oz. glasses.

bag or damp cheesecloth, then strain through several layers of damp cheesecloth without squeezing. Heat back to the boiling point, seal in canning jars, and process in a boiling water bath for 5 minutes. To use, mix equal parts with juice of a low pectin fruit. Use the pectin test (see above) on the mixed juices to determine whether enough pectin is present. Proceed as for other jellies, using ¾ to 1 cup sugar per cup of mixed juice.

MAKING JELLY

Jellies can be made from any clear juice if you use a commercial pectin such as *Sure-Gel* (powder) or *Certo* (liquid). They can be made from the clear juice of a fruit naturally high in pectin without a jell additive. Since commercial pectins are made from apples or citrus fruits, their use is not really "unnatural."

EXTRACTING THE JUICE

Be sure to wash the fruit thoroughly in cold water before using. Never let it soak in the water, however, as you will lose much of the flavor and juice.

Hard fruits such as apples and grapes are cut up or crushed, covered with water and boiled to extract their juice. Soft berries either may be crushed and put through a food mill to draw the juice, or else simmered with little or no water.

When the juicy pulp is ready, it is put into a damp jelly bag, and the juice allowed to drip into a bowl.

For a sparkling clear jelly resist the temptation to squeeze the jelly bag. Just let it drip for several hours. The resultant juice should be perfectly clear and will make the most attractive jelly. The pulp can be turned back into the pan, some water added, and cooked briefly. Then repeat the dripping process. This second extraction will not be as clear as the first but will make satisfactory jelly.

If you are not fussy or if the jelly is to be used in cakes or jelly rolls, you can squeeze to get more juice. This juice can be strained through several layers of damp cheesecloth to remove most of the impurities, or allowed to settle overnight in the refrigerator to get a clearer juice. Since crystals form in grape juice, it always should be allowed to settle overnight. Then carefully pour off the clear juice without disturbing the sediment at the bottom.

The juice may be used immediately, or frozen or canned to be used later. (See Chapter 5 on Fruit Juices for directions on preserving juices.)

COOKING JELLY: THE LONG WAY

Follow these directions if you are *not* adding commercial pectin.

Measure the juice, using only 4 to 6 cups for each batch. Bring the juice to a boil and let boil for a couple of minutes. Then add ¾ to 1 cup of sugar for each cup of juice. Boil rapidly stirring frequently. Stay right with it to be sure it does not boil over. If using a candy thermometer, it should be placed in the kettle, completely covered with jelly, but without touching the bottom.

TESTING FOR THE JELLY STAGE

The jelling point for jelly is 220° F. (or 8° above the boiling temperature of water for the elevation where you live). When your thermometer reaches this temperature, remove the kettle immediately from the heat.

If you are not using a candy thermometer you can tell when the jelly is done by two methods.

The sheet test: With a cold metal spoon, dip out some boiling jelly, hold it well above the kettle and tip it so the juice runs out. Before the jelly is done, it will usually drip off the spoon in two separate drops. When the jelly comes off the spoon in a sheet or when two drops come together before dripping off, the jelly is done.

The refrigerator test: Put some jelly on a plate and place it in the freezing compartment of your refrigerator for 5 minutes. If it is jelled by then, it is done. During this test, remove the rest of the jelly from the heat so it will not overcook.

When the jelly is done, remove from heat, let

APPLE JELLY WITHOUT PECTIN

1. Wash and cut up tart, firm apples, ¼ of them slightly underripe. About 3 pounds will make a batch of jelly. Place in a kettle. Add 1 cup of water per pound of apples. Bring to a boil and simmer 20 to 25 minutes until soft.

4. Add 3 cups of sugar and stir. If desired, add 2 tbsp. of lemon juice. Place on highest heat and boil rapidly until mixture reaches 220° F. Remove from heat and skim off foam with a metal spoon.

2. Pour apples into a jelly bag or into several layers of damp cheesecloth and allow to drip. For less clear jelly, squeeze the bag to remove all the juice. Strain pressed juice through two layers of damp cheesecloth without squeezing.

5. Pour jelly immediately into hot sterilized glasses, leaving ½ inch headroom. For Mason jars, leave ⅛ inch headroom.

3. Measure 4 cups of apple juice into a large kettle.

6. Carefully cover jelly with ⅛ inch of paraffin. Prick air bubbles, then allow to cool undisturbed. Label and store in a cool dark place. For Mason jars, adjust lids. Process in a boiling water bath for 5 minutes to insure a good seal. Remove jars and complete seals if necessary.

GRAPE JELLY—THE LONG COOK METHOD

8 cups grape juice (about 6 pounds
  grapes, ¼ underripe and ¾ ripe)
6 cups sugar

Wash, stem and crush grapes, add a small amount of water (about 1½ cups), cover and bring to a boil over high heat. Reduce heat and simmer 15 minutes. Turn into jelly bag and drip, or squeeze and re-strain through several layers of damp cheesecloth. Let sit overnight in refrigerator, and pour off clear juice or re-strain the next day to remove crystals. Measure juice into kettle and bring to a boil. Add sugar (¾ cup for each cup of juice) and stir. Boil until the jelly stage is reached according to thermometer (8° F. over the boiling point of water) or sheet test or refrigerator test, (see earlier). Remove from heat and skim off foam with a metal spoon. Pour immediately into hot, sterilized containers, leaving ½ inch headroom in jelly glasses for paraffin or ⅛ inch headroom in canning jars, and seal. (See "Sealing Jelly," this page.)

Yield: 7 or 8 eight-ounce glasses

MINT JELLY

3 cups apple juice
2 cups sugar
2 tablespoons lemon juice (if apples
  are sweet)
½-1 cup fresh mint leaves (washed
  and chopped, or cut up fine if you
  plan to leave them in the jelly)
Green food coloring (optional)

Prepare apple juice as you would for apple jelly. Measure juice into kettle and bring to a boil. Add sugar and stir until dissolved. Boil 2 minutes, then add mint leaves. Boil rapidly until the jelly stage is reached according to thermometer (8° F. over the boiling point of water) or sheet or refrigerator test, (see earlier). Add a little green food coloring and lemon juice.

Remove from heat and skim off foam with a metal spoon. Pour through strainer (unless you want the pieces of mint in the jelly) into hot, sterilized containers, leaving ½ inch headroom in jelly glasses for paraffin or ⅛ inch in canning jars, and seal. (See "Sealing Jelly," this page.)

Yeild: 3 or 4 eight-ounce glasses

it settle down and skim off every bit of foam on the surface. A slotted spoon works well for this. Sometimes there is a lot of foam, which seems wasteful. We put it aside and use it on toast; the children call it a special treat. If it is left on the jelly it will spoil the appearance and texture, and make it difficult to seal with paraffin.

SEALING THE JELLY

Immediately ladle or pour the boiling hot jelly into hot sterilized containers, being careful not to spill any on the rim of the jars or on the inside edge of the glasses.

With paraffin: If you are using paraffin, pour the jelly into hot sterilized glasses leaving ½ inch headroom, and immediately cover the jelly with ⅛ inch layer of paraffin. Pour the wax on very slowly in order to prevent it from going too deeply into the jelly. Prick any air bubbles and let it cool undisturbed. You may want to add a second ⅛ inch layer of paraffin after the first cools. Tip the jars carefully so that the wax comes into contact with the edge of the glass all the way around. This will insure a complete seal to keep out mold and bacteria. When completely cooled, cover the glasses with lids, foil or plastic held with tape, and store in a cold, dark place.

With canning jars: Fill hot sterilized jars with boiling hot jelly, leaving ⅛ inch headroom, and wipe the rim with a clean damp cloth to be sure no jelly is left on the rim to spoil the seal. Seal each jar as soon as it is filled. Take Mason lids from hot water and place on jar, then screw the band on tightly (as tightly as an average person can without using a jar tightener). For bail jars put the wet rubber ring on the shoulder, put on the glass lid, complete the seal with both parts of the bail (*unless* you are going to process in a boiling water bath, in which case only pull up the upper wire, leaving the lower wire raised until after processing). Porcelain-lined zinc caps are screwed on tightly (then turned back ¼ inch if processing in a boiling water bath).

Some older recipes and also the directions that accompany the commercial pectin say to invert the jars briefly to help them seal, and to kill mold or bacteria that may be on the lid. This is not recommended by all the jar manufacturers nor by the USDA. So leave the jars upright on a rack or towel in a draft-free spot, and let cool. You may hear a plunking sound that indicates the self-sealing Mason lids are sealing themselves. When cool, remove screw bands if you wish, check for a good seal, label and store in a cold, dark place.

PROCESSING JELLY

If the jar manufacturer recommends it and if your storage facilities are warm (above 70° F.), you will want to process your jelly in a brief, boiling water bath to be extra sure that the jars will seal and the jelly will keep properly. Place the jars on a rack in a kettle full of simmering water, adding more if necessary to bring the level of the water to 1 or 2 inches above the tops of the jars.

Put on cover, bring to a full rolling boil and time for just 5 minutes. When the time is up, remove jars immediately from the kettle and place them on a rack or towel out of drafts to cool. Complete the seal on bail-type and porcelain-lined zinc cap jars. When completely cool, check for a good seal, and if any are not sealed, either refrigerate and use soon, or reprocess after cleaning rim of jar and checking for defects, using a new lid. After 12 hours remove the screw bands from the sealed jars, wash the jars and label.

Attractive labels come with some types of jars or can be bought separately; they will add a personal touch to your jellies. Store in a cool, dark place.

MAKING JELLY WITH ADDED PECTIN

Use fully ripe fruit, and prepare the fruit juice as above. (See also caution note earlier under "Hints.")

Powdered pectin: Add the pectin to the unheated fruit juice, bring to a boil and then add the sugar.

Liquid pectin: Add sugar to the fruit juice, bring to a boil and then add liquid pectin. In

ORANGE-PEACH MARMALADE

5 cups finely chopped peaches (about 4 pounds of peaches)
1 cup finely chopped oranges (about 2 medium-sized oranges)
Peel of 1 orange, shredded very fine
2 tablespoons lemon juice
3 cups sugar

Wash fully ripe peaches, and remove stems, skins, pits and bad spots. Chop or grind them up fine. Remove peel and seeds from oranges. Leave some of the white rind on the oranges as it contains much of the pectin of the fruit. Chop or grind the oranges up fine. Measure the required amount of fruit into kettle and add the remaining ingredients. Stir to mix thoroughly. Bring to a boil rapidly over high heat, stirring constantly. Boil until the mixture thickens, or until it reaches 9° F. above the boiling point of water. Remove from heat and skim off the foam. Ladle into hot, sterilized canning jars, leaving ¼ inch headroom, and seal. (See "Sealing Jelly," opposite.) Process in a boiling water bath for 5 minutes.

Yield: 6 or 7 half-pint jars

AUNT SARAH'S TOMATO MARMALADE

The donor of this recipe says it will please adults and children, and recommends placing homemade bread toast underneath it.

8 pounds plum tomatoes
3 oranges, chopped finely, skin and all, removing only the seeds
3 lemons, treated the same
8 cinnamon sticks
1 tablespoon whole cloves
Sugar (see below)

Skin and chop up tomatoes, to provide 4 quarts. Let stand in bowl until most of the liquid can be poured off and used elsewhere.

Place chopped oranges and lemons in kettle. Add cloves and cinnamon sticks.

Add tomatoes, also adding 1 cup of sugar for each cup of tomatoes. Bring to a boil, stirring as sugar dissolves. Then boil, stirring constantly to prevent burning, until the marmalade sheets off the spoon. (If you are using a candy thermometer, the marmalade is cooked when thermometer registers 220° F.)

Fish out cinnamon sticks and as many of the cloves as can be found. Spoon into hot sterilized jars and top with melted paraffin.

STRAWBERRY JELLY WITH LIQUID PECTIN

1. Crush 2½ quarts of washed, hulled, ripe strawberries.

4. Place over high heat and bring to a boil, stirring constantly. Stir in *Certo* (liquid pectin), bring to a full rolling boil, and boil hard for **1 minute**, stirring constantly.

2. Put pulp into jelly bag or damp cheesecloth. Squeeze bag to extract juice. For clearer jelly, drip, don't squeeze, through cheesecloth again.

5. Remove from heat and skim off all foam with a metal spoon.

3. Measure 3¾ cups juice into large saucepan. Add ¼ cup lemon juice and 7½ cups sugar.

6. Pour quickly into Mason jars, leaving ½ inch headroom and cover at once. Or pour into Mason jars, leaving ½ inch headroom. Wipe rims clean. Adjust lids and process in a boiling water bath for 5 minutes to insure a good seal. Set upright to cool.

both cases follow specific recipe directions for quantities to use.

With both kinds of pectin the jelly is brought to a full rolling boil after all ingredients have been added and boiled hard for exactly one minute, then removed immediately from the heat.

Skim off all the foam and ladle or pour the boiling hot jelly into hot, sterilized containers, and seal with either paraffin or appropriate canning lids as you would for the Long Cook Method.

Please note: Directions and many recipes are included in the booklets that come with the com-

---

JELLY MADE WITH BERRIES

(Blackberry, Boysenberry, Dewberry, Loganberry, Red Raspberry, Strawberry, Youngberry)

1. BERRY JELLY WITH POWDERED PECTIN

3½ cups juice (4 cups loganberry or red raspberry—about 2½ quarts fully ripe berries)
1 box packaged powdered pectin
5 cups sugar (5½ cups for loganberry and red raspberry)

If necessary, wash berries quickly in cold water and drain on paper towels. Do not let stand in the water. Remove stems and caps, and cut out bad spots. Crush thoroughly, place in jelly bag and squeeze out juice. (For clearer jelly let drip only—you will need 1½ to 2 times as much fruit.) Measure juice into kettle. Mix powdered pectin with the juice to dissolve. Bring to a boil on high heat, stirring occasionally. Add sugar all at once, stir and bring to a full rolling boil (a boil that cannot be stirred down); boil hard for exactly one minute, stirring constantly. Remove from heat and skim off foam with a metal spoon. Pour immediately into hot, sterilized jelly glasses, leaving ½ inch headroom for paraffin, or into canning jars, leaving ⅛ inch headroom, and seal. (See "Sealing Jelly," p. 136.)
Yield: 5 or 6 eight-ounce glasses

2. BERRY JELLY WITH LIQUID PECTIN

4 cups berry juice (about 2½ quarts fully ripe berries). For strawberries and blackberries: 3¾ cups juice plus ¼ cup lemon juice, strained
7½ cups (3¼ pound) sugar
1 bottle liquid pectin

Prepare juice as above. Measure 4 cups juice into kettle. Add the sugar and mix well. Bring to

a boil over high heat, stirring constantly. At once stir in liquid pectin and bring to a full rolling boil. Boil hard for exactly one minute, stirring constantly. Remove from heat, skim off foam with a metal spoon. Pour immediately into hot, sterilized containers, leaving ½ inch headroom in jelly glasses for paraffin and ⅛ inch headroom in canning jars, and seal. (See "Sealing Jelly," p. 136.)
Yield: 7 or 8 eight-ounce glasses

3. BERRY JELLY: THE LONG COOK METHOD

8 cups berry juice (blackberries or raspberries only). About 5 quart boxes with berries ¼ underripe and ¾ ripe, plus 1½ cups water
6 cups sugar

Wash berries if necessary and remove stems and caps. Crush, add water, cover and bring to a boil on high heat. Reduce heat and simmer for 5 minutes. Turn into jelly bag and drip only for clearest jelly, or squeeze and re-strain juice through several layers of damp cheesecloth without squeezing. Measure juice into kettle, add sugar and stir well. (For less than 8 cups juice add ¾ cups sugar for each cup of juice.) Bring to a boil over high heat and boil until the jelly stage is reached according to thermometer (8° F. over the boiling point of water) or the sheet or refrigerator test (page 134). Remove from heat and skim off foam with a metal spoon. Pour immediately into hot, sterilized containers, leaving ½ inch headroom in jelly glasses for paraffin or ⅛ inch headroom in canning jars, and seal. (See "Sealing Jelly," p. 136.)
Yield: 7 or 8 eight-ounce glasses

mercial pectin, so we recommend you follow them closely. When using these recipes, it is important to make no more than double the recipe amount at a time, and not to change the amount of sugar or pectin called for. With the liquid type pectin *(Certo)* the recipe book is wrapped around the bottle under the label. A folder comes in the box with the powder type *Sure-Gel.* For some jams and jellies, one bottle of *Certo* will make a doubled recipe; two boxes of *Sure-Gel* are needed for the same quantity. The amount of juice (or fruit with jams) can be adjusted slightly if you prefer a softer (or firmer) jelly or jam. For a softer jelly use ¼ to ½ cup more juice or fruit than the recipe calls for; for a firmer jelly or jam use ¼ or ½ cup less juice or fruit.

MAKING JAMS

Jams are made from crushed fruit with or without added pectin. They are simpler to make than jellies because there is no first cooking and juice extraction. Otherwise making jam is very similar to jelly.

COOKING JAMS THE LONG WAY

The fruit is washed quickly in cold water, care taken not to let it stay in the water long. Then it is prepared for cutting or crushing: peeled, cut-up, hulled or pitted, depending on the variety. Soft fruits then are crushed, hard fruits cut into small pieces, sugar or honey is added (usually ¾ to 1 cup per cup of fruit) and the mixture is brought slowly to a boil.

Sometimes hard fruits are cooked in a water and sugar syrup to soften, or the sugar and fruit are allowed to stand several hours to draw the juices before cooking. Fruits with small seeds that are difficult to remove, such as grapes and raspberries, may be put through a food press or food mill for a seedless jam with a puree consistency.

When cooking jams, the pieces of fruit tend to stick to the pan and scorch unless you stir con-

stantly. The jam is boiled rapidly until it reaches the jellying point, which for a firm jam is 221° F. (or 9° F. above the boiling point of water). This may take anywhere from 15 to 40 minutes, depending on the pectin quantity in the fruit. Rather than cooking the low-pectin fruits too long, you can stop the cooking when they begin to thicken, and be satisfied with a very soft jam, or else use a commercial pectin. If you have no candy or jelly thermometer, the refrigerator test can be used (see "Testing for the Jelly Stage," p. 134), or cook until the jam thickens. The sheet test usually does not work for jams.

When the proper temperature is reached, remove the jam from the heat and skim off all foam on the surface. Then stir and skim constantly for about five minutes, allowing the jam to cool slightly. This will prevent the fruit from floating to the top of the jam. If you are using canning jars rather than paraffin, you may skim off the foam and skip the stirring step; instead shake the filled jars gently several times after sealing.

Pour or ladle the hot jam into sterilized, hot jelly glasses or canning jars, leaving ½ inch headroom if you are sealing with paraffin, or ¼ inch headroom in Mason jars. Then follow the same procedure as for jellies to seal the containers. Paraffin should be used only for stiff jams; it tends to "weep" when used on a soft jam, or when the storage temperature is warm (over 70°). We recommend that jams be processed in a boiling water bath for 5 minutes when sealed in canning jars (not with paraffin!).

Let the jam cool undisturbed, check for good seals, cover paraffined containers with lids or foil, remove screw bands from canning jars (if you wish to reuse them), label and store in a cool, dark place.

JAMS MADE WITH BERRIES

(Blackberry, Boysenberry, Dewberry, Strawberry, Youngberry, Loganberry, Red Raspberry, Gooseberry)

1. BERRY JAM WITH POWDERED PECTIN

6 cups crushed berries (about 3 quart boxes of fully ripe berries)
1 package powdered pectin
8½ cups sugar

If necessary, wash berries. Remove stems and caps and crush completely, one layer at a time. For gooseberries remove stem and blossom end and grind instead of crushing. Part or all of the pulp of the seedy berries may be put through a sieve to remove seeds. Measure crushed berries into large saucepan. Add powdered pectin and stir well to dissolve. Bring to a hard boil over high heat, stirring constantly. Add sugar all at once, and stirring, bring to a full rolling boil (a boil that cannot be stirred down) and boil hard for exactly one minute. Remove from heat, skim off foam with metal spoon. Stir and skim for 5 minutes to cool slightly and prevent fruit from floating. Ladle into hot, sterilized containers, leaving ½ inch headroom in jelly glasses for paraffin or ¼ inch in canning jars, and seal. (See "Sealing Jelly," p. 136.) Process canning jars in boiling water bath for 5 minutes.

Yield: 11 or 12 half-pint jars

2. BERRY JAM WITH LIQUID PECTIN

4 cups crushed fruit—about 2 quarts fully ripe berries (or 3¾ cups fruit and ¼ cup lemon juice for strawberries or other berries that lack tartness)
7 cups sugar (6½ cups for logan-berries and red raspberries; 6 cups for gooseberries)
½ bottle liquid pectin

Prepare fruit as above. Measure 4 cups fruit (or fruit and lemon juice) into large saucepan and add sugar. Mix well. Bring to a full, rolling boil over high heat and boil exactly one minute, stirring constantly. Remove from heat; at once stir in liquid pectin. Skim off foam with metal spoon, then stir and skim for 5 minutes to cool slightly and prevent fruit from floating. Ladle into hot sterilized containers, leaving ½ inch headroom in jelly glasses for paraffin or ⅛ inch headroom in canning jars, and seal. (See "Sealing Jelly," p. 136) Process in boiling water bath for 5 minutes (canning jars only!).

Yield: 8 or 9 half-pint jars

3. BERRY JAM: THE LONG COOK METHOD

4 cups crushed berries (about 2 quarts berries, ¼ underripe and ¾ ripe)
3 cups sugar
2-4 tablespoons lemon juice (optional with strawberries and other berries that are not very tart)

Prepare berries as above. Crush and measure berries and juice into kettle. Bring slowly to a boil over low heat, stirring frequently. Add sugar (¾ cup for each cup fruit), stir constantly and boil rapidly until thick, or for a firm jam until mixture reaches 9° F. over the boiling point of water. Remove from the heat, skim off foam, and ladle into hot, sterilized canning jars, leaving ¼ inch headroom. Seal. (See "Sealing Jelly," p. 136.) Process in boiling water bath for 5 minutes.

Yield: 3 to 4 half-pint jars

MAKING JAM
WITH ADDED PECTIN

As with jellies, be sure you do not substitute the liquid for the powdered pectin or vice versa, since the methods of adding them to the fruit is different. The end results are very similar, however, and both are different from the long way of cooking in that they require more sugar, have a shorter cooking time, and take less guesswork in knowing when they are ready. The colors also are brighter because they are not cooked as much.

Use fully ripe fruit and prepare it as you would for the Long Cook Method.

Powdered pectin: Add pectin and lemon juice, if called for, to the fruit and stir to dissolve the pectin completely. Bring the combined ingredients quickly to a boil over high heat, stirring constantly. When the mixture comes to a full boil (bubbles over entire surface), add the sugar. Stir and again bring rapidly to a full rolling boil. Boil hard for one minute, then remove immediately from the heat.

If you are going to seal with paraffin, skim all foam and stir the jam for 5 minutes to help prevent the fruit from floating. If using canning jars, they can be shaken gently after sealing to prevent floating fruit.

Liquid pectin: Add sugar to measured fruit and lemon juice, if called for, and mix thoroughly. Place over high heat and bring to a full rolling boil, stirring constantly. Boil hard for exactly one minute, then remove from heat and immediately add the liquid pectin. Skim off the foam and stir the jam for 5 minutes to cool slightly and prevent the fruit from floating (unless using canning jars).

Follow the directions for sealing and storing the jams that are included under the Long Cook Method.

PRESERVES, CONSERVES, MARMALADES AND BUTTERS

There are so many variations on fruit preserves that an imaginative cook could provide a different type for every week of the year! At the end of this chapter we are including recipes for a few of the most popular. Have fun looking for other recipes to be found in a multitude of cookbooks, in magazines and newspapers. The important things to remember are to use modern recipes, and follow the same careful procedures for cooking, sealing (preferably in canning jars as these tend to be runnier than the jellies, and paraffin will "weep" on them unless kept very cold), and processing for 5 minutes in a boiling water bath to insure a good seal and longer storage life.

No-Cook Jams and Jellies

For a change you might want to try freezer jams and jellies that require absolutely no cooking. These are made with commercial pectin, either the powder or liquid type, and many recipes are included in the directions that come with the pectin. The color is bright and the flavor delicious—more like the fresh fruit because it has not been cooked. Some drawbacks to this type of jam or jelly are that they must be stored in the refrigerator and used within three weeks, or else stored in the freezer for longer periods. They also require *twice* the amount of pectin needed for ordinary jams and jellies.

STRAWBERRY PRESERVES

6 cups prepared strawberries (about 2
quart boxes of tart strawberries)
4½ cups sugar

Use large, firm tart strawberries. Wash quickly
in cold water, lifting the berries out of the water
so grit will settle to the bottom. Drain and remove hulls. Combine the berries and sugar in
alternate layers and let stand for 8 hours or
overnight in the refrigerator or other cool place.

Heat the fruit and sugar mixture to boiling,
stirring gently. Boil rapidly, stirring often to
prevent sticking or scorching. Cook to 9° F.
above the boiling point of water, or until the
syrup thickens (about 15 to 20 minutes).
Remove from heat and skim off the foam. Ladle
into hot, sterilized canning jars, leaving ¼ inch
headroom, and seal. (See "Sealing Jelly,"
p. 136.) Process in a boiling water bath for 5
minutes.

Yield: about 4 half-pint jars

GRAPE CONSERVE

4½ cups Concord grapes with skins
removed (about 4 pounds)
1 orange
4 cups sugar
1 cup seedless raisins
½ teaspoon salt
Skins from grapes
1 cup nuts, chopped fine

Sort and wash the grapes, and remove from
stems. Slip the skins from the grapes and save.
Measure skinned grapes into a kettle and boil,
stirring constantly, for about 10 minutes, or
until seeds show. Press through a sieve to
remove seeds. Wash and chop the orange up
fine without peeling. Add orange, sugar,
raisins, and salt to sieved grapes. Boil rapidly,
stirring constantly, until the mixture begins to
thicken (about 10 minutes). Add grape skins and
boil, stirring constantly, to 9° F. above the boiling point of water (about 10 minutes). Do not
overcook; the mixture will thicken more on
cooling. Add nuts and stir well. Remove from
heat and skim off foam. Ladle into hot, sterilized canning jars, leaving ¼ inch headroom,
and seal. (See "Sealing Jelly," p. 136.) Process
in a boiling water bath for 5 minutes.

Yield: 8 or 9 half-pint jars

WHAT WENT WRONG?

Most of us who have made jelly have experienced
the frustration of ending up either with syrup or
what might pass for rubber, and yet we don't
know what went wrong. Sometimes the weather
or even the strawberry grower gets blamed!

Syrupy jelly or jam is still good (and messy)
on toast, makes a delicious topping for ice
cream, and with milk can be enjoyed as an interesting milk shake. To avoid it the next time, follow directions to the letter, making small
batches, using a candy thermometer, and (for
the Long Cook Method) fruit that is ¼ underripe
and ¾ ripe.

The weather really *can* be the culprit, since the
boiling point will vary according to the weather.
So, on the day you plan to use it, test your candy
thermometer for the boiling point of water, and
add 8° F. to that for the jelly point and 9° F. for
jams and preserves.

The following are some of the most common
problems people have with jams and jellies, and
ways to avoid them:

1. **Jelly that is too soft.** This may be caused by
   too much juice, too little sugar, too little
   acid or trying to make too large a batch at
   one time. If too soft to use, you can try to
   remake the jelly, doing only 4-8 cups at a
   time.

   Without added pectin: Reboil the jelly
   until the jelly point is reached according to
   your thermometer (8° F. over the boiling
   point of water), or the sheet test or the refrigerator test (see "Testing for Jelly Stage,"
   earlier). Remove the jelly from the heat,
   skim off the foam, pour into hot, sterilized
   containers and seal.

   With powdered pectin: Measure the jelly.
   For each quart of jelly measure ¼ cup sugar,
   ¼ cup water and 4 teaspoons powdered
   pectin. Mix the pectin and water, and bring
   to a boil, stirring constantly to prevent
   scorching. Add the jelly and sugar. Stir
   thoroughly. Bring to a full rolling boil over
   high heat, stirring constantly. Boil mixture

hard for ½ minute. Remove jelly from the heat, skim off foam, pour into hot, sterilized containers and seal.

With liquid pectin: Measure the jelly to be re-cooked. For each quart of jelly measure ¾ cup sugar, 2 tablespoons lemon juice, and 2 tablespoons liquid pectin. Bring jelly to a boil over high heat. Quickly add the sugar, lemon juice, and pectin, and bring to a full, rolling boil, stirring constantly. Boil mixture hard for one minute. Remove jelly from the heat, skim off foam, pour into hot containers and seal.

2. **Jam that is too soft.** Jam may be too soft for the same reasons as jelly, but because of its consistency it is usually still satisfactory to use without trying to re-cook. Next time cook until thicker, or if using a candy thermometer, be sure to stir the jam before reading thermometer, measure the temperature in the middle of the kettle, make sure the jam completely covers the bulb of the thermometer and that the bulb is not touching the bottom of the kettle.

3. **Syrupy jelly.** Using much too much sugar can cause syrupy jelly, and no amount of cooking will make it jell. This may also be caused by too little pectin, acid or sugar.

4. **Jelly or jam that is too stiff.** Overcooking or too much pectin, either added or natural, may cause this. Too much of the fruit may have been underripe. For the Long Cook Method use ¼ underripe and ¾ ripe fruit; use fully ripe fruit when adding pectin. To make a softer jelly or jam, next time you can add ¼ to ½ cup more juice or fruit than called for in the commercial pectin recipes.

5. **Weeping jelly.** Jelly and jam will weep up around the paraffin, breaking the seal, if too soft or stored in a place with warm or fluctuating temperature. If the paraffin is too thick (one layer more than ⅛ inch thick) it may pull away from the sides rather than adjusting to the jelly. Although most other books don't recommend using more than

one layer of paraffin, we have had great success adding a second thin layer after the first cools, tipping the glass around so that the paraffin comes in contact with the entire inside surface of the glass. Too much acid may be another cause of weepy jelly.

APPLE BUTTER

6 pounds apples (24-26 medium apples)
2 quarts water
1 quart sweet cider
3 cups sugar
Cinnamon, ground
Clove, ground

Wash the apples and cut into small pieces, leaving the skins and cores. Add the water and boil the apples until they are soft (about 30 minutes). Put through a food mill or rub through a sieve.

In the meantime, boil down the cider to ½ its volume, add hot apple pulp, sugar and ground spices to taste, and cook until thick enough to spread without running. Stir occasionally to prevent sticking or scorching. Ladle into hot, sterilized canning jars, leaving ¼ inch headroom, and seal. (See "Sealing Jelly," p. 136.) Process in a boiling water bath for 5 minutes.
Yield: 5 or 6 pints

MAPLE SYRUP

Sugaring starts around Town Meeting Day in New England, the first Tuesday in March, and it's a sure sign of spring. Whether you buy or boil your own, you want to store some for later use. The syrup that comes packed in tins is vacuum-sealed, but once it is opened mold, unattractive but not dangerous, can start to grow. The syrup is so high in sugar that it is not a good medium for the growth of bacteria, but if some water separates out to the top, that creates a better medium.

To get rid of the mold, skim off as much as you can and heat the syrup to just below the boiling point (boiling will crystallize the sugar). Then pour the syrup into hot, clean Mason jars for storage. Adjust lids. Process for 5 minutes in a boiling water bath to insure a good seal. Remove jars. Complete seals if necessary.

6. **Tough jelly.** The jelly may have been cooked too long before reaching the jelly stage because too little sugar was used.

7. **Gummy jelly.** This can be caused by overcooking.

8. **Fermentation of jelly.** The jar was sealed improperly, or too little sugar may have been used.

9. **Cloudy jelly.** Speed is important when transferring the cooked jelly from kettle to glasses. It may become cloudy if poured too slowly, or allowed to sit too long in the kettle. Cloudiness also may be caused by improper straining which leaves pulp in the juice, or if it sets too fast as a result of too green fruit.

10. **Mold on jelly or jam.** If the seal is imperfect to begin with or is broken by weeping jelly or mishandling, air and mold will get into the container.

11. **Jelly or jam that darkens** at the top of the container. This can be caused by warm storage or an improper seal that lets in air.

12. **Faded jelly or jam.** Storage that is too warm or long, or exposure to light may cause fading, particularly in red fruits such as strawberries and raspberries.

13. **Floating fruit in jam.** To prevent this, jam is cooled slightly and stirred for 5 minutes before being put in glasses to be sealed with paraffin; or after sealed in canning jars, it is gently shaken. If this was done, other causes of floating may be underripe fruit, fruit that was not sufficiently crushed or ground, or fruit not cooked long enough.

Chapter 7
Pickles and Relishes

Most beginners start with pickling because it is the "fun" part of preserving. Pickling is easy and the results are satisfying. There is variety and room for creativity, but there still are hard and fast rules for safe and successful results.

Pickling refers to adding vinegar and salt, with a variety of spices and sometimes sugar, to fruit and vegetables.

Cucumbers

The pickles most often encountered are made with cucumbers. There are many varieties of cucumbers, and some are "picklers," and others "slicers" or table types. Choose the pickler varieties to grow or buy for use as pickles. Their texture (especially their spiny skin), shape and flavor are superior to table varieties for canning, and they are good for table use, too. The slicers often have a tough, smooth skin developed for its durability in shipping and keeping, but definitely not tender in a pickle.

Picklers can be harvested at any size. They are picked when tiny for use as little dill or sweet gherkins. As they become more mature (4 to 6 inches long) they can be cross-cut for bread-and-butter pickles or dill chips, or sliced lengthwise for spicy or dill spears. This is the stage, before the seeds have had a chance to get very big, when they also are excellent served fresh like a slicer. When you have put-up all you need of these types of pickles and have had your fill of fresh cucumbers, allow the rest to mature to the ripe yellow or white (depending on the type) stage. These big, ripe cukes are peeled and seeded, and the crisp, thick flesh is cut into bite size chunks to be made into sweet "tongue" pickles, "tumerics," "golden glows" or other autumn specialties.

If you don't pressure-can or freeze or if you just want variety, you can look to pickling as a way of preserving your vegetables safely in jars. The addition of the acid vinegar brings the pH level low enough to stop the growth of heat-resistant bacteria. Beans or corn which are pickled are as safe as any cucumber pickle. Try pickled beets, corn relish, dilled beans, pickled carrots or green tomato relish for colorful and tasty side dishes.

Fruits pickle too, and the process adds a whole new dimension to apples, pears and peaches. Watermelon rind, spiced apple slices, mincemeat and chutneys are just samplings of the variety of pickled fruits available.

Processing

First and most important is the question of processing. Pickled vegetables and fruits should receive a boiling water bath for safety, to stop bacteria that cause spoilage, to stop enzyme action and to insure a good seal and high quality. Processing kills the heat-sensitive bacteria that still can grow in high acid foods. Do use new recipes. You may have a favored old family recipe but undoubtedly it will not have a processing time. There are many older recipes that have been adapted to newer methods.

Ingredients

Use a canning salt, which is sold in five-pound bags at most groceries. It is additive-free and is also one of the best buys around. Table salt should not be used for pickling, as the additives that prevent caking can cause clouding. Do not use rock salt, since it is impure.

Vinegar is the key ingredient in pickling, providing flavor and storing qualities. The prime consideration with vinegar is acidity. Check the label, as 5-6 percent acidity is necessary. Homemade vinegars may vary in strength, so save them for salads. Use either the cider type or distilled white vinegar. Don't use commercial wine vinegars. And again *don't* use old recipes.

They may have been geared to a less- or more-acid vinegar which would throw your proportions off. White vinegar makes a clearer pickle juice and has a sharp, tart taste while cider vinegar has a mellower, fruity flavor. Buy vinegar in bulk (gallons) if you're doing many pickles, as you will use large quantities. Don't be tempted to water down your vinegar if you should run short, for this will lower the acidity and possibly compromise the quality.

Crispness is a part of good pickles. *Alum* used to be recommended to make them crisp, but if you follow the recipe carefully, it won't be necessary. If you do want alum, you'll find it at the pharmacy in a powdered or lump form. Simply adding grape or cherry leaves also will help maintain crispness.

Spices are the flavor-makers, and their use allows for creativity in pickling. Quantities and varieties can be varied with no danger except to taste. Always use fresh spices, since they lose quality when stored from one year to the next. The use of a cheesecloth pickling bag for mixed spices will distribute the flavor evenly without causing bland or hot spots. Some pickling spices come ready-mixed.

Recipes often call for peppercorns, cinnamon stick, cloves, ginger, tumeric (which produces a yellow color), hot pepper and large quantities of

mustard seed. Don't forget to grow your own garlic, which is far superior fresh and is called for in many pickle recipes. The same is true of dill flower and onions. Small onions grown from sets are ideal and go far in saving on expense.

You can use either brown or white sugar, although brown makes a darker pickle. You can substitute honey for part of your sugar. If a recipe calls for two cups of sugar, use one cup of honey and one cup of sugar.

Soft water is a luxury in some areas but it is a necessity for pickling, since hard water interferes with fermentation. Boil hard water, skim off the scum and let it sit for 24 hours before using it.

Dill, the key ingredient for dill pickles, is difficult to find fresh locally, but it is as easy to grow as a weed and will frequently re-seed. Usually it matures before the cucumbers, unless it is planted late. Dill is easy to air-dry or freeze. To freeze, don't wash it. Just put the dill heads in a container, freeze until pickling time. Fresh dill seems to have more of a wallop than commercial, dried dill seed, so you may want to adjust for that.

Equipment

Don't use brass, copper or iron utensils, which react with the salt and vinegar, and can affect the color in your pickles. Use enameled, aluminum, glass or stainless steel pots instead.

Wide-mouth jars are a great convenience in pickling. Dill spears go in and come out far

easier than with a regular jar. However, don't pack your cucumbers so tightly that they won't be completely surrounded by the juice.

There are several slicers on the market that adapt to the uniform slicing of cucumbers, but a good chopping knife is perfectly adequate.

NEW GIANT PERA CUCUMBER

Recipes

Recipes are the heart of good pickling. There is only one way to freeze or can properly but there are hundreds of options in pickling, so it's impossible to come up with one classic example. Whole books even have been written on the subject.

Remember pickles improve with age, the flavor mellows (but try to use them up within a year). The shriveling often encountered in dill beans will disappear after several weeks on the shelf. So be patient and wait for a month to six weeks.

Do try more than one recipe the first year. You may find you made a great pickle but not a family favorite. Also mark your recipes so you remember which ones to try again.

PICKLE RECIPES

DILL PICKLES

4 pounds of cucumbers, washed
    and cut into spears
3 cups white vinegar
3 cups water
⅓ cup pickling salt
    Optional: 12 peeled sliced garlic
    cloves. Remove garlic before
    packing into jars.

Combine liquids and salt and heat to boiling point. Pack cucumbers into hot clean jars. Add 2 tbs. dill seed or one dill head and 3 peppercorns to each jar.

Fill the jars with the hot pickling syrup, leaving ½ inch headroom. Adjust lids. Process in boiling water bath—quarts for 20 minutes. Remove jars. Complete seals if necessary. Yield: 7 pints.

SPICED APPLE SLICES

6 cups sugar
2 cups vinegar
4 sticks cinnamon in small pieces
2 teaspoons whole cloves
5 lbs. firm apples, peeled, cored
    and in thick slices

Boil sugar, vinegar and spices, add apples and simmer uncovered until apples are tender *but not broken.*

Pack in clean, hot pint jars, leaving ½ inch headroom, and process in a boiling water bath for 10 minutes. Remove jars; complete seals if necessary. Yield: 3-4 pints.

SHORT-CUT BREAD AND BUTTER PICKLES

½ gallon of your own
    or store-bought dill pickles
1 clove garlic, cut into pieces
4 cups sugar
2 cups cider vinegar
2 sticks cinnamon
2 tbs. celery seed
1 tbs. dry mustard

Drain pickles and cut them into ½ inch slices. Put them back into jar with cut garlic.

Combine sugar and vinegar and boil. Add cinnamon, celery seed, mustard and pour over pickles. Keep in refrigerator for one week before serving.

These are not to be resealed.

CORN RELISH

8 cups raw corn cut from cob
3 cups chopped onions
½ cup chopped green pepper
½ cup chopped sweet red pepper
¾ cup packed brown sugar
½ cup white corn syrup
7 teaspoons salt
1 tablespoon dry mustard
3 cups cider vinegar

Mix all ingredients thoroughly. Cover and boil for 15 minutes, stirring often. Pour into clean, hot pint jars, leaving ½ inch headroom, and process in a boiling water bath for 15 minutes. Remove jars; complete seals if necessary. Yield: 4-5 pints.

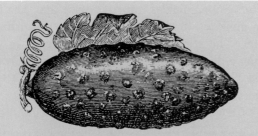

TWO-DAY MUSTARD PICKLES

This recipe is a gardener's delight, since when he eats it, he can exclaim with pride, "That's from my garden—and that, and that." It demands vegetables from six different rows, all of which can be found in most gardens in August.

1 head cauliflower (about 1½
    quarts) broken into florets
1 quart small white onions, peeled
1 quart small cucumbers
1 quart small green tomatoes
2 large green peppers, chopped
    and with seeds removed
2 large sweet red peppers,
    treated in like manner, and
    giving a total of 4 cups
    chopped peppers. (The taste
    will be the same if the ratio
    of green to red peppers varies.)
2 quarts cider vinegar
6 tablespoons prepared mustard
1½ cups light brown sugar
⅔ cup flour
2 tablespoons tumeric

First day: Tidy up vegetables, place them in large bowl and cover them with a brine made of three quarts of cold water to which ½ cup of salt is added. Cover and let sit for 24 hours.

Second day: Using a colander and large pan, drain salt solution from vegetables, catching them in colander and it in saucepan. Heat solution to boiling and pour over vegetables in colander, this time discarding it. Let vegetables drain.

Combine vinegar, mustard, brown sugar, flour and tumeric. Stir, then heat gradually, stirring constantly, until mixture is thick and smooth. Add drained vegetables and cook gently until they are tender but have not lost their individuality. Stirring (with heavy wooden spoon) is necessary to prevent scorching.

Pack into hot sterilized pint jars, leaving ½ inch headroom. Process in boiling water bath 10 minutes. This will produce more than five quarts of pickles— excellent gifts for fellow gardeners.

MAKING CROSS-CUT PICKLES

1. Wash 4 quarts (6 pounds) of cucumbers thoroughly. Slice unpeeled cucumbers into ⅛ inch to ¼ inch slices or use slicer. Remove skins and wash 1½ cups (1 pound) of onions. Slice into ⅛ inch slices.

2. Combine cucumbers and onions. Add 2 large peeled garlic cloves and ⅓ cup canning salt. Mix thoroughly.

3. Cover with 2 trays of ice cubes. Let stand 3 hours. Drain completely. Remove garlic.

4. Combine 4½ cups sugar, 1½ tsp. tumeric, 1½ tsp. celery seed, 2 tbs. mustard seed and 3 cups white vinegar.

5. Add drained cucumbers and onions and heat 5 minutes.

6. Pack hot pickles into clean, hot jars, leaving ½ inch headroom. Adjust jar lids. Process in boiling water bath—5 minutes for pints, 10 minutes for quarts. Remove jars. Complete seals if necessary.

MIXED PICKLES

4 qts. cucumbers
1 qt. onions
3 cups cauliflower
1 green pepper
3 cloves garlic
⅓ cup pickling salt
  ice cubes
5 cups sugar
2 tablespoons mustard seed
½ tablespoon celery seed
1 qt. cider vinegar

Slice onions and pepper and cucumbers thin. Break up cauliflower. Combine vegetables with garlic and add salt. Cover with ice cubes, mix and let stand for 3 hours. Drain well.

Combine remaining ingredients and pour over vegetables. Bring to boil. Put in clean, hot pint jars, allowing ½ inch headroom. Seal and process in a boiling water bath for 15 minutes. Remove jars and complete seals if necessary. Yield: 8 pints

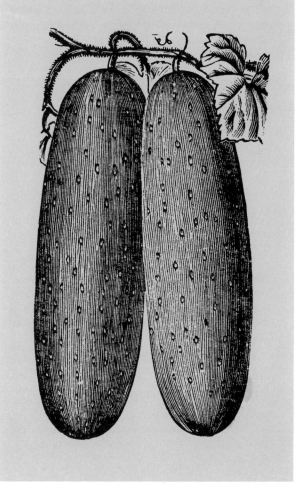

GREEN TOMATO MINCEMEAT
WITHOUT MEAT

2 qts. chopped or minced
   green tomatoes
1 orange
2½ qts. chopped apples
1 tablespoon salt
1 lb. seeded raisins
3½ cups brown sugar
2 teaspoons cinnamon
1 teaspoon cloves
½ teaspoon ginger
1 teaspoon nutmeg
½ cup vinegar

Wash and drain tomatoes, orange and apples. Grind up tomatoes in a meat grinder, sprinkle with salt and let stand for 1 hour.

Drain and cover with boiling water for 5 minutes. Drain again. Grate rind and chop pulp of orange. Core, pare and chop apples.

Mix all ingredients and boil slowly until tender. Pour into hot pint jars and seal, allowing ½ inch headroom. Process in boiling water bath for 25 minutes. Remove jars and complete seals if necessary. Yield: 6 pints.

Ideal in pies or cookies.

GREEN TOMATO RELISH
WITH HONEY

12 green tomatoes
1 red and 1 green sweet pepper
4 large onions
1 tablespoon salt
1 cup dark honey
1 cup vinegar
1 tablespoon mustard seed
1 tablespoon celery seed

Chop tomatoes, onions and peppers coarsely. Drain. Add remaining ingredients and mix. Cook slowly until tender, about 20 minutes. Put into hot clean jars, leaving ½ inch headroom. Adjust lids. Process in a boiling water bath.

Pints................ 10 minutes
Quarts .... 15 minutes

As you may have noticed, several of these recipes call for large amounts of honey which is still more expensive than sugar. This might be discouraging unless you keep your own bees.

MAKING DILL PICKLES

1. Wash cucumbers and cut into spears. Four pounds of cucumbers yield 7 pints.

2. Combine 3 cups white or cider vinegar, 3 cups water, ⅓ cup pickling salt and heat to boiling. (Optional: Add 12 peeled, sliced garlic cloves. Remove garlic before packing into jars.)

3. Pack cucumbers into hot, clean jars.

4. Add 3 peppercorns and 2 tbs. dill seed or 1 dill head to each jar.

5. Fill the jars with the hot pickling mixture, leaving ½ inch headroom.

6. Adjust lids. Process in a boiling water bath 20 minutes for quarts. Remove jars. Complete seals if necessary.

TUMERIC PICKLES

4 qts. chunked ripe yellow
  cucumbers (about 1½ ×
  ½ inch pieces)
4 large onions sliced
1 tbs. salt
1 tbs. celery seed
1 tbs. tumeric powder
4 cups white sugar
2¾ cups cider vinegar
¼ cup water

Mix all but onions and cucumbers together in a kettle. Bring to a boil. Put in onion mixture, stirring occasionally until cukes turn transparent. Don't overcook. Pack in hot clean jars. Cover to within ½ inch of rim. Adjust lids. Process pints 10 minutes in a boiling water bath. Remove jars. Complete seals if necessary. These pickles can be used immediately if desired.

FANCY PICKLES

CABBAGE & BEET RELISH

3 pints shredded cabbage
3 pints cooked sliced beets
1 cup chopped onions
¾ cup grated horseradish
2 tablespoons canning salt
2½ cups vinegar
1 cup sugar

Mix vegetables and salt. Heat vinegar and sugar until dissolved. Add to vegetables and boil 12 minutes. Pack into hot, clean pint jars, leaving ½ inch headroom. Adjust lids and process in boiling water bath 15 minutes. Remove jars and complete seals if necessary.

ZUCCHINI PICKLES

4 quarts sliced zucchini
6 sliced, large onions
2 chopped green peppers
2 chopped sweet red peppers
2 garlic cloves
½ cup pickling salt
5 cups sugar
3 cups cider vinegar
1½ tsp. tumeric powder
2 tbs. mustard seed
1 tsp. celery seed

Make a syrup of sugar, cider vinegar, tumeric powder (this will create a clear, yellow color), mustard seed and celery seed.

Put vegetables in a kettle and cover with cracked ice. Let sit for 3 hours. Drain. Boil syrup and add vegetables. Cook 15 minutes. Pack into hot, clean pint jars, leaving ½ inch headroom. Process in a boiling water bath for 5 minutes. Remove jars. Complete seals if necessary.

PICCALILLI

2 qts. green tomatoes
3 sweet red peppers
3 green peppers
10 small onions
3 cups cider vinegar
1¾ cups sugar
⅛ cup salt
¼ cup mustard seed
⅓ tablespoon celery seed
½ teaspoon cinnamon
½ teaspoon allspice

Wash, seed and quarter peppers. Wash and quarter tomatoes. Peel and quarter onions. Put all through a food mill. Drain of extra liquid.

In a large kettle add vegetables and ½ of vinegar. Boil for ½ hour, stirring often. Drain and discard liquid.

Add remaining vinegar, sugar and spices, and simmer for 3 minutes. Pour into clean pint jars, allowing ½ inch headroom, and process in boiling water bath for 5 minutes. Remove jars and complete seals if necessary. Yield: 6 pints.

Ideal with hamburgers or mixed with catsup for relish, or in potato salad.

PROBLEMS

Soft pickles: vinegar too weak.

Hollow pickles: too mature or poorly developed cucumbers, or too long between harvesting and pickling.

Dark pickles: iodized salt, too much spice or the use of iron, copper or brass utensils.

Shriveling: sweet pickles in a too-heavy syrup or a too-strong vinegar, over-cooking or over-processing.

Soft and slippery pickles: due to growth of bacteria from a poor seal. Throw away.

QUICK-BRINED PICKLES

20 pounds cucumber
¾ cup whole mixed pickling spices
3 bunches fresh dill
2½ cups vinegar
1¾ cups pickling salt
2½ gallons water

Never use overripe cucumbers. Be especially careful to wash completely, removing the blossom end.

Put half the pickling spice and a layer of dill in a 5 gallon crock or glass jar. Fill with cucumbers, leaving 3 to 4 inches headspace. Put remaining dill and spices on top.

Mix vinegar, water and salt and pour on. Cover with a plate, using a canning jar filled with sand or water to keep the pickles below the brine surface. Cover crock with a clean cloth. Leave at room temperature.

Remove scum every day, being sure cucumbers are completely covered. First scum forms in about 3 days. In about 3 weeks pickles will be ready to process. The brine may be cloudy, and if you wish a clear brine replace with ½ cup salt and 4 cups vinegar to 1 gallon water. Pack in clean, hot, quart jars, adding some of the dill. Cover with boiling brine, leaving ½ inch headroom. Process in boiling water bath for 15 minutes. Remove jars and complete seals if necessary.

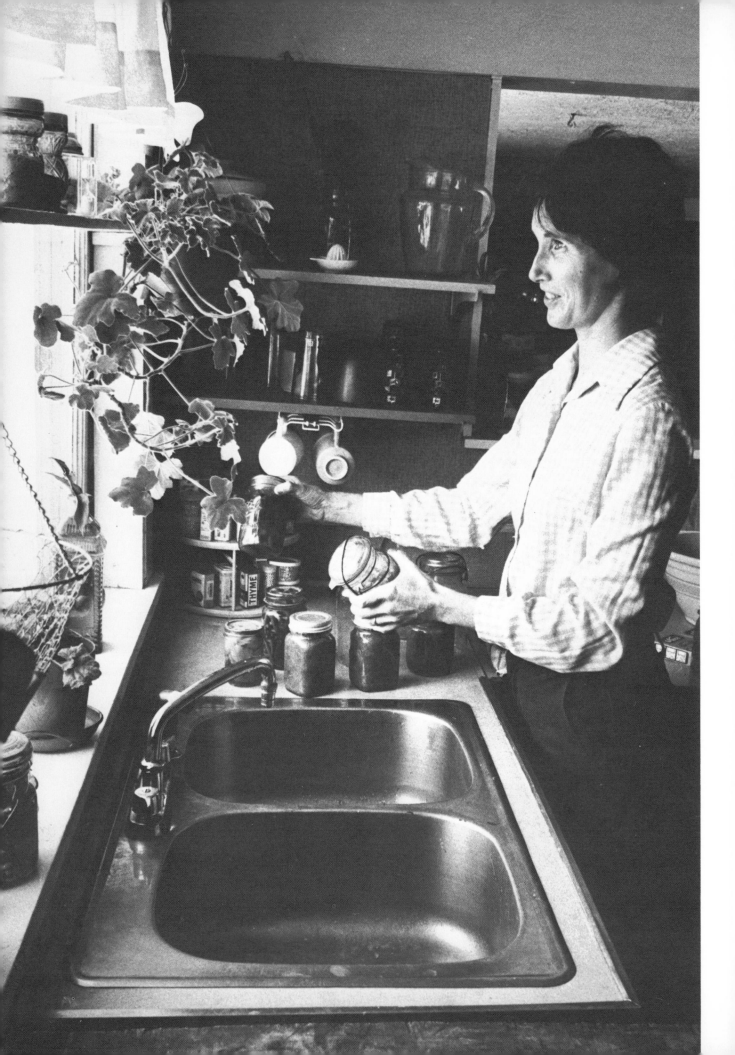

Chapter 8 Curing With Salt

Salting, a very ancient method of preserving, is based on the discovery that large amounts of salt will inhibit spoilage. However, using a great deal of salt means that the food is not fit to eat until it has been desalted and freshened by soaking it in several changes of water. When this is done, however, many of the nutrients are dissolved and lost.

Fermentation occurs when *small* amounts of salt are used. The bacteria change the sugars of the vegetables to lactic acid, and the acid (with the salt) prevents other spoilage organisms from growing. This lactic acid fermentation is the method used in making sauerkraut and other "sour" vegetables. Since the salting is so mild both vegetable and juice may be eaten, while nearly all the nutrients are preserved.

The Chinese may have been the first to preserve food by the fermentation process. The present-day Yen Tsai—meaning vegetables preserved in brine—is prepared with mixtures of various vegetables that have been available since ancient times. Turnips, radishes, cabbage and other vegetables are used in these preparations and, if available, salt is added.

Some of the vegetables which may be fermented in the home with success are cabbage, Chinese cabbage, turnips, rutabagas, lettuce, green tomatoes and snap beans. Cucumbers also are fermented when brined the long way for pickles.

When properly prepared, all of these foods will be crisp but tender. They are pleasantly acid and salty in flavor; therefore (except for sauerkraut) they are good in salads, or served whole on the relish tray, without freshening. They also are good when cooked with meat.

General Directions

1. As with all kinds of storage, choose only fresh, healthy, tender young produce for the best results.

2. Use pure "pickling" salt, which also is called "canning" salt. Ordinary table salt usually has iodine and starch added to it. Neither of these additives is harmful if used in salting, but the iodine may cause an off-color and the starch may interfere with the fermenting process and settle to the bottom of the jar, giving a cloudy appearance. Canning salt also is much cheaper than table salt. "Flaky" and medium salts, such as dairy, cheese and kosher salts, also may be used, but be careful when measuring, (see salt chart following). Pound for pound these are the same as the granulated pickling salt, but by *measure* almost 1½ times as much is called for. Coarse salt is *not* recommended for use, because it dissolves too slowly and is harder to distribute evenly.

3. Weigh or measure the vegetables and salt accurately and follow directions exactly.

4. Keep the vegetables completely immersed in the brine at all times, both during fermentation and storage.

5. Never add fresh vegetables to a batch that has already started curing.

The Vandergaw Cabbage. The Best Second Early and Summer Cabbage. Equally as Good For Winter. COPYRIGHTED 1887. BY W. ATLEE BURPEE & CO PHILADA.

6. Clean the cloth and cover regularly and remove scum from surface of brine. A piece of cloth tied over the curing container will help keep insects and dust off the cover and out of the brine.

7. Discard without tasting any material that is slimy, soft or has an off-odor or off-color. It is not fit to eat.

Equipment Needed

Household scales to weigh vegetables and salt.

Kraut-cutting board, or a large, very sharp knife and cutting board (for sauerkraut).

Large pans for making brine and mixing vegetables and salt. These should be of stainless steel, glass, unchipped enamel or plastic. Never use copper, brass, galvanized or iron utensils for mixing or heating acid or salty solutions. They may react with the metal causing undesirable compounds and color changes.

Curing containers. For small quantities use glass quart-to-gallon-size wide-mouth containers with lids. Do not use zinc lids. For large quantities use stone jars, crocks, paraffined wooden barrels, large casserole or kettle of unchipped enamel ware.

Cover for large containers: a round, flat board or china plate that will fit snugly *inside* the top

of the container; or a large, waterproof plastic bag suitable for use with food.

Weight to hold cover and vegetables below the level of the brine: something that can be washed thoroughly such as a glass jar filled with sand or water.

Clean white cheesecloth or muslin to put on top of the vegetables. For small jars, pieces of wood slightly shorter than the width of the jar opening to be used to hold the vegetables under the brine. Popsicle sticks or wooden ice cream spoons work well.

Wooden tamper, potato masher or a clean, heavy bottle to tamp down cabbage and turnip.

Canning jars and lids for processing fermented vegetables.

All equipment should be scrupulously clean. Containers that have been used before should be aired thoroughly and scalded. Do not use wooden containers or covers made of yellow or pitch pine, or the vegetables will develop a piney flavor. To paraffin wooden containers or covers, warm them and be sure they are thoroughly dry. Melt paraffin and apply with a brush, thinly but thoroughly. Dry well before using.

Sauerkraut

The health-giving properties of sauerkraut have been well-recognized for 200 years or more, and before vitamin C was discovered, it was a preventative or cure for scurvy. This was, of course, because cabbage ranks high among foods for vitamin C value. Even though two-thirds of the vitamin C is lost in fermenting and processing, there are still 16 mg. in a four-ounce serving, and only about 20 calories. Sauerkraut also happens to be very inexpensive to make. You can use Chinese cabbage in this recipe as well as regular cabbage.

One pound of salt is needed for 40 to 50 pounds of cabbage; approximately 45 pounds of cabbage will fill a 5-gallon crock. About 8 pounds of cabbage will fill a one-gallon jar. For each 5 pounds of cabbage you will need 3 tablespoons of pickling salt.

1. Choose heavy, firm heads of cabbage of the long-growing, late variety. Let them stand at room temperature for several hours to wilt and the leaves will become less brittle and less likely to break in cutting. Trim off the outer leaves and wash the heads. With a sharp knife cut the heads into quarters. The core may be cut out or left on and sliced thinly with the rest of the cabbage. It contains as many nutrients as the rest of the cabbage, but is tough and somewhat bitter.

2. Cut five pounds of cabbage at a time into thin shreds. If using a kraut-cutting board, set the blade to cut shreds about the thickness of a dime. Mix five pounds of cabbage with 3 tablespoons of salt in a large pan, and let it settle for ten to 15 minutes or more while shredding the next batch. The salt will start working on the cabbage during this time, reducing the bulk (which makes it easier to pack), drawing juices (so less tamping is required), and softening it somewhat (helping to prevent breakage of the shreds when packed).

3. Pack the cabbage into clean containers, pressing firmly with hands or tamper to remove air pockets and to draw the juice. Fill large containers to within 3 or 4 inches of the top with salted cabbage, pressing and tamping down after each layer. Leave about 6 inches space above the cabbage when using a plastic bag for the cover.

Do not tamp so hard that you bruise or tear the shreds, for this can result in undesirable softening of the kraut. Juice should cover the surface of the kraut within 24 hours.

4. Wipe stray pieces of cabbage from around the edge of the container. Cover the cabbage with several layers of clean white cheesecloth and tuck it down the sides. Then put on your cover. The size of the cover is important: it should fit snugly within the container to seal out air, preventing the growth of undesirable yeast and aerobic bacteria that can spoil the kraut. It should also be flat, so that no air will be caught under it.

On top of the cover place a weight of such heft that the juice will rise just above the cover. It

Strength of Brine (Percent)	oz./qt.	By Weight oz./gal. All Types of Salt	lb./gal.	By Volume cups/gal. Granulated	cups/gal. Flake or Medium
2½	1 oz.	3½ oz.	¼ lb.	⅓ cup	½ cup
5	1¾	7½	½	¾	1
10	4	16	1	1½	2¼
15	6¼	25	1½	2½	3¾
20	9	36	2¼	3½	5¼

AMOUNT OF SALT NEEDED FOR DIFFERENT STRENGTHS OF BRINE

Amount of Salt to Water

MAKING SAUERKRAUT

1. Remove outer leaves from firm, mature heads of cabbage. Wash and drain. Remove core and shred with a knife or shredder. Weigh 5 pounds carefully to insure correct cabbage-salt proportions.

2. Measure 3 tbs. canning salt and sprinkle over 5 pounds prepared cabbage. Mix well with spoon or hands. Allow a few minutes for cabbage to wilt slightly.

3. Pack cabbage into a 1 gallon jar. Press firmly with wooden spoon or hands until juice is drawn out to

cover shredded cabbage. Put a heavy-duty plastic bag on cabbage and fill with water until it sits firmly, allowing no air to reach the cabbage.

Ferment for approximately 5 to 6 weeks. Gas bubbles indicate that fermentation is occurring. Temperatures between 68° and 72° are ideal for fermentation.

4. After fermentation has ceased, put kraut into kettle and heat to simmering. Pack hot sauerkraut into clean, hot jars. Cover with hot juice, leaving ½ inch headroom. Adjust lids. Process in a boiling water bath—pints for 15 minutes, quarts for 20 minutes. Remove jars. Complete seals if necessary.

may take several hours for this to happen. If the juice has not risen over the cover within 24 hours, add enough 2½ percent brine to bring it to this level.

Instead of using cloth, cover and weight, a large plastic bag of a type suitable for freezing food may be placed directly on the kraut, and filled with enough water to keep the juice over the top of the kraut. A second or third bag may be put inside the first to avoid leakage. The bag should be big enough to cover the kraut completely and fit tightly against the inside edge of the container. This will seal out air effectively. After putting cold tap water into the bag to the level of the top of the container, close it with metal twisties or rubber bands.

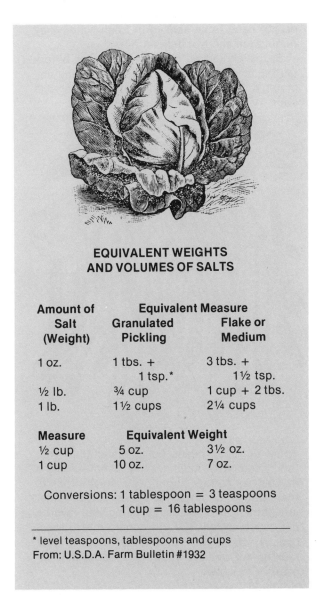

EQUIVALENT WEIGHTS AND VOLUMES OF SALTS

Amount of Salt (Weight)	Equivalent Measure	
	Granulated Pickling	Flake or Medium
1 oz.	1 tbs. + 1 tsp.*	3 tbs. + 1½ tsp.
½ lb.	¾ cup	1 cup + 2 tbs.
1 lb.	1½ cups	2¼ cups

Measure	Equivalent Weight	
½ cup	5 oz.	3½ oz.
1 cup	10 oz.	7 oz.

Conversions: 1 tablespoon = 3 teaspoons
1 cup = 16 tablespoons

* level teaspoons, tablespoons and cups
From: U.S.D.A. Farm Bulletin #1932

5. Room temperature of 68°-72° F. is recommended for fermenting cabbage, which will usually be ready in 5 to 6 weeks. Fermentation will be faster at 75°-80° F., and at 85° F. it will be ready in about two weeks. However, the chances of spoilage are much greater at these high temperatures.

Unless air is completely sealed out a white scum will appear on the brine surface within a few days. This should be taken care of promptly by removing the cover and carefully lifting off the cloth, then skimming off any scum that does not adhere to the cloth. Replace the cloth with a clean one, scald and replace the cover and weight. Check the kraut daily, removing the scum and cleaning the cloth and cover as often as the scum forms. Adjust the weight to keep the brine level up above the kraut. Add more 2½ percent brine if the level becomes too low. After a couple of weeks there may be a dramatic drop in the level of the juice (meaning fermentation is ceasing). Then add enough 2½ percent brine to cover the kraut.

Bubbles will be visible on the surface of the kraut as long as fermentation continues. When no bubbles are seen, fermentation is complete.

SMALL-BATCH KRAUTING

If you have just a few heads of cabbage, you may want to ferment it in individual containers. You could use these small batches to experiment with such seasonings as garlic or caraway. (See under Hot Pack Canning.) If you are fermenting your kraut in quart or pint-sized jars, proceed according to the directions, cutting and mixing five pounds of cabbage with 3 tablespoons of salt. Let it settle for 20 or 30 minutes, then pack tightly into jars. Insert two or three wooden sticks, cut slightly shorter than the width of the jar mouth, into the jar, catching the ends up under the shoulders of the jars. This should hold the kraut down under the juice.

Add more 2½ percent brine to cover if enough does not form spontaneously in 24 hours. The tops should be placed on the jars loosely so that gas formed during fermentation can escape. Place the jars on trays or newspapers to catch the juice that oozes out with the gas. The level of the kraut may sink enough in a week or two to make it necessary to combine the kraut from several jars—about one quart of kraut will be needed to supplement the contents of four other quarts. Do *not* add fresh vegetables to a batch of already-started sauerkraut or other salted vegetables.

If scum forms in these small containers, remove it with a spoon. If the level of the brine is so low that it is difficult to reach the scum, add more 2½ percent brine. The scum will rise to the surface of the brine where it can be reached more easily.

After about two to six weeks the fermentation process will cease. The kraut should have a pleasantly acid taste and have changed color to a slightly translucent pale gold-white. At this point kraut packed in large containers may be transferred to smaller canning jars to be processed for storage, or it can be stored for several months in the original container in a cold (38°) place. For storage, put on a fresh cloth, be sure the brine covers the surface of the kraut, and cover with a tight-fitting lid.

SAUER BEANS OR GREEN TOMATOES (SLICED)

Wash young, tender snap beans, snip off the ends and cut into short lengths. Blanch them for five minutes in boiling water or steam. Cool promptly in ice cold water and drain. Wash green tomatoes, remove stem and core, and slice thickly.

Mix, as evenly as possible 4 ounces salt and 4 ounces (½ cup) vinegar with each 5 pounds of vegetables. If not enough brine forms to cover the vegetables completely within 24 hours, add 5 percent brine. Pack firmly and proceed with each step as for making and processing sauerkraut.

Vegetables prepared by this method will be attractive in appearance, crisp in texture and both slightly salty and acid in flavor. Since they do not need to be soaked in fresh water, they retain a fair share of their nutrients.

Beans should be boiled 10 minutes before tasting or serving. Discard without tasting any material that is soft or has an objectionable odor.

TOO MANY?

When the snap beans come faster than your family can pick—much less eat them—and the freezer has had its quota, try a small crock of them brined, or better yet put up pint or larger jars of them as dilled beans, using your favorite dill pickle recipe. The dill comes into flowers usually when your first bean crop is just running out, and everybody's had enough fresh beans for a while.

KRAUT PROBLEMS

Here are some of the common causes of spoilage in sauerkraut, and the reasons the U.S. Department of Agriculture gives for them.

Softness: Insufficient salt, too-high temperatures during fermentation, uneven distribution of salt, or air pockets caused by improper packing.

Pink kraut: Certain types of yeast grow on the surface of the kraut, because of too much salt, an uneven distribution of salt, or when the kraut is improperly covered or weighted during fermentation.

Rotted: Usually found at the surface where the cabbage has not been covered sufficiently to exclude air during fermentation.

Dark kraut: Unwashed and improperly trimmed cabbage, insufficient juice to cover fermenting cabbage, uneven distribution of salt, exposure to air, high temperatures during fermentation, processing and storage, or too long a storage period.

CANNING

For longer or warmer storage, can the kraut as follows:

Hot pack canning. Place the kraut in a kettle and heat to simmering (185°-210° F.) in its own juice. Stir gently so the kraut will heat evenly, but do not boil. Add more 2½ percent brine if there is not enough juice to cover the kraut. Pack into clean hot canning jars, press down to release air bubbles and cover with hot juice, leaving ½ inch headroom. Adjust lids and process in a boiling water bath.

Pints . . . . 15 minutes
Quarts . . . . 20 minutes

Remove jars, complete seals if necessary, and place on a towel or rack several inches apart to cool. If allowed to remain hot for too long a time, the kraut will darken and soften. When canned and cooled properly kraut will have much the flavor and texture of the fresh product.

For a change of pace, sauerkraut can be made more interesting by adding herbs (carraway or dill) or garlic cloves to small batches of the cabbage before fermenting. Remove the garlic before cooking or serving the finished kraut. A few sliced carrots, whole green tomatoes or pieces of cauliflower or broccoli may be scattered within the cabbage to ferment with it. Or try a whole cabbage, for use as stuffed cabbage leaves, pickled in the kraut.

Put salt into the cavity left by cutting out the core—about 2 teaspoons salt per pound of cabbage. Bury the whole cabbage, cavity side up, in the center of the shredded cabbage.

LETTUCE KRAUT

Head lettuce of the Los Angeles or iceberg types may be made into kraut in the same manner as cabbage. It is milder in flavor than cabbage kraut, and is an excellent product if properly made.

Brine-Cured Pickles

Curing cucumbers and other vegetables in a brine "strong enough to float an egg" is as much a part of our food heritage as salt pork or apple pie. A 10 percent brine will float a fresh egg, and in it we cure many vegetables that are then used for sour, spiced and sweet pickles: cucumbers, green tomatoes, green beans, onions and cauliflower.

1. Prepare vegetables by washing, trimming, and removing stems and blossom ends. Use whole, immature cucumbers—from tiny gherkins up to 7-inch size. Wipe rather than wash, unless very dirty. Beans should be blanched in boiling water or steam for 5 minutes. Small green tomatoes and onions are left whole. Cut cauliflower into flowerets.

2. Weigh vegetables and pack into a clean container. Cover with a cold brine "strong enough to float an egg" (1 pound granulated salt per gallon of water). A gallon of brine will be needed for each two gallons of vegetables.

3. Cover the vegetables with a wooden cover or plate weighed down to keep the vegetables under the brine.

4. The following day add additional salt at the rate of ½ pound for each 5 pounds of vegetables. This is necessary to keep the brine strong enough despite the liquid drawn from the vegetables by the salt. Place the salt in a mound on top of the cover rather than directly into the brine, so it will not sink to the bottom.

5. At the end of the first week, and for 4 or 5 succeeding weeks, add ⅛ pound salt for each 5 pounds of vegetables. To help remember when and how much salt to add, tape a timetable to the crock, marking off each time the the salt is added.

6. Remove any scum that forms, and be sure to keep every pickle completely submerged in the brine. Add more 10 percent brine if necessary.

7. Fermentation will continue 4 to 8 weeks, indicated by a few bubbles rising to the surface. The speed will depend on the storage temperature—68°-72° F. is safest to avoid spoilage though 80°-85° F. is faster.

More vegetables *may* be added in this recipe for the first couple of weeks of the brining process, provided the brine is kept strong enough—at 10 percent. Go ahead and test it with an egg!

The cucumbers are ready when they are a consistent olive green color, translucent throughout and without white spots. Before using for pickles, they should be de-salted by soaking for several hours in large quantities of fresh water which is changed several times, or in equal parts water and vinegar.

166

Weak Brining with Salt and Vinegar

This is a method of preserving some vegetables if you have no other means. You also might try it since it offers interesting flavor changes. Several vegetables may be stored by this method. When preparing to serve them they do not need to be soaked to remove the salt. But if the flavor is too tart they can be rinsed well or soaked a short time before cooking.

Vegetables that may be used are snap beans, beets, beet tops, carrots, cauliflower, mustard and turnip greens, kale, rutabagas, turnips and small, whole green tomatoes.

1. Prepare the vegetables as for table use by trimming and washing. Cut the cauliflower or break it into flowerets, and slice or dice turnips and rutabagas. Wash greens thoroughly in several waters to remove all traces of grit. Wash small carrots, beets and green tomatoes, remove stems (leave ½ inch of stem on the beets), do not cut into pieces. Wash very tender snap green or wax beans and blanch for 5 minutes in boiling water or steam, and cool promptly. They may be cut into pieces crosswise or left whole.

2. Prepare a 5 percent brine. The amount needed will be about half the volume of the vegetables to be packed. To each gallon of water, add and dissolve ½ pound of salt. Add one cup of vinegar that has a 4 to 6 percent strength of acetic acid.

3. Pack the vegetables firmly into clean containers to within 3 or 4 inches of the top. Cover with several layers of clean white cheesecloth or muslin and tuck in around the edge. On top of this place a weighted cover. Pour the brine over the vegetables until it comes up over the cover.

4. Store the containers in a cool place. Follow directions given for sauerkraut about removing scum and washing the cloth and cover frequently. After fermentation for 10 days to two weeks, hot pack the vegetables in

SAUERRUBEN (SOUR TURNIP)

Select young, sweet, juicy purple-topped turnips for this specialty. Rutabagas also may be used.

Peel, shred and mix 3 tablespoons of granulated pickling salt with each 5 pounds of turnips. Pack into clean containers, press down gently after all of it has been packed, to remove air pockets. Tamping layer-by-layer should be unnecessary if the turnips are juicy. Cover and weigh down as you would sauerkraut. Enough juice should form to cover the turnips within 24 hours. If not, add more 2½ percent brine to cover.

Kept at room temperature (68°-72° F.) it may take from a month to six weeks for the turnips to ferment. Be sure they remain covered with brine, and remove scum as it forms. Replace the cloth with a clean one and scald the cover daily.

When fermentation is complete, heat the sauerruben to simmering, and hot pack into clean, hot canning jars. Cover with its own juice, leaving ½ inch headroom. Adjust lids and process in a boiling water bath.

Pints . . . . 15 minutes
Quarts . . . . 20 minutes

canning jars and process in a boiling water bath the same way as sauerkraut. If necessary, make more 5 percent brine to cover the vegetables in the jars, leaving ½ inch headroom.

Other Methods

There are methods of heavily salting or brining vegetables, using a 20 percent brine, but in order to prepare them for table use it is necessary to soak them for a long time in fresh water. Since this does a pretty good job of pouring nutrition down the drain, we do not recommend these methods unless you have absolutely no alternative. Any of the other storage or preserving methods in this book are nutritionally superior.

Chapter 9
Drying

Drying, one of the oldest forms of food preservation, has been generally neglected in the last few generations. It wasn't until the publication of *The Foxfire Book*'s chapter on drying that many of us gave it much thought. Then we heard of some of the old-time techniques of air-drying: *leather britches*, for instance, in which you string tender green beans on a thread, hang them in the shade to dry and then store them in a paper bag. Having tried other techniques, we have found better and tastier alternatives, but the idea gives food for thought if nothing else.

Leather britches demonstrate how little equipment you will need. Freezing and canning are certainly more expensive and time-consuming.

Other than that, why dry foods? If you are a hiker and have purchased freeze-dried foods done in a drying chamber (in which food is frozen and then vacuum heat is applied to evaporate the ice into water vapor—a complicated and expensive undertaking) you will know their expense, lack of variety and tastelessness. Your own dried foods will be cheaper, more flavorful and you can be assured of no chemical preservatives. We reconstitute ours in soups and stews, and nibble the dried fruits. And don't forget fruit leathers which are so expensive in the delicatessen departments. They are made of dried fruit purees and provide a healthful snack at any time.

But you don't need to be a hiker to appreciate dried foods. They are convenient to use, have a long shelf life (up to a year), and require little space, since they are reduced to a third or less of their original bulk. In addition, you can take a little out of your storage container and simply screw down the lid or re-tie the bag without worrying about the seal. Since drying extracts the water and spoilage organisms can't grow,

there is not as much danger of bacterial growth as there is in canning.

But don't expect dried foods to have true flavors or an enticing appearance. Until reconstituted, their looks leave much to be desired. The flavor is different, but children, once they have tasted dried apples for instance, will demand more.

Starting

Where to start? Don't be put off by elaborate instructions or equipment. Probably herbs are the simplest and most satisfying place to start, and with nothing more elaborate than a paper bag. Remember that much of what you do will be experimental, and there are few definitive texts on drying.

Perhaps you should start with air-drying apples, which for generations have been air-dried by being cut into wedges and strung, or cut into rings and dried on a pole over a fireplace or wood stove. Try cutting, peeling and laying apple wedges, each separated, on a cookie sheet in the sun. But remember that sanitary standards several generations ago were not the same as ours. If flies bother you, cover your trays with cheesecloth.

WHY DRY FOODS?

"Of all the methods of preserving food, drying is the simplest and most natural. It is also the least expensive, in energy expended, equipment and in storage space. Compared to canning, which requires special lids and processing equipment and a great deal of shelf space, or freezing, which requires special containers and a constant source of electricity, drying foods is the least complicated method of storing food for the winter months. You simply cut the food into small pieces and spread it out in the sun. When the drying is completed, you put it into a small container—almost any container—and store it in a cool, dark place."

Phyllis Hobson
Home Drying Vegetables, Fruits and Herbs
A Garden Way publication

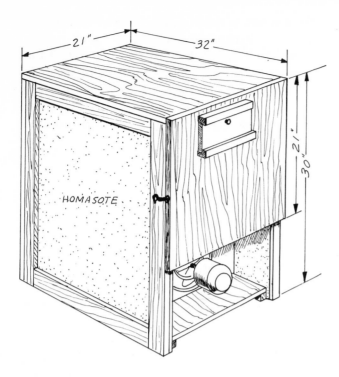

Construction details and dimensions for an electrical home-made dryer. Detail shows heating unit.

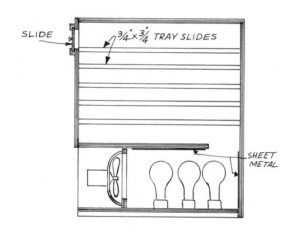

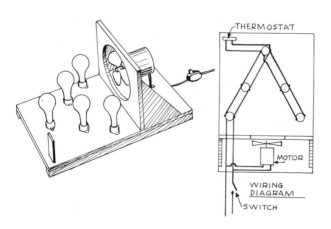

Sun drying is easy and practical only in those parts of the country where the air is dry and the sun is hot. It just isn't the thing for northern and damp areas, where you are lucky to have two sunny, dry summer days in a row. If you do sun dry, however, use wooden frames with cheese-cloth bottoms. Again don't neglect to lay cheese-cloth over the food to protect it from insects. Take the frames in at night before the dew falls or if it looks like rain. If bad weather persist, you can finish off in the oven at very low heat.

Electric dehydrators are a possibility and plans are included (opposite) for building one at home. Commercial dehydrators on the market are expensive and they are large, which makes their storage a problem. Try someone else's dehydrator before deciding on such a large investment.

Oven drying seems by far the most sensible approach for most climates, unless you plan to dry food in large quantities. Most people look upon drying as a supplement to other methods of food preservation, and they rely on it for special, lightweight foods or a change of taste or for snacks.

For oven drying, there is little or no initial investment. The only equipment are drying frames built to fit your oven, and cheesecloth (as in air-drying). You can use cookie sheets or, simpler still, stretch cheesecloth over your oven racks for ready-made frames.

But remember that drying is the process of removing water from the food *without cooking it,* so set your oven heat as low as possible, between 80° and 120°. Leave the oven door ajar. It is possible to oven dry in a gas stove with nothing more than the pilot light.

Stove-top dryers, another alternative, are best used with a wood stove. They can be home-made or mail ordered. The principle behind them is simple and seems to work very well. Water is heated in the bottom "box," which dries the food spread on top. Care must be taken to see that it doesn't burn out.

People air-dry fruits and vegetables successfully using no more than the heat from a fur-

170

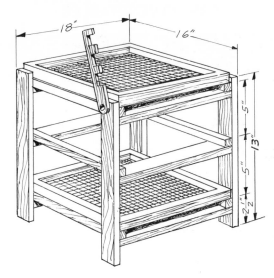

A home-made oven dryer.

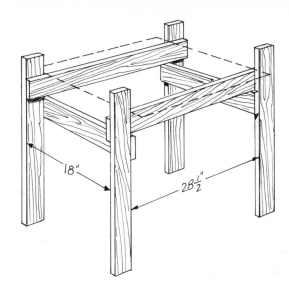

A simple wooden stand for converting an on-stove dryer to an oil-heater dryer.

nace, the top (or bottom) heat vent of the refrigerator or a radiator heat register—but beware of dust and dirt. Improvise and use your imagination.

As important as the heat in the drying process is air circulation, which is aided if the dried food is spaced far enough apart so that air flows between the pieces. Sun drying and dehydrators provide for circulation, but with an oven you have to leave the door ajar or completely open. Therefore you won't want to oven-dry on a hot, hot summer day.

MORE HELP ON DRYING

For further detailed information on drying (by sun or otherwise) a variety of fruits and vegetables, we recommend Phyllis Hobson's *Home Drying Vegetables, Fruits and Herbs* (Garden Way Publishing). This little book also contains directions for re-constituting the dried foods, as well as recipes for their use.

Another recommended book on drying foods is Gen Macmaniman's *Dry It! You'll Like It.*

Construction details and dimensions for a stove-top dryer.

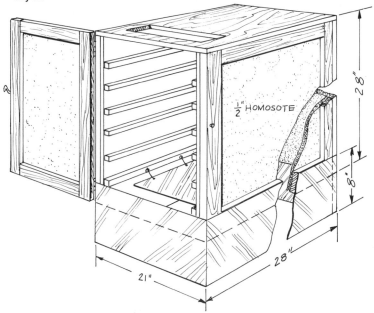

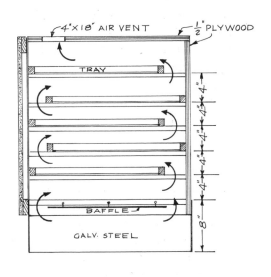

Drying Fruits and Vegetables

As in all other preserving methods, use only the best and freshest produce. Process it as quickly as possible and under the most sanitary conditions.

First wash all foods thoroughly, drain and cut into pieces as small and as uniform as possible. Uniformity is important so that none will be over-dried while others are still moist.

Blanch vegetables first in water at 212° F. (see page 174.) The arguments for it are that blanching fixes color and flavor and stops enzyme action, which will continue to mature the foods beyond the optimum. Blanching may actually hasten the drying process, contrary as this may seem. Vegetables do benefit from blanching more than fruits. Dry the blanched produce with paper towels before air or oven drying.

We have had excellent results in drying with blanching. There is much evidence showing the distinct advantages of blanching.

Drying is one of the "fun" parts of home food preservation, and one where there is some margin for experimentation.

Oven drying vegetables takes around 6-10 hours, while wet fruits will take longer. Turn pieces often for even drying. Once food is well dried, it can be removed to the back of the stove or a cupboard to finish air-drying. Or after oven drying, you can "condition" it for absolute dryness by placing the produce into a deep container and stirring once a day for 10 days before storing.

How can you know when food is fully dried? A good test for fruit is to cut a cooled slice and squeeze. If no moisture comes out, it is dried. Most fruits will have a leathery, pliable quality, while vegetables on the whole become crisp or brittle. More moisture can be successfully left in fruits, since they are high acid foods and consequently more resistant to damage. Vegetables must be thoroughly dried.

Blanching sliced vegetables.

Sun-drying pieces of four items on a screened tray.

Dried corn, apple, carrot, and celery in jars.

172

Nancy Thurber plucking the leaves off dried herbs for packaging.

Store the finished product in plastic bags, screw-top jars or coffee cans with plastic lids, perhaps even in the mayonnaise or peanut butter jars that can't be used for canning. A perfect seal is not necessary—just a good screw-on lid. Be sure your product is cool or it will sweat. Check jars in a few days for condensation and moisture which will lead to mold. If moisture shows, open and dry the produce further.

Label all containers and store in a cool, dark, dry place.

To reconstitute the vegetables, soak them in cold water until they have regained their original texture, as nearly as possible. Remember to cook them in the water that they were soaked in so as not to lose vitamins.

THE HICKORY NUT HARVEST

"Hickories like Pecans are encased in four-parted husks from which they drop. Rake or gather them into piles and do this often, for Hickories are notoriously attractive to squirrels which know a good thing when they see it. Store the nuts at room temperature in any cool, dry place and they will keep for months. The hard shells will never get any softer, but I have found that a hot water bath will make the shelling task easier. I soak them for 10 to 15 minutes. You will derive about one pound of nutmeats (or about four cups) from three pounds of nuts in the shell."

Louise Riotte
Nuts for the Food Gardener
A Garden Way publication

VEGETABLE DRYING CHART

Use only the best and be sure never to process more than one kind at a time.

Beans, green: Wash, cut and blanch for 3 minutes before drying.
Carrots: Wash, peel and cut in thin sections. Blanch 5 to 6 minutes before drying.
Corn: Husk, blanch ears 3 minutes and cool quickly. Cut off kernels and dry.
Peas: Shell, blanch for 4 minutes before drying.
Peppers: Wash, core and slice thin or dice. Don't blanch.
Potatoes: Wash. Boil in jackets, cool, peel and slice thin before drying.
Tomatoes: Wash and dip into boiling water to slip skins. Cool quickly. Cut in half and scoop out juice and seeds. Cut pulp into sections and dry. Or do unpeeled, unblanched in wedges.
Zucchini: Wash, and cut into thin slices. Blanch 3 minutes. Excellent when dried with dips.

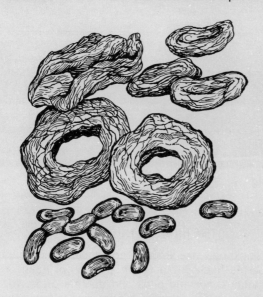

DRYING PEAS

"Pick when peas are at their green best. Carefully pick over and remove any pods that are mildewed or spotted. Do not wash. Spread pods on trays or racks in the sun. After several days, the peas inside the pods will be so dry you can hear them rattle when you shake them. Shell and store peas in clean, dry jars."

Phyllis Hobson
Home Drying Vegetables, Fruits and Herbs
A Garden Way publication

Many dried vegetables can be added directly to soups or stews where they will absorb moisture.

Fruit generally is eaten as is, dried, but can be soaked in enough cold water to cover for several hours, adding more water if necessary. Use any remaining liquid in your recipe. For stewed fruit, cover the dried food with water in a saucepan and simmer for 10 minutes, adding water if necessary. Add sugar after cooking, and cool. Chill before serving.

Fruit leathers—a whole drying topic in themselves—are very easy. Use apples, peaches, apricots, plums or berries to make a puree. Make your own imaginative recipes from combinations, such as cranberry-apple. Purees are made by washing the fruit, peeling skins if necessary, quartering larger fruits, and simmering with just enough water to keep from scorching. Then put through a food press, mill or blender. We much prefer fruit leathers without the addition of sugar. This is optional, but remember that the sugar in the fruit becomes more concentrated as the moisture evaporates, and so you have a natural candy substitute.

Line a cookie sheet with a clear plastic wrap and spread the puree approximately ¼ inch thick. Oven-dry or air-dry, covering with cheesecloth that is elevated so it doesn't come in

FRUIT DRYING CHART

Apples: Wash, peel and section into wedges or rings. Recommended to treat with an anti-oxidant (see Chapter 3). Consider leaving apples in cold storage until harvest is past and then dry. A friend says there is nothing better than apple pie made with dried apples.
Bananas: Peel and slice into "coins" (which stick less than slices). They have little eye appeal but taste like banana candy. Dry.
Blueberries: Wash and spread to dry.
Cherries: Wash, pit and spread to dry.
Figs: When completely tree-ripened, wash, leaving whole and dry.
Peaches: Wash, dip in boiling water to slip skins, pit, section and dry. An anti-oxidant (Chapter 3) is recommended.
Pears: Use very ripe pears. Wash, peel and cut into strips. Dry.

174

contact with the puree. Drying takes 24 hours to several days. When the fruit can be peeled off the plastic wrap, it is done and ready for storage. Roll it up with the plastic. Then wrap the roll in more plastic wrap.

Last comes the controversial question of sulfuring, which is the commercial method used to prevent the darkening of fruit and to inhibit mold growth. No fruit that we have dried has been unpleasantly dark, and sulfuring is a tricky and irritating process (it must be done out-of-doors). We expend too much energy in acquiring additive-free food to want to sulfur, but this is a matter of personal preference. For sulfuring instructions, consult the USDA pamphlet on the subject. Other methods to prevent darkening are discussed in Chapter 5 on Fruits.

Drying Beans

(kidney, navy, pea, horticultural, etc.)

Since market supplies have dwindled and prices skyrocketed, more and more people are growing their own beans for baking. Let the plant and pods dry right in the garden, if you are having a dry fall. Then shell and store in jars with a good tight lid. However, if the plants' pods look moldy, pull them by the roots and hang to dry in a garage or attic. Then shell and store when dry.

You also can shell ripe beans before they dry and then dry them on drying racks or cookie sheets in the oven until ready for storage.

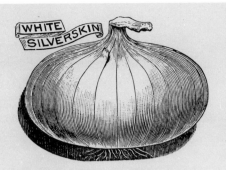

KEEPING ONIONS

Stored onions can be decorative as well as useful, if they are braided.

When pulled in the fall, they should be dried in the garden for a few days. This cures them, and without this treatment they cannot be stored for many months. Use quickly (don't store) the thick-stemmed ones.

Braided onions will fall apart as the tops dry if the braid is not given some reinforcement. Cut three pieces of baler twine about three feet long. Tie them together at one end. Then braid twine and onion tops together, until within six inches of the end of the twine. Wrap one piece of twine fast around the onion stems, then tie to the other two, and hang in a dry, cool place. They may be clipped off with scissors as needed.

There's a practical advantage to braiding onions. A spoiled onion in a bag is a smelly nuisance, but it is a dried and hardly noticed part of a braid of onions.

GRINDING CORN MEAL

"For corn meal, let the (sweet corn, yellow or white) ears dry until a kernel feels good and hard between your teeth. Remove the kernels (there are several hand-held shellers on the market now) and store in covered jars in a dry place. Then grind as you need white or yellow cornmeal. A grain mill is preferred, of course, but a kitchen blender will do a fine job if you grind small batches at a time."

John Vivian
Growing Corn for Many Uses
Garden Way Bulletin O

175

Clipping herbs with help from a friend.

Drying Herbs

Herbs (and herb gardens), a part of American history as far back as the Pilgrims, were used to vary a monotonous diet, to camouflage odors and to make medicines. Currently there has been a resurgence of interest in herbs, which are easy to grow or often can be found in the wild (such as mints) and are very easy to dry. Most are picked just before the flowers open or when the leaves are still young and tender. As the plants mature, the oils which produce the odors and flavors become less intense. Wash picked herbs only if dirty or if they've been treated with chemicals.

Herbs with long stems can be cut and hung in a paper bag. Put the head end toward the bottom of the bag and gather the top of the bag around the stems and secure with a string. Poke

Herbs drying on the rafters. See page 178 for step-by-step instructions.

HERB CHART

Anise: Dry seeds for use in breads, cakes, cookies; fresh stalks in soups and stews.

Basil: Use fresh with tomatoes and dried leaves with almost all main dishes.

Bay: Dry leaves for use in dressings, stews and soups.

Carraway: Dry seeds for use in breads and vegetables.

Chives: Use fresh or dried in salads, dips, sauces.

Dill: Use fresh or dried in pickles, salads.

Marjoram: Use fresh or dried leaves in stews, salads and stuffing.

Mint: Use fresh in teas or in jellies.

Oregano: Use fresh or dried leaves in Italian, Spanish, and Mexican cooking.

Parsley: Use leaves fresh or dried in salads or cooked dishes. Consider keeping a parsley plant growing on your window sill all winter.

Sage: Use leaves fresh or dried in stuffing.

Savory: Use leaves fresh or dried in stuffing, stews and soups.

Tarragon: Use dried leaves in fish dishes, salads. It is difficult to grow.

Thyme: Use fresh or dried leaves in stuffing, salads, and cooked dishes. Very strong.

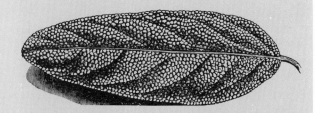

Remember that herbs go a long way. Usually one plant of each is sufficient for the home gardener. Consider adding sprigs of fresh herbs to bottled vinegar and let age for several months. These are interesting additions to salads and make novel gifts for friends.

DRYING HERBS

1. Pick herbs early on a warm, sunny day after the dew has dried. Choose tender young leaves and stems.

4. Hang herbs in a warm, shady, well-ventilated spot away from dust. They should be brittle in 2 or 3 weeks.

2. Tie handfuls of herbs together gently.

5. Herbs may also be dried on a screen in the sun. Be sure that the herbs are well separated and that the screen is elevated so that air can circulate underneath.

3. To protect them from sun and dust, put the herbs into paper bags with holes cut for ventilation.

6. Remove dried leaves from the stem with your fingers.

7. For best flavor, the dried leaves may be stored whole, or they may be cut (above) or ground up with mortar and pestle (right) to take up less space.

8. Store herbs in airtight, opaque containers.

holes in the bag for ventilation and then hang in a warm but well-ventilated area. Remember that herb leaves will fade when exposed to light, so dry in a dim place. For smaller leaves, make a drying rack, spread out the herbs, and air-dry in a well-ventilated place.

When herbs are dry and brittle they are ready for storage. Shake the bags or strip the leaves by hand from the stem. The leaves may be stored whole in jars or crushed into a powder with a rolling pin or mortar and pestle. Seeds can be shaken off in the paper bags.

Remember that herbs are much more potent dried than fresh. To store, put in jars with lids, label and keep in a dry, dark area.

HARVESTING BLACK WALNUTS

"There are a number of ways for handling Black Walnuts in order to remove them from the husks, and you can take your choice. . . . Place the nuts on the driveway and drive the pickup truck over them slowly, forward and then back several times. If two people work at this and the second member of the team keeps shoveling the nuts (a square shovel is handy for this) under the wheels, the work goes faster. The abrasive action of the tires usually is sufficient. . . . After the hulls are off, the nuts should be thoroughly washed and spread out to dry away from direct sunlight for two or three weeks. The nuts then can be stored in a cool, dry place until needed."

Louise Riotte
Nuts for the Food Gardener

179

Chapter 10
Common Storage and Grains

Common storage is the oldest, easiest and least costly method of keeping vegetables and fruits. It includes any method of storing produce that does not require processing. Storing carrots in a root cellar, parsnips in the garden or braids of onions in the pantry all are forms of common storage.

Crops that will store successfully are the root vegetables, potatoes, winter squash, pumpkins, dry legumes, grains, green tomatoes, celery, cabbage and (briefly) peppers. Among the fruits, apples and pears store the best. Grapes and citrus fruits will store for some time, given the right storage conditions.

There are many ways to store fruits and vegetables, including the "ideal" way and the "practical" way. The table following lists the ideal storage temperatures and humidity for a variety of crops, and if you have or can build the facilities to provide these perfect conditions, you should have little problem with storage.

On the other hand if you are like most of us and make use of space and temperatures already available, you will have better luck with some crops than others—and each year your experience may be different. The trick is to locate places in your home or outbuildings that are naturally suitable for storage and then hope for cooperation from Mother Nature!

You may be lucky enough to live in an older home that has a root cellar, or at least a basement that is cool (35°-50° F.) and damp. A dirt floor is even better, especially when there is no furnace in the vicinity. Given these conditions you can store potatoes (in simple bins or slatted boxes), root crops (in plastic bags or packing material), and fruit (in a separate area, in closed containers or plastic bags). There will be little need for alterations in order to be successful.

Upstairs or nearer the furnace there may be areas that are somewhat warmer (45°-65° F.) and drier, and more suitable for winter squash and pumpkins. Pantries, hallways, under the beds in cool bedrooms, closets, a big chest in the mud room, an attic room or garage that is partially heated—all of these areas may be used for some crops with varying success.

11 Practical Storage Hints

Assuming you are going to try to store the "practical way" by using the places available, here are a few suggestions. These hints also apply to more scientific storage, which you may find you want to get into after a year or two. Experience in your own home and geographic area will be the best teacher.

1. Generally, later maturing, longer growing vegetables and fruits are the most suitable for storage. Harvest should be delayed until as late as possible in the fall when the weather has cooled, but before the first heavy frost.

2. Do not try to store immature vegetables. The obvious exception is green tomatoes, which ripen during storage. Winter squash are mature when your thumbnail cannot pierce their rinds; potatoes when a thumb pushed across them will not slip the skin. Onions with wide necks and green stalks will not store. Cabbage heads should be solid and heavy for their size. Root crops should have been in the ground long enough to mature, as indicated on the seed package. See Chapter 4 on vegetables for detailed harvesting information on each crop.

3. Vegetables and fruits should be handled as little and as gently as possible. Those that

STORING APPLES

"Apples freeze at about 28.5 degrees F. Hence it is necessary to keep them above this temperature. A storage temperature of 32 degrees F. is usually maintained in commercial storages. Ripening and softening of apples in storage is twice as rapid at 40 degrees F. as at 32 degrees F.; at 50 degrees it is almost double that at 40 degrees. Therefore, for extended storage, prompt cooling of picked apples is essential, since they will ripen as much in one day at 70 degrees as they will in ten days at 30 degrees. For the home grower without refrigeration the recommended 32-34 degrees storage temperature is usually unattainable in the fall. The best alternative is to keep the apples as cool as possible in unheated basements, or specially-built, insulated fruit storage rooms. By regulating openings to the outside, advantage can be taken of the cooling effect of night air."

Lawrence Southwick
Dwarf Fruit Trees for the Home Gardener
A Garden Way publication

APPLE KEEPERS

**Normal and maximum storage periods
for some common apple varieties***

	Storage period	
	---	---
Variety	**Normal months**	**Maximum months**
Gravenstein	0-1	3
Wealthy	0-1	3
Grimes Golden	2-3	4
Jonathan	2-3	4
MacIntosh	2-4	4-5
Cortland	3-4	5
Spartan	4	5
Rhode Island Greening	3-4	6
Delicious	3-4	6
Stayman	4-5	5
York Imperial	4-5	5-6
Northern Spy	4-5	6
Rome Beauty	4-5	6-7
Newton	5-6	8
Winesap	5-7	8

*From Canada Department of Agriculture Publication 1532, *Storage of Fruits and Vegetables*, by S. W. Porritt. 1974

are blemished or damaged in harvest will not store well. Washing before storage usually is *not* recommended and not necessary; instead wash just before use. An inch or more of stem should be left on just about every vegetable and fruit that has one—especially squash, pumpkins and beets. This helps keep juices in and infection out.

4. Crops should be cool and their surfaces dry before storing. For many crops "curing" is necessary in order to dry and harden the skins before storing. Putting away vegetables fresh from the garden covered with moist soil is a sure invitation to molds, disease and insects.

5. Vegetables needing dry storage conditions (squash, pumpkins, onions) store best if kept up off the floor, and not touching each other—so air can circulate freely around them. Onions can be braided or tied, then hung up. Large squash and pumpkins are more of a problem. If cramped for space you may have to pile them up. If so, you should inspect them regularly and remove any that show signs of rot or mold.

   The mold on squash can double overnight if not kept in check. If mold appears, rubbing each squash with a cloth dampened with vegetable oil may help them keep.

6. Vegetables and fruits requiring moist conditions should be kept *in* something, rather than exposed to the air. Roots traditionally are stored in fresh-cut sawdust, sand or leaves. Plastic bags or linings for boxes; plastic garbage cans; metal cans lined with cardboard—these are all ways of keeping moisture in. Cut a few holes in plastic bags to allow some air circulation, to avoid mustiness.

7. Strong-smelling vegetables such as cabbages should be wrapped closely in several layers of newspaper to keep in the odor as well as the moisture, or they can also be stored outside in pits or a shed. Odors from vegetables can permeate fruits, which is probably why it is usually recommended that fruits and vegetables be kept separately.

8. Boxes, shelves and the area used for food storage should be cleaned and aired thoroughly before and after use. Molds and diseases can be harbored over the summer months, waiting to ruin your next year's harvest. Do not reuse packing material such as sawdust or cardboard boxes. Both can be put on the garden or compost pile.

9. Do not allow temperatures to go below freezing in your storage area, as this can ruin many crops. Also avoid fluctuations in temperature. Cool temperatures are needed for successful storage, so it is usually recommended to open windows or vents when it gets cold outside in the fall. This is fine, except when you forget to close them the next day when it warms up. It is better to have a closed room with constant temperature, than irregular drafts of cold and then warm air. Proper ventilation is part of the "ideal" method of storage, but may not always be practical.

10. Storage should be in the dark.

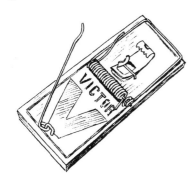

11. Protect your stored vegetables from rodents and dust. Mice will feast on potatoes and grain if given the chance. Keep them away by using a closed room or sealed containers when possible; or use traps or poison. Vegetables and canned foods stored in the open in a cellar gradually will become covered with grime. Covering with newspaper or cloths will help.

Our experience one year with sunflowers was a good example of how not to store. The sunflower heads were cut from the stalks and put immediately—warm and moist—into the root cellar, to avoid the birds. Within days they were covered with mold. We

CARROT KEEPING

Garden Way gardener Dick Raymond recommends storing carrots in sawdust.

"I try to get fresh sawdust—the kind that is still light colored and unweathered," he writes in *Vegetable Gardening Know-How.* "Then I take a regular cardboard box; put two or three inches of sawdust in the bottom; add a layer of carrots, making sure that the carrots are at least two inches from the sides of the box; and cover them with a half-inch layer of sawdust. I keep adding layers of carrots and sawdust until the box is full."

Raymond points out that if the boxes are to be kept in an unheated area, such as a garage, a large box should be used, permitting a layer of the insulating sawdust at least five inches thick around the bottom and sides. Turnips and apples can be stored this way, too.

Giving a Hubbard squash the thumbnail test for maturity.

moved them outside on the lawn to dry out, and soon the crows were eating them and (worse) the neighborhood dogs were using them as markers. So we again moved them, this time to the floor of our tool shed. There they dried, protected from the birds, dogs and mold—and were completely eaten by mice!

The sunflowers would have been safer dried on the stalk, protected from the birds by cheesecloth or paper bags with holes cut in them for ventilation. Or they could have been cut and hung up out of reach in an airy shed.

Storage Containers

Any clean container, uncontaminated by previous use with diseased vegetables, can be adapted for storage. Vegetables and fruits requiring moist conditions can be kept in closed containers. Heavy-duty plastic trash or leaf bags or sheets of polyethylene can be used alone or inside most containers to maintain a moist atmosphere. Dry storage is best provided by containers that are open and airy. Some container suggestions include:

> wooden barrels or nail kegs
> fruit crates
> cardboard boxes
> garbage or trash cans
> milk boxes
> mesh bags
> grain bags
> baskets
> simple bins made from slats of wood

BEBE'S CORN, CHEESE AND ONIONS

Sauté chopped onions until transparent in a small amount of butter. Prepare corn meal mush. Cut up cheddar cheese into small pieces and melt in the mush. When melted add the onions. Serve in a bowl with seasonings to taste.

STORING ONIONS

Your onions didn't keep well?

The most common reason for this is failure to dry them well after harvesting. Onions should be cured for several weeks in a warm, dry and well-ventilated place. They're ready for storage when the skins rustle. After that the best place for them is a location that is barely above freezing, but where they will not freeze.

Here's one way to dry onions before storing. Spread them in the sun on a bed of sawdust.

MATERIALS FOR PACKING ROOT CROPS AND FRUITS

Root crops and fruits can be packed in layers in:

> freshly cut sawdust
> clean, washed builders' sand
> dry leaves
> peat moss
> newspapers
> straw or hay
> burlap

Freshly cut sawdust can be hauled from a saw mill or lumber yard. It keeps vegetables especially well, for the same reasons that ice was preserved in it during the summer months in the days before refrigeration.

Sand or leaves may be easier to acquire and also work well, though sometimes sand lends an undesirable flavor to the vegetables. It should not be too moist (or the crops will root and grow), or totally dry, (in which case they may wither).

Packing Root Crops and Fruits

For storage in a cool cellar or room: Put a 4 inch layer of packing material in the bottom of a container. We use fresh-cut sawdust and cardboard boxes, since they are light and easy to handle. Put in a single layer of root vegetables or fruit. The root crops should have been left out in the sun several hours, long enough for the dirt to dry and fall off. Cut their tops to about 1 inch from the root. The roots may touch each other, but do not wedge them tightly together. Leave 4 inches of room for sawdust all around the sides. Cover the vegetable or fruit layer with 2 to 3 inches of sawdust, then repeat. Fill in around the sides with sawdust, and cover the top with 4 inches more. The box is ready to store in a cool place. When some carrots or apples or whatever are needed, dig down to a layer and remove, covering over what's left.

KEG-OF-THE-MONTH PLAN

Ruth Harmon, a practical Kentucky gardener, harvests a keg full of assorted fresh vegetables every month throughout the winter. In the fall, she places a layer of straw in the bottom of a nail keg, then lays the keg on its side. She adds more straw, then half-fills it with white potatoes. Next come carrots, more straw, beets, and still more straw. Finally, she adds a layer of lettuce or another favorite vegetable — except any member of the cabbage family — and packs straw around it. She fills ten of these kegs, sets them all in a deep trench, and covers them with dirt.

STORAGE BIN

A two-feet-deep storage bin, preferably built on sloping ground for good drainage. A covering of hardware cloth will keep out rodents, and a styrofoam lining will provide excellent insulation. Cover the top with boards and hay bales for easy access. Place sand between layers of vegetables.

For storage where the temperature may dip below freezing occasionally, such as in a garage or shed: Use a bigger box and put at least 6 to 8 inches of sawdust. Or pack the box as in paragraph above, then place that box into a bigger one in which sawdust is placed 6 inches thick in the bottom, around the sides and over the top.

Boxes of root vegetables or fruit should not be stored directly on a concrete or dirt floor, since they might become too moist on the bottom. Set them on a shelf or lay several boards on the floor under them to allow air to circulate. If the boxes are stacked on top of each other, place boards in between.

Building a Root Cellar

The serious gardener who wants to achieve the best conditions for storage will want to build or improvise a root cellar. It can be a simple, small room in a corner of a cellar, or it can be an automatically ventilated, multi-chambered underground combination root cellar and emergency shelter. We are including here plans for a simple root cellar. For more complex plans contact your state extension service at your state agricultural college, or for information about where to get plans write the Cooperative Farm Building Plan Exchange and Rural Housing, Building 228, ARC-East, Agricultural Research Service, U.S. Department of Agriculture, Beltsville, Maryland, 20705. Or send for Garden Way Bulletin I on how to build a root cellar.

If your house has an unused outside stairwell or bulkhead into the basement, this area can be used for some storage with relative ease and small expense. Install an inside door to the steps to keep out basement heat; bank the doors to the outside with hay to prevent freezing cold or unseasonal hot sun from spoiling the stored food. If you want to create a larger storage area around the stairwell, build inward into the basement, taking care to insulate the extra space well. Temperatures in the closed stairwell will go down as you go up the steps (during cold weather). A little experimenting with a thermometer will help you determine the best levels for the different crops you are storing. If the air is too dry, set pans of water at the warmest level for extra humidity.

For small storage areas, window area wells can be utilized by covering the well with boards banked with bales of hay. If basement windows open inward, access can be convenient and simple during the cold winter months.

A simple but effective root cellar was made by a friend of ours when he was building a new home. He chose the northeast corner of his basement, the coolest area, with no heating ducts running through it. If there had been, he would have insulated them.

He planned a 6 by 8 foot area, with an 8 foot ceiling. Using the corner gave him two concrete walls, which he did not cover; and he put up 2 × 4 studding for the other two walls which were made of homasote board, inside and out. These could have been further insulated with rolled fiberglass insulation. The ceiling was also insulated. A snug-fitting door completed the room, and movable shelves of rough, cheap lumber were built inside. An outside window, darkened, provided outside cooling and ventilation.

Plans for a similar type of simple root cellar are shown opposite.

The layout of your basement will dictate the size and location of your root cellar. No matter what size it is, there are some guidelines that you will want to follow.

1. Locate the root cellar in the coldest area of the basement away from furnace and heaters. The north or east sides of the house are preferred.

2. If heat pipes or ducts cannot be avoided, insulate them carefully so heat will be kept out of the root cellar area.

3. Interior walls and the ceiling should be insulated to keep out basement warmth; the exterior wall(s) of concrete, block or stone can be left uncovered so the coolness from the earth can penetrate.

4. Shelves built for the cellar should be in movable sections to make it easy to clean under and around them. Slatted rather than solid shelves provide the best air circulation.

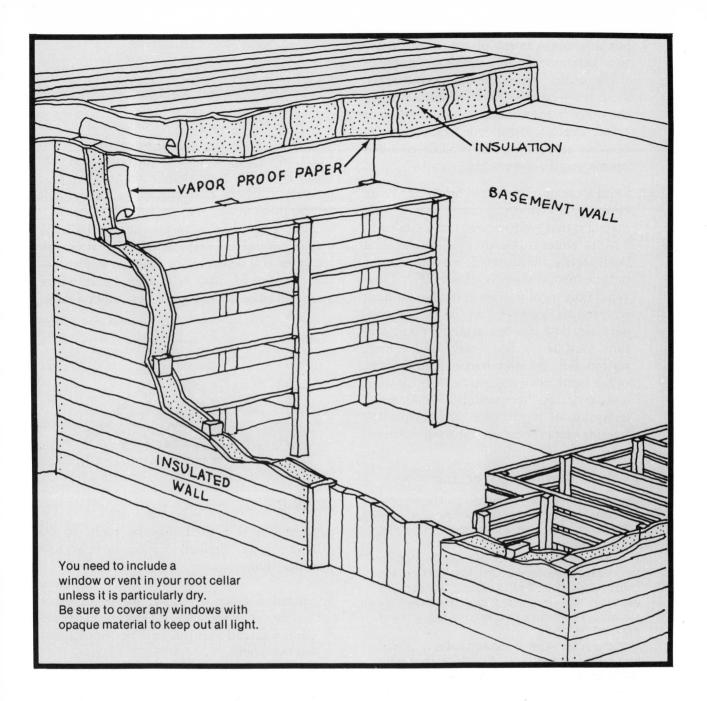

INSULATION

VAPOR PROOF PAPER

BASEMENT WALL

INSULATED WALL

You need to include a
window or vent in your root cellar
unless it is particularly dry.
Be sure to cover any windows with
opaque material to keep out all light.

5. The door to the root cellar should be insulated with a mouse-proof threshold, and wide enough to allow easy access to the room with large storage containers and crocks.

6. For added moisture the floor can be covered with sawdust or sand, and sprinkled with water. Or pans of water can be kept under the ventilator.

7. Ventilation to the room can be provided by means of a window or vent. If a window is used, it should be covered to exclude all light from the room. It can be boxed in, with the adjustable air flow directed to the floor to avoid cold drafts on the food.

8. With colder air entering and concentrating close to the floor, the temperature will be warmest close to the ceiling. With this in mind, plan your storage so that crops requiring the coldest temperatures are close to the floor, reserving the upper areas for those requiring warmer storage.

9. For scientific control of the temperature, two thermometers are helpful, preferably of the kind that record minimum and maximum temperatures. Place one outdoors and the other in the coldest section of the root cellar. Regulate the indoor temperature by opening and closing the window or other opening used as the ventilator.

10. Outdoor temperatures well below 32° F. are necessary to cool storage air to near 32° and maintain that temperature. Once cooled to 32° the indoor temperature will rise again if ventilators are kept closed, even though the outside temperature is about 25°. Close ventilators tightly whenever the outdoor temperature is *higher* than the storage temperature. Both indoor and outdoor temperatures must be watched closely, and in most regions daily (or more frequent) adjustment of the ventilator is necessary. A brisk wind and very low temperatures could bring temperatures in the root cellar below the freezing point for the vegetables stored there.

OUT OF THE ROOT CELLAR

Use vegetables and fruits as quickly as possible after taking them out of cold storage. They will not keep as long as will the freshly harvested produce.

A warning signal is moisture condensing on the surface of produce when it is taken from the cold storage room. This "sweating" encourages decay. It can be avoided to some extent by allowing the produce to warm up gradually in a dry location.

Some years none of the squashes or pumpkins keep very well. Look for this, says master gardener Dick Raymond, when there was an unusually warm autumn, which set the vegetables to growing again. Watch your cold cellar carefully, and if there are signs of deterioration, process, freeze or can them now.

POTATO CELLAR-LOCKER

John Zircke has a simple way to keep potatoes at earth temperature throughout the winter. He buried a metal wall locker in the dirt floor of an old shed. The door faces upward to give easy access. An old rug or some straw is thrown over the top. Any cabinet or box would do as well. His potatoes keep fine this way.

Outdoor Storage

There are cheap and simple methods of outside storage that are useful for winter apples and pears, as well as for root crops, celery and cabbage. However, they should not be attempted unless you live in a climate where the outdoor temperatures in winter average 30° F. or below.

Also, if you live in an area where the snow can get several feet deep, remember that shoveling snow will be necessary to get at your produce. Be sure to mark with high stakes where your vegetables are hidden so you can find them.

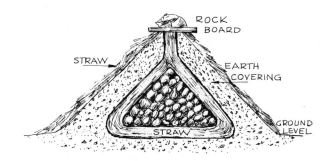

MOUNDS

A cone-shaped mound may be built on the ground in a well-drained location, or in a 6 to 8 inch-deep hole.

1. Spread a layer of straw, leaves or other bedding on the ground. A length of hardware cloth is spread over this to deter winter feasting by rodents.

2. Stack the vegetables or fruits on the hardware cloth in a cone-shaped pile. Different types of vegetables can be stored together, separated by bedding. Do not store fruits and vegetables together.

3. Cover the pile generously with more bedding, and pack well.

4. Cover the whole pile with three or four inches of soil. Firm the soil to make the mound waterproof.

5. Cover everything with a thick layer of straw or hay to keep the soil from freezing too hard.

6. Dig a shallow drainage ditch around and sloping away from the mound.

Small mounds containing only a few bushels of vegetables or fruits will get sufficient ventilation if you let the bedding material that surrounds the produce extend through the top of the pile. Cover the top of the pile with a board or piece of sheet metal to protect the food from rain. A stone will hold the cover in place.

It may be difficult to dig out the produce from these mounds in cold weather, and once the mound is opened all the contents will have to be removed. Trying to rebuild the mound with frozen earth after exposing the contents to the cold air might do more harm than good. So it is better to have several small mounds than one large one.

When vegetables and fruits are brought into the house from outdoor storage they first should be inspected for decay. Cut out any blemished areas and use that produce first. The rest should be put in plastic bags and stored in the refrigerator or a chilly area of the house until needed.

When spring comes, clean out the mounds, put the bedding on the compost pile or garden, and use a different place next year to avoid contamination.

OTHER OUTSIDE STORAGE

Another simple type of outdoor storage shown is a barrel covered with several layers of straw and earth. Cover the barrel opening with a lid or boards, and be sure the bedding is layered thickly on all sides.

If you have nine bales of hay or straw, you can build a storage pit with them. Arrange six of the bales as the walls of the pit. Line the pit with hardware cloth or store the produce in closed wooden boxes (leave some air holes for ventilation) to keep out the mice. Cover the produce with loose bedding, and place the last three bales over the top.

Another method is to bury a box or other container in a pit dug in a well-drained area. An old refrigerator or freezer set in with its door facing upwards would work well. Or build a box to fit the size of the pit that is dug. The pit

Root crops can be stored in an ordinary barrel covered with a blanket of earth and mulch.

should be two to four feet deep, depending on the depth frost penetrates the ground in your area and how well you insulate your box.

To build the box, make a framework of rough lumber. Staple hardware cloth to the inside of this framework, then line the inside with styrofoam about two inches thick. The hardward cloth keeps out rodents and the styrofoam insulates. The top is finished with a solid wooden lid.

At harvest time, select the vegetables to be stored. Put a layer of clean, washed builders' sand or fresh-cut sawdust on the bottom of the box. Then place a neat layer of root vegetables or fruit in the pit and cover that layer with sand

THE OTHER WAYS OF STORAGE

Jerry Belanger, editor of *Countryside & Small Stock Journal*, has some suggestions for people beset by shortages in jars and lids and by the high cost of buying and runnning freezers.

"I'm more interested than ever in drying," Belanger writes. "And we have a root cellar, which will be stocked with carrots, beets, squash, potatoes, pumpkins, onions and other staples. We'll have plenty of dried beans, open-pollinated corn for corn meal mush, corn muffins, bread and so on. We'll have Jerusalem artichokes and turnips and some carrots under mulch in the garden, witloof chicory for winter salads and dried herbs for condiments.

"And we'd better be ready. It'll be much easier in this year of transition than it will be a few years down the pike, when it's too late to learn the basics of survival."

or sawdust. Handle the vegetables gently; do not just dump them into the box.

Continue in this manner until the box is filled. Making a map as you work can be helpful in finding the different vegetables later. Bales of hay or straw can be laid on the cover, and a plastic sheet can be thrown over them, weighted with stones, to keep off the snow. The insulation provided by the straw and styrofoam not only keeps vegetables from freezing in winter, but keeps them cool during the warm days of Indian summer and early spring. When the weather becomes drier in the summer, the box should be thoroughly cleaned out, then left open to the fresh air and sunshine until fall.

A tile or piece of drainage pipe also can be used for in-ground storage. If a tile 18 inches in diameter and 30 inches high is buried upright in the soil, three bushels of vegetables or fruit can be stored in baskets in it. The tile should be located in a well-drained area, away from possible overflow from downspouts and eaves and where it will be shaded. Have the tile extend slightly above ground and cap with a board or plastic to keep out rain and ground water. Cover with a deep mulch of straw, hay or leaves.

GARDEN STORAGE

It is possible to leave some of your root crops in the ground where they grew, until spring. When the ground begins to freeze in the late fall cover such crops as carrots, turnips and beets with a heavy (18 inch thick) mulch of hay or straw. Except where the cold is severe (0° F. and below) you should be able to pull back the mulch and dig up the crops throughout the winter. Mark where you stop digging each time so you will know where to start again.

If you are not sure about your climate, try leaving just a few roots in the ground, digging the rest in the fall to store elsewhere. That way

A box, too, can be sunk into the earth to make a fine storage container. Remember, though, that the entire contents must be removed at the same time, making smaller boxes more practical.

Master gardener Dick Raymond picking kale in winter.

some will be safe for sure, and if you are lucky you also will have fresh, crisp vegetables right out of the garden in mid-winter.

Traditionally, parsnips, horseradish, and salsify are best left in the ground long enough for thorough freezing, which improves their flavor. Harvested in the late winter or early spring, they provide a great taste treat. With parsnips be sure to harvest them before they begin their second growth, because they become poisonous at that time.

Kale, a hardy green that is rich in vitamins A and C, withstands extremely cold weather. If the plants are mulched before snow falls, they will keep throughout the winter and be the first crop to grow in the spring. We have pushed snow and mulch aside from the kale and harvested a crop in late winter. This can be an important crop for your family's nutrition, since in late winter and early spring your root crops are beginning to lose large amounts of vitamin C.

Celery or Chinese cabbage plants of late-maturing varieties also may be stored in the garden for one or two months. Bank a few inches of soil around the base of the plants at the end of the growing season; then build the bank up to

191

the top of the plants before severe freezing occurs. As the weather becomes colder cover the banking with straw or corn stalks held in place with boards.

Celery and Chinese cabbage also may be dug up, keeping a good-sized clump of soil attached to the roots. Place these plants in a trench, a hot bed, a cold frame or on a dirt or concrete floor in a root cellar. Provide protection from the weather and insulate with some kind of bedding for the outside storage, and you may have success keeping these plants until Christmas. Endive can be brought inside like celery with roots on and kept for a month or two. Tie the leaves together to help blanching. The celery and Chinese cabbage also will blanch in the dark.

Cabbages can be stored in mound-shaped or long pits. Their odor is penetrating, so store alone to avoid spoiling the flavor of other food. When stored this way they should be dug up with their roots intact, and placed head down in the mound and covered with bedding and soil.

Another way to store cabbage plants is upright in a shallow trench, covered by a framework made of boards and stakes driven into the ground, or a very thick covering of hay. Cabbages can also be hung up by their roots in a shed where they will not freeze, or kept wrapped in newspaper in the root cellar.

For healthy, large green tomatoes ready to harvest just before frost, take the suckers off new plants 2 to 3 weeks after planting in the spring. Put them in a glass of water for several hours and then plant, watering liberally. These late plants will produce tomatoes timed just right for cold storage.

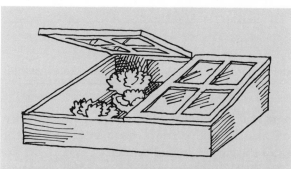

FREEZING POINTS, RECOMMENDED STORAGE CONDITIONS, AND LENGTH OF STORAGE PERIOD OF VEGETABLES AND FRUITS

Commodity	Freezing point °F.	Place to store	Storage conditions Temperature °F.	Humidity	Length of storage period
Vegetables:					
Dry beans and peas	—	Any cool, dry place	32° to 40°	Dry	As long as desired
Late cabbage	30.4	Pit, trench, or outdoor cellar	Near 32° as possible	Moderately moist	Through late fall and winter
Cauliflower	30.3	Storage cellar	,,	,,	6 to 8 weeks
Late celery	31.6	Pit or trench; roots in soil in storage cellar	,,	,,	Through late fall and winter
Endive	31.9	Roots in soil in storage cellar	,,	,,	2 to 3 months
Onions	30.6	Any cool, dry place	,,	Dry	Through fall and winter
Parsnips	30.4	Where they grew, or in storage cellar	,,	Moist	,,
Peppers	30.7	Unheated basement or room	45° to 50°	Moderately moist	2 to 3 weeks
Potatoes	30.9	Pit or in storage cellar	35° to 40°	,,	Through fall and winter
Pumpkins and squashes	30.5	Home cellar or basement	55°	Moderately dry	,,
Root crops (miscellaneous)	—	Pit or in storage cellar	Near 32° as possible	Moist	,,
Sweet Potatoes	29.7	Home cellar or basement	55° to 60°	Moderately dry	,,
Tomatoes (mature green)	31.0	,,	55° to 70°	,,	4 to 6 weeks
Fruits:					
Apples	29.0	Fruit storage cellar	Near 32° as possible	Moderately moist	Through fall and winter
Grapefruit	29.8	,,	,,	,,	4 to 6 weeks
Grapes	28.1	,,	,,	,,	1 to 2 months
Oranges	30.5	,,	,,	,,	4 to 6 weeks
Pears	29.2	,,	,,	,,	

(From U.S.D.A. Bulletin No. 119.)

Springtime Preserving of Stored Crops

After several months the quality of stored crops may begin to deteriorate, particularly when not stored under "ideal" conditions. As long as they are firm, crisp and have good flavor and color, their nutritive value is close to that of the fresh crop. But when they begin to wither their food value decreases.

Rather than letting these crops continue to deteriorate you may want to preserve them in midwinter or early spring by canning, freezing or drying. The rush of the harvest season is over. There should be plenty of empty canning jars available now, if you have been eating vegetables canned in the fall, and space in the freezer is opening up.

Now is the time to make and preserve strained pumpkin, squash or turnip, applesauce, pickled beets or what have you. Crops wintered in the garden or outside storage also should be preserved now. These winter vegetables and fruits then will be usable throughout the spring and summer—until the next harvest.

GRAINS

Grains such as wheat, oats and corn are simple to store and will provide your family with an inexpensive source of nutritious food. Grains are high in protein, and when served in combination with another type of protein food such as dairy products, nuts, dried legumes or small amounts of meat, help provide the complete protein needed for body growth and maintenance. They are especially rich in the B vitamins. Baking bread from home-ground whole wheat flour is a labor of love that will give you satisfaction and your family good health.

WHEAT

The home gardener can try growing grains, especially if there is plenty of garden space. Our neighbor, who has homesteaded for several years, has grown wheat on a small scale, (a 4 to 5 bushel crop) in both a rectangular area (100 × 100 feet) and in wide rows in the garden. Weeds were less of a problem in the rows where they could be pulled, and the crop more manageable. Weather, she warns, is the worst impediment. If the wheat ripens during a prolonged wet spell you may have difficulty harvesting it.

Types of Wheat. There are several different types of wheat. Hard red spring wheat is usually recommended for bread-making because it has

BURPEE'S MAMMOTH SILVER KING

4¾ POUNDS

COPYRIGHTED BY W. ATLEE BURPEE & CO.

194

the highest protein content. It also is high in gluten, which is the sticky substance that holds bread dough together when it rises. Our neighbor likes to use hard white winter wheat with the spring wheat to make a softer, better loaf. She grinds the two together, 3 parts winter to 1 part spring, to make her flour for bread.

Harvesting. Wheat is ready to harvest when all but a few stalks have turned yellow, and the grain will separate from its husks fairly easily when rubbed in your hand. The grain should not be thoroughly ripe or else it will scatter when cut.

Our neighbor found that it was easier to pull the plants than to cut them. This will depend on the size of your crop and your expertise with a scythe. A "cradle" is the best hand tool to use; it has a blade similar to a scythe, but up along the handle are bars that stick out to catch the grain as it is cut. The stalks are slid neatly to the ground when enough accumulates on the cradle.

After cutting or pulling the plants they are tied into bundles. The pioneers used several stalks twisted together to tie the bundles; twine might be more convenient. Then several of the bundles are stood up together in "shocks," which are left to stand in the garden for about two weeks, during which time the grain will finish ripening and start to dry. The wheat then is taken under cover to finish drying. The harvesting is obviously best done during dry weather. The grain is removed from the stalks by threshing when both grain and stalks are completely dry.

Clear a large area of floor—a canvas or plastic covering aids in cleaning up. Untie and lay out a bundle of stalks. Then beat them with a flail or flexible stick until the grain breaks free. Remove the stalks and repeat until all the bundles have been threshed. The grain is gathered up and winnowed to remove the chaff. To winnow the grain, pour it from one container to another on a windy day.

Storage. Wheat can be stored in clean, dry, airtight containers, such as plastic trash cans with lids or large glass jars. These containers should be kept in a cool dry place. Do not store

on concrete, especially if using metal containers or they may sweat.

The drier the wheat the better it will keep. Insects cannot reproduce in wheat with a 10 percent or less moisture content. But it is difficult to tell just how dry the wheat is unless you buy it with a guaranteed moisture content, and even then it can pick up moisture from the air during wet weather. It should never be washed before storing, as this also increases the moisture content.

If you live in a humid climate or if you suspect insects are present, dry the grain before storing. Put it in shallow pans no more than ¾ of an inch deep and heat in a 130°-150° F. oven for 20-30 minutes. Leave the oven door ajar to allow air to circulate and prevent overheating. Stir occasionally to dry evenly. Do *not* heat wheat to be planted or sprouted.

Wheat is best aged at least a month before using, and then just the amount needed should be ground. Even a week's storage of the ground whole wheat flour will reduce its vitamin content, although refrigeration will help keep the flour fresh. Your home-ground flour has all the nutrients of the whole wheat, and you do not want to lose these by improper storage. Enriched white flour bought from the store will keep longer because the wheat germ has been removed (the same is true of store-bought corn meal processed the "new" way, removing the germ to increase its storage life). Some vitamins lost with the germ and bran have been returned to the enriched flour, but not all the vitamins and not in their natural proportions.

If the wheat needs cleaning, sift it to remove dirt and debris, then wash quickly in several changes of water. Dry thoroughly in the oven at 150° F. for 20 minutes if you are in a hurry. Then grind soon.

Grinders. There are many types of grinders available in a wide range of prices, both hand-crank and electric. Not all are suitable for use with corn, so check before buying if you plan to make corn meal. Some of the electric ones can be converted for use with a hand crank in the event of a power failure. The family that has a supply of wheat safely stored and the means to grind it can feel confident in any emergency.

The perfect accompaniment? Home-made butter and tangy slices of cheddar cheese.

SHORT-CUT WHOLE WHEAT BREAD

This bread tends to be heavy, but the flavor is delicious and it is quick to make.

> 5 cups hot water
> ⅔ cup melted butter, lard, or
>   cooking oil
> ⅔ cup honey
> 4 teaspoons salt
> 3 tablespoons (packages) dry yeast
> 10-11 cups whole wheat flour (7 cups
>   unground wheat)

Grind 7 cups of wheat berries. Set an electric grinder on "fine"; by hand you may need to grind the wheat through three times to get it fine enough.

Put hot water, shortening, honey and salt into a large bowl. A hand-turned bread maker or electric mixer works well with this recipe. Add 6 cups of whole wheat flour and mix thoroughly. Add yeast and mix again. Then add the rest of the flour.

Mix for 10 minutes—this dough is too sticky to knead by hand. Then with oiled hands remove ⅓ of the dough at a time and form into loaves. Place in oiled bread pans and let rise in a warm place for 20 to 60 minutes or until doubled. A warm oven with a pan of hot water in the bottom is a good place to put the rising bread.

Place bread in a preheated 350° F. oven and bake for 45 minutes. Remove from pans and cool on a rack. For a crisp crust brush with butter or oil. For a soft crust cover with a towel while cooling.

What could be more delicious than home-made bread baked from dough made from home-grown grains!

MARYET'S WHOLE WHEAT AND OATMEAL BREAD

1 cup oatmeal
1 cup molasses
⅓ cup honey
3 tablespoons margarine or
  other shortening
1 tablespoon salt
4 cups hot water
2 tablespoons dry yeast
  softened in ½ cup warm
  water
6 cups whole wheat flour (or 5
  cups ground wheat berries)
5-6 cups all-purpose flour

Put oatmeal, molasses, honey, margarine and salt into a large bowl and add 4 cups very hot water. Allow to cool to lukewarm, then add yeast softened in water. Grind whole wheat three times. Add the flours, and mix thoroughly.

Knead the dough on a floured board for about 10 minutes, or until elastic and no longer sticky.

Place dough into oiled bowl, turn over so the top is oiled, and allow to rise in a warm place until doubled (about 2 hours).

Knock down, pinch off loaf-sized pieces and form into loaves. There should be enough dough for three loaves plus some left over for a few rolls. Place in oiled bread pans and allow to rise again until double.

Place in oven preheated to 400° F., turn down immediately to 350° F. and bake for 50 minutes. Turn out of pans as soon as removed from oven and place on a rack to cool. Brush with melted shortening for a shiny, crisp crust. Cover with a towel while cooling for softer crust. When completely cool place in plastic bags. Freeze extra loaves.

OTHER GRAINS

Other grains such as oats, rye, barley and buckwheat can be grown and harvested somewhat like wheat. Ask for advice on the type to use and culture of all grains from your seed supplier or local Extension Service.

CORN

Corn, called maize by the Indians (which means both "bread-of-life" and "grain-of-the-gods,") was a staple in the diet of the American Indians and the early settlers in America. More corn is grown in the world today than any other grain except wheat. Corn meal is a popular use of corn that can be made easily in the home. It is used for breads, johnny cake and mush, and in Mexico and South America it is used extensively as the base for the unleavened tortillas. Corn treated with lye to remove the rough outer skin results in *hominy*, used extensively in the South.

Parched corn, made from dried sweet corn heated in a little butter or fat, is a nutritious food mostly enjoyed by people with good, strong teeth. Serving a few kernels to everyone at Thanksgiving dinner is an effective reminder of the hardship endured by our ancestors during their first lean years on this continent.

Our neighbor has found that the best type to grow for corn meal is *flint corn*, which is a multicolored corn similar to that grown by the Indians. In the North the best variety to grow is the *Hard Northern Flint*. It is planted and cultivated in the same way as sweet corn and will mature in 120 days. *Flour corn*, which is softer

BASIC CORN MEAL MUSH

For each serving add about ¾ cup boiling water very slowly to ¼ cup freshly ground corn meal, stirring rapidly. Cook for 2 to 3 minutes. The amount of water will depend on how thick or thin you like it. Serve as a hot cereal with cream and honey or as a side dish with salt, pepper and butter. Or put mush into soup or orange juice can, cover and chill. Then push out, slice and fry the slices in butter.

197

SPROUTING

The seeds that you store, such as the grains and dried legumes, can be sprouted to provide fresh vegetables for salads, casseroles and soups. Sprouts can be roasted, ground up and used to enrich breads, cookies and other baked goods. Sprouting greatly increases the food value of the seed and its digestibility, because some of the fats and starches are converted to vitamins and sugar. A dry seed becomes a home-grown vegetable in your kitchen any time of the year.

Sprouting is simple. We have found the easiest method is to put a few seeds into a clean quart-size canning jar. Use about ½ cup of large seeds, such as beans, fewer of the small seeds like alfalfa. Cover the top of the jar with a piece of cheesecloth or fine screen wire, held in place by a screw band. Fill with water and soak overnight.

The next day pour off the water and rinse the seeds with cool, fresh water. The cheesecloth acts as a sieve on top of the jar. Pour off all water and put the jar in a dark place, such as a kitchen cabinet. The temperature should be warm but not hot; seeds may turn rancid at over 80° F.

Rinse the seeds several times a day with fresh water, always pouring it off, leaving the seeds damp but not soaking. In three or four days you will have nutritious sprouts ready to serve raw in salads or in cooked dishes. Store unused sprouts in the refrigerator to keep them fresh for several days.

Large bean sprouts such as kidney beans, soybeans and garbanzos, will need to be steamed for 10-15 minutes before using to

At left, seeds just starting to sprout. Once they do (right), they must be kept moist by adding water through the cheesecloth-covered jar top.

tenderize them. Sprouted grains to be used in recipes such as breads may be roasted and ground before using.

Seeds will not sprout well if they have been heated at over 130° to dry them or to destroy insects. If you intend to use some of your wheat or other grains for sprouting or for planting do not use this heat treatment on them.

When buying seeds for sprouting be sure that they are pure, untreated seeds suitable for eating. Many seeds sold for planting have been treated with fungicides that are poisonous.

and easier to grind by hand, is grown by the Southwest Indians, but it requires too long a growing season for cool climates.

Unlike sweet corn, which is picked at the immature milk stage for all uses, including drying, the flint corn is allowed to mature and dry thoroughly on the stalk. Harvest the ears after frost in October or November. Pull down the husks and braid or tie the ears together. Then hang them out of reach of mice or birds in a dry, cool place.

The corn should be completely dry, so wait several more months before shelling. Then, as you have the time, shell the kernels from the cobs. Store the kernels like grain in airtight containers in a dry place. The corn can be ground for meal as needed.

Index

Page numbers in brown include canning and freezing information, as well as harvesting, preparation and storage where appropriate. For recipes, see specific vegetables or fruits.

200

Suggested Additional Reading

A good library is essential for the person or family raising and storing food. No one can remember all of the information this requires, and a good library will provide it, at your fingertips. New ideas, techniques and theories are always being put forth, and the best way to keep up with them all is to keep your library up to date. There are many good books available; here are some that are excellent choices.

Down-to-Earth Vegetable Gardening Know-How, featuring Dick Raymond. 160 pp., 8½" x 11", quality paperback, $4.95. A treasury of vegetable gardening information.

The Sprouter's Cookbook, by Marjorie Blanchard. 144 pp., quality paperback, $3.95. The wonder food—how to create, prepare and serve it.

Home-Drying Vegetables, Fruits and Herbs, by Phyllis Hobson. 60 pp., quality paperback, $2.95. Practical methods you can use with ease.

Vegetable Garden Handbook, by Roger Griffith. 120 pp., spiral bound, $3.95. Take it into your garden, for information and your own record book.

Making Breads with Home-Grown Yeasts and Home-Ground Grains, by Phyllis Hobson. 48 pp., quality paperback, $2.95. You'll be delighted. Information you can't find elsewhere.

The Home Gardener's Cookbook, by Marjorie Blanchard. 192 pp., deluxe paperback, $4.95; hardback, $6.95. Mouth-watering recipes using your garden produce.

Secrets of Companion Planting for Successful Gardening, by Louise Riotte. 226 pp., quality paperback, $4.95; hardback, $8.95. For bigger, more luscious crops.

Cash from Your Garden: Roadside Farm Stands, by David W. Lynch. 208 pp., quality paperback, $3.95. Turn a big garden into a profitable family business.

Treasured Recipes from Early New England Kitchens, by Marjorie Blanchard. 144 pp., quality paperback, $4.95; hardback, $8.95. Yesterday's favorite recipes, adapted to today's kitchens.

These books are available at your bookstore, or may be ordered directly from Garden Way Publishing, Dept. HS, Charlotte, Vermont 05445. If order is less than $10, please add 60¢ postage and handling.